What They Didn't Teach You in American History Class

OTHER BOOKS BY THE AUTHOR

Black History: More than Just a Month

What They Didn't Teach You in American History Class

Mike Henry

ROWMAN & LITTLEFIELD
Lanham • Boulder • New York • Toronto • Plymouth, UK

Published by Rowman & Littlefield
4501 Forbes Boulevard, Suite 200, Lanham, Maryland 20706
www.rowman.com

10 Thornbury Road, Plymouth PL6 7PP, United Kingdom

British Library Cataloguing in Publication Information Available

Library of Congress Cataloging-in-Publication Data
Henry, Mike, 1952–
   What they didn't teach you in American history class / Mike Henry.
        pages ; cm.
   Includes bibliographical references.
   ISBN 978-1-4758-0845-2 (cloth) — ISBN 978-1-4758-0846-9 (paper) —
ISBN 978-1-4758-0847-6 (electronic)
   1. United States—History—Miscellanea.   2. United States—Biography—Miscellanea.
I. Title.
   E179.H53 2014
   973—dc23

                                                                2013045610

Printed in the United States of America

This book is dedicated to two guys named Paul:
Paul Eugene Rexer and his grandson, Paul B. Hammond

Table of Contents

Preface

$\mathcal{I}$ was a history teacher for thirty-one years, and if I had a dollar for every time somebody said to me, "History . . . I hated history!" I could have retired a very wealthy man.

My interest in the past evolved as I made my way through secondary school during the 1960s. At the time, I didn't realize that the news that I watched on television with my family during dinner would become a part of the subject that I would teach for three decades. During that time, I witnessed events unfold and the public's reaction to the assassinations of John F. Kennedy, Martin Luther King, and Robert Kennedy; the near nuclear conflict stemming from the Cuban Missile Crisis; the ongoing war in Vietnam; the fall and rise (and fall again) of Richard Nixon; the counterculture movement; and Americans landing on the moon.

Over the years, I wasn't exactly sure from a historical point of view what I was witnessing, but I did know that it was profoundly interesting. As time passed and more information about these events became known, I became more intrigued. My curiosity surrounding the nation's history continued to grow from my changing roles of student to educator. My retirement from the classroom in 2008 has allowed more time to research events in detail that are often neglected by many texts.

Today most teachers and students are caught up in the testing game. They are under pressure from administrators to pass their standardized state tests, whether or not the students learn anything along the way. A great deal of that content is dry and boring.

In every aspect of life, there is always another story behind a major event. It was those additional items that my students always enjoyed hearing about and helped many of them to actually appreciate history.

On these pages, I wanted to share some of those true stories with you. If you're a young teacher, perhaps you'll find some material to help you get through those less-than-exciting areas of the textbook. If you hated history as a student, maybe you'll find some of this stuff entertaining. For those of you who are history buffs, hopefully you'll come across a few things that are new to you.

The story of America is interesting and exciting but it's those lesser-known parts of our history that make it special.

In the Beginning: The Early Arrivals and the Young Colonies

History teaches us that men and nations behave wisely once they have exhausted all other alternatives.

—Abba Eban

In June 1579, California was discovered by the English explorer Sir Francis Drake. Like most of the leaders of his time, the Englishman made the act official by planting his native flag on the newly claimed territory. Drake did so at Point Reyes Peninsula.

However to this day, the explorer's claim to the land has never been challenged in court and the British have never officially ceded the area to the United States.

While studying Jamestown, we've learned much about John Smith, Pocahontas, and the Virginia Company. Something that may not have been taught is that a prolonged drought struck the colony from 1606 to 1612. Only 38 of the original 104 colonists survived the first year (1607) at the settlement, and of the 6,000 people that came there between the years 1608–1624, only 3,400 survived. Most of them died of malnutrition.

Jamestown was the first permanent English settlement in the New World. Some textbooks have given the impression to readers that everyone in the colony lived happily ever after.

But the truth was that three years after its founding, the Virginia colony was an abject failure. So a few dozen starving settlers packed some meager possessions and sailed from Jamestown on June 7, 1610, to begin the journey back to England. The next morning, to their surprise, they spotted a fleet coming toward them carrying a new governor, Lord De La Warr, and a year's worth of supplies.

If not for his appearance, Jamestown might have gone the way of so many other lost colonies.

Much is made about Pocahontas and her role with the habitants at Jamestown. But the name "Pocahontas" was given to her by the settlers. Her actual birth name was Natoaka.

Everyone who has studied the history of Jamestown knows about the famous tale of Pocahontas saving the life of Captain John Smith. But according to the English adventurer, this wasn't the first time that he was saved by a compassionate female.

In 1602, Smith was captured by Turks in a battle in Hungary, and a Turkish princess saved his life after he was captured. No doubt, the captain was one lucky guy.

When Pocahontas married John Rolfe in 1614, her name was changed once again—this time to Rebecca. At age eighteen, she moved to England with her new husband and never returned to her homeland.

First Lady Edith Wilson, the wife of President Woodrow Wilson, was a direct descendant of Pocahontas.

Students in an American history class are issued a textbook to use during the school year. But who wrote the first American history textbook? In 1647, Governor William Bradford completed *Of Plymouth Plantation*. It tells the story of the Pilgrims' departure, the *Mayflower* voyage, and the founding of the colony. It also contains the oldest known copy of the *Mayflower Compact*. The manuscript of Bradford's book disappeared but was found over two hundred years later in England and was finally published in 1856.

Another early work was *Notes on the State of Virginia*, which was produced by Thomas Jefferson in 1785. It describes the history, geography, economy, and social institutions of the area known as the Old Dominion.

Squanto was a native Indian who helped the Pilgrims survive during the rough winters in their new homeland. But what ever happened to him?

Squanto was kidnapped and taken to Europe. He served seven years there as an indentured servant before returning to his native land, only to find that all of his people had been killed by disease.

The Pilgrims celebrated the first Thanksgiving in 1621. But they probably didn't eat turkey during the feast.

Instead of the old gobbler, they dined on venison and shellfish. There was also no cranberry sauce, pumpkin pies, or sweet potatoes. However, there are actually twelve claims to where the "first" Thanksgiving took place: two in Texas, two in Florida, one in Maine, two in Virginia, and five in Massachusetts.

So, take your choice.

Most know about the history surrounding Thanksgiving, but unless you were schooled in Hawaii, you probably don't know about Makahiki. It was the ancient islanders' version of a day of grace to honor the god Lono. The holiday covered four consecutive lunar months, from October or November through February or March.

Many religious ceremonies happened in this period. The islanders halted work, and making war was forbidden during those weeks.

The legend of the Thanksgiving holiday may have begun with the Pilgrims, but while it was a big hit with the new arrivals, another well-known celebration was not. They ignored Christmas because of their ongoing disagreements with the Church of England. In 1621, Governor William Bradford took the step of banning game-playing on Christmas Day in Plymouth Colony, while thirty years later, the Massachusetts General Court ordered a fine of five shillings for "observing any such day as Christmas."

The first person, other than a Native American, to view Niagara Falls is believed to have been the French explorer Etienne Brûlé before his death in 1633.

What he would never know was that the flow of water was stopped completely over both falls for several hours on March 29, 1848, due to an ice jam in the upper river. It is the only time this is known to have occurred. The falls did not actually freeze over, but the flow was stopped to the point that people walked out and recovered artifacts from the riverbed. Niagara Falls did freeze over in 1911 and 1932.

Americans have been writing letters for a long time. In 1639, Richard Fairbanks's Tavern in Boston was the first official mail depot for communiqués arriving from or sent overseas. But credit must also be given to William Penn, who established the first official post office in the colony of Pennsylvania in 1683.

Figure 1.1 In 1896, Niagara Falls' Cave of the Winds became a winter wonderland. *Albert Breistadt and the Niagara Falls Public Library*

It is important for individuals to patent their inventions. The first patent in North America was issued in 1641 to Samuel Winslow from the colony of Massachusetts for his process of making salt.

The Sixteenth Amendment of the Constitution, which gives the government the right to levy an income tax, was ratified in 1913. But back in 1643, a faculty tax was adopted in New Plymouth, Massachusetts.

This tax was the ancestor of today's income taxes and was applied to a person's "faculties"—a term used to judge one's earning power from property, trade, or a skill. In time, most of the colonies established faculty taxes.

For many years, parents have read Mother Goose stories to their children. What many don't know is that there really was a Mother Goose. Her name was Mary Goose, and she lived in Boston as the wife of Isaac Goose.

Mary used to sing songs to her grandchildren throughout the day, and other kids in the neighborhood would gather to listen. Thomas Fleet, her son-in-law, collected the little jingles and printed them.

Mary died in 1690 and was laid to rest at the Granary Burying Ground in Boston. Among other well-known individuals who are also buried at

Granary along with Mother Goose are Samuel Adams, Crispus Attucks, John Hancock, and Paul Revere.

Benjamin Franklin's famous *Poor Richard's Almanack* circulated from 1732 to 1758. But the first newspaper in the colonies was published decades earlier on September 25, 1690.

Boston printer Benjamin Harris produced the first issue of *Publick Occurrences, Both Forreign and Domestick*, the first newspaper published in Britain's North American colonies. Readers were enthusiastic, but the governor was not. Under English law, "no person [was to] keep any printing-press for printing, nor [was] any book, pamphlet or other matter whatsoever" to be printed without the governor's "especial leave and licence first obtained."

In short, it was illegal to publish any document without the government's approval, and Harris had failed to obtain it. Within a few days, the governor and council had banned publication of the paper. Authorities collected and destroyed every copy they could find. The one edition known to have survived is preserved in the British Library in London.

Almost everyone has heard of the Cadillac automobile. It is a luxury vehicle produced by General Motors in Detroit.

What isn't included in the information contained in the owner's manual is that the car was named in honor of Antoine Laumet de La Mothe, sieur de Cadillac (1658–1730). He was the founder of Detroit and served as governor of Louisiana from 1710 to 1716. The auto also bears his family coat of arms as its emblem.

During the colonial era, white, male property-owners who were twenty-one years of age or older were eligible to vote.

But in 1715, Connecticut imposed the first personal-property rights for voting. Non–land owners could still vote if they could show possession of personal property worth at least £40.

By 1790, states began dropping the land-ownership requirement to vote because so many of the American soldiers who had fought in the Revolutionary War didn't own property.

There were many famous members of the House of Burgesses of Virginia such as Thomas Jefferson, Patrick Henry, and George Washington. But during this period, the Lee family was probably the most powerful in Virginia politics. Among family members who served in the House of Burgesses were Thomas Lee; his sons Richard Henry, Thomas Ludwell, and Francis Lightfoot Lee; his nephew Henry Lee II; his father Richard Lee II;

and his grandfather Richard Lee I. Among their descendants was Civil War general Robert E. Lee.

In 1732, King George II granted a charter for creating Georgia and named James Oglethorpe as one of twenty-one trustees to govern the new colony. Oglethorpe is known for his creation of the city of Savannah. Eleven years later, he returned to England to pursue a military career. The former Georgia resident rose to the rank of colonel and fought in several European battles. At the outbreak of the American Revolution, Oglethorpe was asked to command a British force against the colonists.

But the man who had once created the beautiful city of Savannah declined the offer.

Savannah is the oldest city in Georgia. It was founded in 1733, and although it is now only the fourth-largest city in the state, the community has been visited by eighteen U.S. presidents. The most recent was Barack Obama in March 2010.

The Liberty Bell was originally cast in London, England, in 1752 at the Whitechapel Foundry. This is the same neighborhood where Jack the Ripper murdered his victims in 1888.

In 1755, British general Edward Braddock was killed in battle during the French and Indian War. The command of his troops was taken over by a young lieutenant colonel named George Washington.

It was this instance that would eventually lead the Virginian to a brilliant military career. But what is rarely mentioned is the fact that Washington inherited the command by default because he was the only officer on Braddock's staff who wasn't killed in the battle.

Fifteen years later, in 1770, Washington returned to the same Pennsylvania woods. A respected Indian chief, having heard that the former adversary was in the area, traveled a long way to meet with him.

He sat down with Washington, and face-to-face over a council fire, the chief told the future president, "It was on the day when the white man's blood mixed with the streams of our forests that I first beheld this chief [Washington]. . . . Our rifles were leveled, rifles which, but for you, knew not how to miss—'Twas all in vain, a power mightier far than we shielded you."

"The Great Spirit protects that man [pointing at Washington], and guides his destinies—he will become the chief of nations, and a people yet unborn will hail him as the founder of a mighty empire. I am come to pay homage to the man who is the particular favorite of Heaven, and who can never die in battle."

It was during those battles that Washington emerged uninjured, but there were some close calls. His coat was pierced by four bullets, and two horses were shot from beneath him.

As time has progressed, it has become more expensive for politicians to get elected to public office. One of the early candidates who understood the cost of an election was George Washington.

During his 1758 campaign for the House of Burgesses, Washington hosted a political event known as "Swilling the Planters with Bumbo."

At the gathering, candidate George served 160 gallons of rum to about four hundred guests. Most were wealthy, white landowners, like himself, so everyone was quite comfortable.

On December 16, 1773, members of a group calling themselves the "Sons of Liberty," disguised as Indians, carried out the famous Boston Tea Party. They did it by throwing cases of taxed tea into Boston Harbor from the decks of three ships.

Among the fifty-eight protesters was a member of the Sons of Liberty who was also disguised as an Indian but became well known for his actions years later. His name was Paul Revere.

Bostonians enjoyed the Tea Party so much that they repeated the protest in the spring. On March 7, 1774, once again disguised as Indians, a group of patriots tossed sixteen chests of tea from British merchant Davison, Newman & Co. into Boston Harbor from the deck of the merchant ship *Fortune*.

John Kendrick was one of the participating patriots at the first Boston Tea Party. He went on to serve in the Continental Navy, and when the war was over, he returned to his original profession of whaling.

After the Revolution, Kendrick arrived in Fairhaven (now Honolulu) on December 3, 1794. Two other British ships were also there: the *Jackal* and the *Prince Lee Boo*.

When Oahu was invaded by natives from another island, the ships' captains sent men to successfully aid in the defense of the locals.

To celebrate their victory, on the morning of December 12, 1794, Kendrick's ship the *Lady Washington* fired a thirteen-gun salute, to which the *Jackal* answered with a return blast. But one of the *Jackal*'s cannons was loaded with live ammunition and the shot smashed into the American ship, killing Captain Kendrick on deck along with several other men.

The fifty-five-year-old had survived the naval battles of the Revolutionary War but was eventually killed at sea during peacetime by the cannon of a British ship.

Freedom: What a Revolutionary Idea!

War is when the government tells you who the bad guy is. Revolution is when you decide that for yourself.

—Unknown

*P*atrick Henry gave the well-known speech that included the famous line "Give me liberty or give me death."

But the inspirational Founding Father also forgave his enemies. During his second stint as Virginia's governor, Henry supported amnesty for British Tories after the war was over.

The Continental Army was in desperate need of soldiers. But even with that, commander in chief George Washington took an unprecedented step by insisting that no recruit could join the army until he was vaccinated against smallpox. Washington had suffered from the disease when he was nineteen years old and understood that an outbreak could decimate his forces.

The midnight ride of Paul Revere took place at the beginning of the American Revolution. But who knew that the famous rider didn't own a horse?

Revere had to borrow a steed to make the historic jaunt. It was a Narragansett Pacer named Brown Betty, a small chestnut mare. The animal was loaned at the request of Deacon John Larkin, an ordained minister of the First Congregational Church in Charlestown, Massachusetts.

Before Revere could reach Concord, the horse was confiscated by British troops and never returned to its owner.

The signals for Paul Revere's midnight ride were sent to him by lanterns hung in the steeple of Boston's Old North Church.

The building survived the American Revolution, but years later it took a beating from Mother Nature. The original historic steeple was destroyed by a storm in 1804 and had to be replaced. Then on August 31, 1954, the restored tower was toppled by Hurricane Carol.

Many have heard the well-known poem "The Midnight Ride of Paul Revere" by the renowned poet Henry Wadsworth Longfellow.

What the author failed to mention was that there were several other riders who were also alerting the public about the impending arrival of the British. Among those was twenty-five-year-old mail carrier Israel Bissell.

On April 19, 1775, he rode from Watertown, Massachusetts, the same day that Paul Revere and William Dawes made their historic treks. Bissell escaped capture and galloped his mount the thirty miles to Worcester in just two hours. It was a remarkable feat as the journey was considered a two-day ride.

In Worcester, his horse collapsed and died of exhaustion. Bissell climbed aboard another mount and continued to ride for a total of 345 miles in five days, averaging 69 miles a day. His original goal was to reach Connecticut but he rode on to New York City and then to Trenton, New Jersey, before finally arriving in Philadelphia, where the Continental Congress was meeting.

There was also a sixteen-year-old girl named Sybil Ludington who rode over forty miles in just six hours as the British neared Danbury, Connecticut. Another dramatic gallop took place on July 1, 1776, when Caesar Rodney of Delaware rode seventy miles through a thunderstorm to Philadelphia. He arrived just in time to join the other members of the Continental Congress to vote in favor of the resolution for independence.

However, there are no famous poems about any of the other riders of history. By the way, Craigie House in Cambridge, the home of Henry Wadsworth Longfellow, was among the first homes in America to have indoor plumbing, installed shortly after his marriage in 1843.

The British wore bright red jackets as part of their military attire, which earned them the nickname "redcoats," while the Americans were clad in blue uniform jackets.

The Continental Army wore blue due to the fact that indigo was one of the major cash crops grown in the South, thus it was one of the only colors that was readily available to the colonists.

The first two battles of the American Revolution were fought at Lexington and Concord. British General Thomas Gage, who was in Boston, was ordered to seize a cache of arms in Concord, a small town fifteen miles away and, if possible, capture the outspoken American patriots John Hancock and Samuel Adams.

How badly did Gage want the patriot pair? He issued a proclamation granting a general pardon to all who would demonstrate loyalty to the British crown except for Adams and Hancock. But his effort was futile as the wanted duo remained free.

General Israel Putnam became best known at the Battle of Bunker Hill when he told his troops, "Don't fire until you see the whites of their eyes."

Putnam was also a veteran of the French and Indian War, where he was scalped in combat. He is the only American general to suffer such a personal attack during a battle and survive.

America's first submarine, the *Turtle*, was used in the Revolutionary War. George Washington was a major proponent of submarine warfare but couldn't get Congress to appropriate funds for its further development.

Thomas Paine wrote *Common Sense* in 1776 to persuade the colonists to fight for their independence. But the story of the well-known writer began in England.

In September 1774, Paine met Benjamin Franklin in London who advised him to emigrate to the British colonies in America and who wrote letters of recommendation on his behalf. Paine left England in October, arriving in Philadelphia on November 30. Just before he departed, Thomas and his second wife (with whom he did not get along) were legally separated.

The soon-to-be colonist barely survived the transatlantic voyage. The drinking water on the ship was so bad that typhoid fever killed five passengers, and Paine was too ill to leave his cabin when he arrived in Philadelphia. Franklin's personal physician, Dr. John Kearsley, met the ship upon arrival and carried him off. It took the doctor six weeks to nurse the future patriot author back to health.

As commander of the Continental Army, George Washington was in constant danger. On June 28, 1776, Thomas Hickey became the first American soldier to be executed. He had plotted to have Washington kidnapped.

Hickey was court-martialed and found guilty of mutiny and sedition. A crowd of twenty thousand witnessed his hanging at Grand and Chrystie streets in New York City. That's about the same number of spectators that gather today just a few blocks away for a sold-out event at Madison Square Garden.

The Declaration of Independence was a written statement adopted by the Continental Congress on July 4, 1776, which announced that the thirteen American colonies, then at war with Great Britain, had become independent states and were no longer a part of the British Empire.

The document was engrossed on parchment, which is an animal skin specially treated with lime and stretched to create a strong, long-lasting writing support.

Even with that, the Declaration underwent a conservation treatment in 1942 while it resided at Fort Knox during World War II.

Many people have seen a copy of the Declaration of Independence. What they may not have noticed is that there is a blank space between the signatures of Edward Rutledge and Thomas Heyward Jr. It was intended for the signature of Thomas Lynch Sr., who never signed the historic document.

Lynch Sr. fell ill and died in December 1776. His son, Thomas Lynch Jr., joined Arthur Middleton, Rutledge, and Heyward Jr. as the signers from South Carolina. But after that, bad luck followed the foursome.

In 1779, Lynch Jr. and his wife were lost at sea. The following year, Rutledge, Heyward, and Middleton were all captured while defending Charleston and imprisoned in Florida.

Thomas Jefferson wrote most of the Declaration of Independence in Philadelphia. The patriot author did a great deal of his composing at Graff House where he resided and complained about the houseflies from a stable that was located across the street while he was putting pen to paper.

In the years that followed, the place where Jefferson drafted the famous document became a print shop and later a Tom Thumb Diner. Today, it's a part of Philadelphia's Independence National Historical Park.

The events surrounding the Declaration of Independence took place on July 4, 1776. But the day had to be one of mixed emotions for General George Washington. On that date, exactly twenty-two years earlier in 1754, the then strapping, twenty-two-year-old militia commander had surrendered to an enemy for the first and only time in his career.

That low point came at the battle of Fort Necessity during the French and Indian War. As part of the surrender, Washington was forced by the French to sign a murder confession.

The Founding Fathers approved the Declaration of Independence on July 4, 1776, at Philadelphia's Independence Hall. But because of the heat and humidity, the windows of the famous meeting place were open. As delegates debated the details of the historic document, a swarm of horseflies invaded the hall.

That concluded the debate as a motion was quickly made and seconded to approve Thomas Jefferson's work. The motion passed without delay as the delegates rapidly made their way outside to avoid the pesky non-British intruders.

It's likely that when students are studying the American Revolution, on the page that highlights Washington troops crossing the Delaware, they see the painting illustrated in figure 2.1.

It is the famous work *Washington Crossing the Delaware*, by Emanuel Leutze.

The original hangs in the Metropolitan Museum of Art in New York City. It is a wonderful depiction of the Continental Army's journey to Trenton, but there are a few things about the depiction that are usually not mentioned. Leutze (1816–1868) was born in Germany and painted the piece in 1851 in Dusseldorf, using the Rhine River as his model for the Delaware.

The actual crossing was done in the dead of night, during a driving snowstorm, and was completed around three in the morning. But the glorification of the general leading his troops requires a lighted sky spotlighting his impressive figure.

The flag shown in the picture did not exist at the time of the historic crossing. It was not adopted until June 14, 1777, some six months later. But it's still a nice painting.

Figure 2.1 *Washington Crossing the Delaware* . . . made in Germany! *Emanuel Leutze*

George Washington and his troops crossed the Delaware on Christmas night 1776 and attacked the enemy at Trenton, New Jersey, the following morning. But was a chess game the key to the mission's success?

A British informant sent a small boy to Colonel Gottlieb (Johann) Rall with a message that Washington's troops were about to cross the Delaware River. But the colonel was so engrossed in a Christmas chess game that he put the unopened note in his pocket and continued to play the pieces on the board.

Rall had a force of 1,500 Hessians (Germans) stationed in Trenton, but most were busy celebrating the holiday. Besides, no one believed that the outmanned and under-supplied American troops would dare stage an attack during the Christmas holiday while ravaged by inclement weather.

Washington tried to cross the river at three locations but couldn't find a suitable docking area. He eventually chose a spot nine miles away from Trenton and marched his soldiers in the darkness through sleet and rain. The crossing took ten hours and involved 2,400 troops. At around 8:00 am on the day after Christmas, the commander attacked Trenton in broad daylight as most of the enemy slept inside their quarters.

Rall and forty men were killed as the others surrendered. The note of warning which Rall had ignored because he was busy playing chess was found as the German officer lay mortally wounded after being shot from his horse.

George Washington crossed the Delaware and eventually became president of the United States. But there was a second future U.S. president among the soldiers who were headed to Trenton.

James Monroe served in the Continental Army from 1776 to 1778 and rose to the rank of major. He crossed the Delaware with Washington and is depicted in Leutze's painting as the soldier holding the American flag.

Monroe was wounded at the Battle of Trenton and nearly died from his injuries as a bullet grazed the left side of his chest then hit his shoulder and injured the major artery bringing blood to the arm, which bled profusely.

Monroe's life was probably saved by a doctor who stopped the bleeding by sticking his index finger into the wound and applying pressure to the artery. Surgeons later attempted to remove the bullet but could not find it. Monroe recovered from the wound in eleven weeks but carried the bullet in his shoulder the rest of his life.

Among the other famous individuals in the boats were a future chief justice of the United States Supreme Court (John Marshall), a future vice president (Aaron Burr), and a future secretary of the treasury (Alexander Hamilton).

At that juncture, Burr and Hamilton were shooting at the enemy and not at each other . . . yet.

The British defeated the Americans at the Battle of Brandywine Creek near Chadds Ford, Pennsylvania. On September 11, 1777, an army of 12,500 British troops that had recently landed at the northern end of the Chesapeake Bay marched through the Keystone State toward the patriot capital of Philadelphia.

Among the masses was Captain Patrick Ferguson, a thirty-three-year-old Scotsman who was reputed to be the redcoat's finest shot. He commanded the British marksmen, who were equipped with fast-firing, breech-loading rifles of Ferguson's own design.

They were on the lookout for American officers, and the sharpshooting captain soon had one in his sights. Ferguson called out, leveling his rifle toward the target, but the American only gave a simple glance back before slowly riding away.

The following day, after being seriously wounded, Ferguson learned that the American officer whom he let ride off was most likely General George Washington. "I could have lodged half a dozen balls in or about him, before he was out of my reach," Ferguson recalled. "But it was not pleasant to fire at the back of an unoffending individual, who was acquitting himself very coolly of his duty—so I let him alone."

But the generosity would not be reciprocated. Three years later, Ferguson was killed atop his horse by a gunshot wound delivered by a member of General Washington's Continental Army at the Battle of Kings Mountain in South Carolina.

Food was scarce for George Washington's troops during the winter of 1777–1778 at Valley Forge. But when the soldiers of the Continental Army were starving to death at their encampment, it was a band of Oneida Indians who carried six hundred bushels of corn to sustain them. The Oneida had walked some four hundred miles from their home in central New York to help the troops.

One of those Oneida was a woman by the name of Polly Cooper. She showed the soldiers how to get the most value out of their preparation of the corn. For this she was awarded a shawl by Martha Washington which is still in the possession of her family and occasionally displayed by the Oneida Nation.

Congress sent John Adams to France in 1778 to aid in negotiating an alliance. But the voyage, which was expected to be a pleasant crossing, included an unpleasant experience.

While aboard the Europe-bound frigate *Boston*, Adams helped hold down the ship's 1st lieutenant William Barron as the vessel's surgeon amputated Barron's right leg below the knee. His gun had burst while he was firing a warning shot to halt a French brig. The officer died a few days later.

Soldiers on both sides were captured and taken as prisoners of war during the American Revolution. Among that group was a future U.S. president. In 1780, thirteen-year-old Andrew Jackson had joined a local regiment as a courier. However, he and his brother Robert were gathered up by the British and held, nearly starving to death during captivity.

On one occasion when young Andrew refused to clean the boots of a British officer, the irate redcoat slashed at him with a sword, giving Andrew scars on his left hand and head, as well as an intense hatred for the British. While imprisoned, the brothers contracted smallpox. Robert died just a few days after their mother had secured their release.

But he wasn't the family's only loss. On June 20, 1779, Jackson's older brother Hugh died of heat stroke after the Battle of Stono Ferry, South Carolina. Jackson's entire immediate family eventually died from war-related hardships which he blamed on the British and never forgot.

These events might explain why Old Hickory went after the Brits with such ferocity as a U.S. general during the War of 1812.

The British were engaged in hostilities with the United States, but how many other countries was England fighting during the American War for Independence?

By 1780, the redcoats were not only battling the Continentals and their ally France, but also Spain, the Netherlands, and the Kingdom of Mysore in India. The other conflicts were not all related to American independence, but they did keep the British busy on many fronts, which proved to be an asset to the U.S. cause.

John Paul Jones was the first great naval hero in the history of the United States. After the American Revolution, he became a rear admiral in the Russian Navy in their war against the Turks. Following his service in 1790, the former Revolutionary War hero retired to Paris, where he died two years later.

Jones was buried at Saint Louis Cemetery in Paris, but the property was sold a few years later and became unkempt. In 1905, his remains were identified by U.S. Ambassador to France General Horace Porter, who had searched for six years to track down the body.

Jones's remains were returned to the United States aboard the USS *Brooklyn* with full military honors. In April 1906, he was reburied on the grounds of the U.S. Naval Academy where among those delivering tributes was President Theodore Roosevelt.

His final internment came seven years later when Jones's remains were moved to a crypt at the naval academy chapel.

There was a smallpox outbreak during the Revolutionary War. At least 130,000 North Americans died during the period.

Because of the possible spread of the illness, General George Washington decreed that letters from Boston had to be dipped in vinegar to kill any germs. The general had recalled that in 1763, during the French and Indian War, the British had deliberately infected natives who were threatening the safety of Fort Pitt.

Washington believed evidence presented to him during the Revolution proved that the British were deliberately spreading smallpox to American troops.

Thomas Jefferson was one of America's Founding Fathers. As such, he was always a target for the British troops.

Figure 2.2 Revolutionary War hero John Paul Jones heads for his final resting place at the U.S. Naval Academy after he died 121 years earlier. *C. R. Miller*

On June 3, 1781, a plot to kidnap Jefferson was foiled by twenty-seven-year-old Captain Jack Jouett of the Virginia Militia. He had overheard the details from soldiers of the famed British colonel Banastre Tarleton at Louisa's Cuckoo Tavern while they discussed the plan. The mission was to capture Jefferson, who was the governor of Virginia, along with other members of the state legislature.

After catching details of the scheme, Jouett dashed out and rode forty miles through the night to Monticello in order to warn Jefferson, which allowed the statesman time to escape to safety. Tarleton, clad in his distinctive green uniform, made his way to Charlottesville a few hours later. However, the British troops were too late, arriving at Monticello just after Jefferson had escaped.

While their primary target was nowhere to be found, Tarleton's Green Dragoons did not come away empty handed. They captured a few legislators along with the celebrated trailblazer Daniel Boone. The British released them on parole several days later.

The final major battle of the American Revolution took place at Yorktown, Virginia. General George Washington fired the first cannon into the town to begin the battle. It turned out to be a good omen.

The cannonball went straight through the dining-room window of British headquarters and blew up a general and his officers who were just sitting down to dinner. Nice shot, George.

British General Charles Cornwallis surrendered on October 19, 1781, following the Battle of Yorktown, which effectively ended the war.

This humiliating defeat was not the end of Cornwallis's career, however. He went on to become governor general of India (1786–1794) and viceroy of Ireland (1798–1801).

The British surrendered to the United States during an elaborate ceremony. Everyone was present for the ritual except for one of the primary participants—redcoat commander Charles Cornwallis.

The British leader did not attend the formal surrender, saying that he was not feeling well. His substitute, General Charles O'Hara, first tried to offer his sword to the Comte de Rochambeau, figuring it was less of a disgrace to give in to the redcoats' long-time enemy—the French. But Rochambeau directed the British officer to General Washington, who in turn pointed him to his subordinate Major General Benjamin Lincoln (not related to the sixteenth president).

To this day, no one who is quite sure what became of that famous sword of surrender. Some say that General Lincoln allowed O'Hara to retain the weapon while others claim that it is on display somewhere inside the White House.

During the ceremony a British band played the song "The World Turned Upside Down." Upon hearing that, American general the Marquis de Lafayette had his musicians play "Yankee Doodle" to drown out the tune of the defeated troops.

Earlier, Lord Cornwallis had contacted General Henry Clinton asking him to send help to Yorktown, and he did, but it was five days after the surrender.

As in all wars, captured soldiers were sent to prison camps. During the American Revolution, some prisoners of war were put aboard prison ships. One of the most notorious was the *Jersey*. It was a former hospital vessel that was in poor condition and anchored in New York's East River.

The boat was used by the British to hold captured American soldiers. The *Jersey* was overcrowded and filthy. By war's end, it was estimated that over ten thousand prisoners of war died on prison ships—a higher number than those killed in individual battles.

The Treaty of Paris of 1783 formally acknowledged the United States as a free and independent nation. That one came after the Treaty of Paris of 1763, which ended the French and Indian War.

And that wasn't the end of it as there were many more treaties of Paris. The others included treaties in 1814—the first abduction of Napoleon; 1815—the end of Napoleon's return; 1856—the end of the Crimean War; 1898—the end of the Spanish-American War; 1919 and 1920—the end of World War I; 1947—the end of World War II; and 1968—the end of the war in Vietnam.

So the next time that someone mentions the "Treaty of Paris," you can ask, "Which one?"

The survivors of the Revolutionary War enjoyed the distinction of being the first citizens of the new country that they had helped to create.

They included Daniel Frederick Bakeman, who may have been the last surviving veteran of the War for American Independence. He was born on October 10, 1759, and he died on April 5, 1869—four years after the conclusion of the Civil War.

The last veteran of the American Revolution is buried in an appropriate location—Freedom, New York.

• 3 •

Welcome to the New Nation

> We are all born ignorant, but one must work hard to remain stupid.
>
> —Benjamin Franklin

*D*uring the eighteenth century, the ultimate punishment for a crime, be the convicted a man or a woman, was to be hanged. On January 3, 1786, twenty-seven-year old-Elizabeth Wilson was scheduled to be executed in Chester, Pennsylvania, for killing her two out-of-wedlock infant children.

But many of the locals believed that she was innocent, including the sheriff, who thought that she would be pardoned. However, when there was no word, the proceedings got underway. At noon, Wilson was hanged from the back of a cart at the intersection of Edgmont and Providence avenues.

After it was over, a rider galloped onto the scene with a document from Philadelphia. Elizabeth had been granted a reprieve, but it arrived twenty-three minutes too late. The stay had been issued by the Supreme Executive Council of the Commonwealth of Pennsylvania and its president, Benjamin Franklin.

Before they each became president, John Adams was minister to Britain and Thomas Jefferson served as minister to France.

In April 1786, the American statesmen became common sightseers and visited William Shakespeare's birthplace at Stratford-upon-Avon. But when they arrived at the historic dwelling, they proceeded to act more like undisciplined tourists rather than dignitaries as they took as souvenirs a few wooden chips that they had cut from one of Shakespeare's chairs.

21

In 1787 the Constitutional Convention took place in Philadelphia, but there was another historic event occurring just a few miles away from the assemblage that same year.

The first dinosaur fossil found in the United States was discovered by Dr. Caspar Wistar in Gloucester County, New Jersey. It was a thigh bone that has since been lost, but more fossils were later found in the area.

Wistar was a distinguished Philadelphia physician. He and Thomas Jefferson were friends and had worked together on a collection and identification of the bones of the megalonyx (giant ground sloth), as well as on several other scientific projects.

Along with building a new nation, the third president had a serious interest in prehistoric studies and fossils.

Philadelphia's Independence Hall was where the Declaration of Independence was adopted. It was there that the Constitution of the United States was debated, drafted, and signed. It is truly a place where history was made.

It is not as well known that Pennsylvania delegate and practical joker Benjamin Franklin would occasionally trip other delegates from his aisle seat. During the nineteenth century, this historical landmark went to the dogs as its basement served as the city's municipal pound for lost canines.

George Washington was sworn in as the nation's first president on April 30, 1789. But there was another event taking place south of the inauguration in New York City.

On June 14, Elijah Craig, a Baptist minister, founded the first bourbon whiskey distillery in the president's home state of Virginia (in the area that would later become Kentucky). It was made from corn and some of it probably made its way north to the politicians of the new nation.

Many Americans enjoy eating pasta. During his tenure as American ambassador to France, Thomas Jefferson developed an appetite for the great foods of Europe.

In 1789 on his return home, he brought the first "macaroni" maker to America. As was often the case, Jefferson's inventive nature took over and led him to create his own version of a pasta-making machine.

Though Jefferson had a personal taste for pasta, it was first produced commercially in the United States in 1848 by Frenchman Antoine Zerega in Brooklyn, New York.

In 1791, a decade after the American Revolution ended, the federal city was incorporated into the District of Columbia.

This agreement wasn't struck in some grand meeting room or palace. The deal was reached at Suter's Tavern, which was located in the federal city and was a favorite watering hole of George Washington and other notables.

Before becoming president, Thomas Jefferson served as secretary of state. He was always interested in architecture, having designed his sprawling estate at Monticello along with the first buildings at the University of Virginia.

In 1792, Jefferson entered a competition to design the White House, submitting his sketches under a pseudonym—A. Z. His participation was unknown until it was uncovered in the 1930s.

Even though Jefferson's covert effort was commendable, the winner of the contest was a well-known Irish-born architect, James Hoban of South Carolina.

Kentucky became the nation's fifteenth state in 1792. It was also the first to be located on the western frontier. One of the state's favorite sons is Fred Vinson, who was born in 1890 in the front part of the building that housed the Lawrence County Jail in the town of Louisa.

His birthplace wasn't such because his mother was a criminal; it was due to the fact that his father served as the Lawrence County jailer. Perhaps there was an omen in Fred's birthplace being inside a facility that enforced the law.

When Fred grew up, he became chief justice of the Supreme Court.

Before the creation of Washington, D.C., Philadelphia served as the capital city of the United States.

But when the Yellow Fever Epidemic of 1793 struck the City of Brotherly Love, President Washington and his cabinet fled the capital ten miles to the northwest to Germantown. From November 16 to November 30, Washington lived in the historic Deshler-Morris House, which is sometimes referred to as the "Germantown White House."

In the presidential election of 1796, John Adams defeated Thomas Jefferson. It was also the only time in U.S. history when two brothers got electoral votes for president in the same election.

Federalist Party candidates Charles Pinckney and his younger brother Thomas (both from South Carolina) each received electoral votes, but Adams won the presidency with seventy-one ballots. Charles earned fifty-nine electors (good for third place behind runner-up Jefferson), while Thomas Pinckney got one.

The minimum-age requirement to become a member of the House of Representatives is twenty-five years old. William Charles Cole Claiborne was born in 1775 (the exact date remains questionable) and was elected from Tennessee in 1796 then reelected in 1798, in spite of the fact that he was still under the constitutional age requirement of twenty-five years.

Chalk that one up to errors of the records administrator in Sussex County, Virginia, where Claiborne was born.

John Adams's term as president began in 1797 and ended in 1801. But it wasn't all work and no play for the nation's second chief executive.

Beginning in 1798, Adams resided for seven months at his farm in Quincy, Massachusetts. Much of his time was spent tending to his ill wife, Abigail. Some believed the rumors that he had abdicated, but the young nation's second president returned to Philadelphia in November.

Meanwhile, Vice President Thomas Jefferson was also unavailable, spending ten months away from the capital. He had begun rebuilding his Monticello estate in 1796 and was devoted to overseeing the task. It was a project that continued until 1809.

So who was actually running the government during the Adams administration? Most of the time, it was the president pro tempore, Senator William Bingham of Pennsylvania.

The White House was designed by architect James Hoban. But what served as the prototype for the executive mansion?

Hoban was an Irish immigrant so he modeled his design after that of Leinster House in Dublin. The building was completed in 1748 and served as the residence of the Duke of Leinster. Since 1922 it has been the seat of both houses of the Irish parliament.

While Hoban used the Irish structure as his guide, it was George Washington who wanted the newly built residence constructed of stone to symbolize the permanence of the nation.

Like the White House, the U.S. Capitol first opened in 1800. But the building's grand structure wasn't designed by an architect. Its creator was Dr. William Thornton, a British subject who had been born in the Virgin Islands. He was the son of wealthy sugar planters from the Caribbean island of Tortola and had done his medical training in London and Scotland.

He was not a trained builder, but rather his knowledge of architecture came from books which he had read.

Figure 3.1 Dublin's Leinster House served as James Hoban's model for his design of the White House. *James Malton*

Most are aware that Thomas Jefferson was a man of many talents. He was an architect and designed his beautiful estate at Monticello, Virginia.

What many don't know was that the dome on Jefferson's home concealed a billiard room. In that era, billiards were illegal in Virginia.

Newspapers have a long history of endorsing political candidates, but the *Hartford Courant* opposed the presidential campaign of Thomas Jefferson in 1800. However, there were no hard feelings as in 1993 the paper's editors offered a formal apology for their decision.

Alexander Hamilton was the first secretary of the treasury, and he established the country's banking system. He also founded the *New York Post* in 1801, which is now the thirteenth-oldest newspaper published in the United States and is generally acknowledged as the oldest to have been produced continually as a daily.

Unfortunately for Hamilton, he was unable to reap the rewards of his business venture. When he died in 1804 during that famous duel with Aaron Burr, the coauthor of the *Federalist Papers* was $55,000 in debt. But over the years, Hamilton's former enterprise grew, and in 1976 the *Post* was sold for $30 million.

Thomas Jefferson was sworn in for his first term as president on March 4, 1801, succeeding John Adams.

The outgoing president was still upset over his electoral loss. He resented that, unlike his predecessor George Washington, the voters had cast him aside without an opportunity to serve a second term.

It was a difficult transition period for the nation's second president. One month after Adams lost the election, his son Charles, only thirty years old, died from the ravages of alcoholism. In mid-February 1801, First Lady Abigail Adams made an early departure for the family home in Quincy, Massachusetts. The angry spouse believed that God had punished the United States "for our sins and transgressions" by allowing Jefferson to defeat her husband in the election.

Before he left the White House for the last time, Adam's final act in office was to send his nomination to the Senate for John Marshall to become chief justice of the Supreme Court.

At 4:00 am on inauguration day, the president's carriage quietly pulled away from the mansion and into the darkness. Thomas Jefferson was sworn-in without Adams being present at the ceremony.

In 1801, Thomas Jefferson took the oath as the nation's third president. But his inauguration didn't resemble the pageantry that would be displayed for his successors. Jefferson walked from Conrad and McMunn's boarding house to the still-unfinished Capitol Building to be sworn-in at noon. After that, he strolled back to the lodging establishment in time for an unceremonious inaugural lunch which he partook with his fellow boarders.

When he arrived, Jefferson's usual seat was taken by a guest so the new commander in chief stood and waited patiently until a female diner volunteered her chair.

Thomas Jefferson was a man who believed in freedom and independence and those ideals carried over to other aspects of his life. When he entered the White House in March of 1801, it was still a work in progress. Among the first acts of the new president was to have proper water closets (early toilets) built on the upper floor to replace the outdoor privy (aka, outhouse).

After Benedict Arnold left America, he never returned. Upon his death in 1801, the nation's most infamous traitor was buried in the crypt at St. Mary's Church Battersea in London wearing his old uniform from the Continental Army.

In 1804, Aaron Burr killed Alexander Hamilton in the nation's most celebrated duel. But for many who heard the news about the showdown, it must have seemed like déjà vu.

Back on November 20, 1801, Hamilton's nineteen-year-old son Philip had come to his father's defense against George I. Eacker, a twenty-seven-year-old lawyer. Eacker had given a speech that was critical of the nation's first secretary of the treasury.

Three days later, the two men faced each other at the dueling site of Weehawken, New Jersey, just across the Hudson River from New York City. The location had been chosen because New York had banned dueling.

As each man fired, young Hamilton was mortally wounded while Eacker was uninjured. Philip died the following day. His sister Angelica suffered a nervous breakdown from which she never recovered.

Three years later, Philip's father died on the same dueling grounds. He and Burr used the very same pistols that Philip Hamilton and George Eacker had employed in their clash.

The weapons are on display on the 50th floor of the J.P. Morgan Chase & Co. Building in New York City, the place where dueling had been banned.

Meriwether Lewis and William Clark brought maps to Thomas Jefferson that they had drawn up during their exploration of the Louisiana Territory. But those weren't the only items secured by the frontiersmen.

They presented the nation's chief executive with some grizzly bear cubs, which Jefferson kept as pets. He was often seen walking them around the grounds of the White House.

Lewis and Clark were sent by Thomas Jefferson to map the Louisiana Territory which had been bought from France. But that was only part of the reason for the expedition.

In 1781, General George Rogers Clark (William's big brother) had sent a fossilized tooth from Big Bone Lick, Kentucky, to the then Virginia governor. It stirred Jefferson's quest to find a living mammoth and confirm his belief of a prehistoric westward migration.

When Congress approved the Corps of Discovery funding in February 1803, it opened the door for Jefferson to conduct a paleontological expedition. By the spring of 1804, the explorers had gathered a large shipment of fossils from Big Bone Lick, which were crated and sent down the Mississippi River, but eventually they were lost when the boat transporting the valuable cargo sank near Natchez.

Undaunted by the unfortunate accident, the determined Jefferson, who was now in his second term, sent William Clark back to Big Bone Lick in

1807. A year later, the president finally received his long-awaited shipment of fossils from the location. He unpacked three hundred specimens and arranged them on the floor in a room of the White House where he studied them as if he were in a museum.

Meriwether Lewis and William Clark formed the most famous exploration team in American history. But many are unaware of the mysterious questions surrounding Lewis's death.

On September 3, 1809, Meriwether Lewis set out for Washington, D.C., where he hoped to resolve issues regarding the denied payment of drafts he had drawn against the War Department while serving as the first American governor of the Louisiana Territory.

On October 10, 1809, he stopped for the night at the Grinder House, an inn on the Natchez Trace located about seventy miles from Nashville, Tennessee. After he excused himself from dinner, the former trailblazer went to his room.

At some point in the night, Mrs. Grinder heard multiple gunshots and what she believed was someone asking for help. But in a strange happenstance, she took no action.

The next morning she sent Lewis's servants for him, and they found the explorer on the floor bleeding but still alive. His wounds proved severe, however, and he died a few hours later.

When Clark and President Thomas Jefferson were informed of Lewis's death, both accepted it as a suicide, but his family contended it was murder. To this day, the exact cause of his death has never been resolved.

In 1806 Zebulon Pike discovered a mountain in Colorado which became known as Pike's Peak. After his discovery, he attempted to climb the ridge but failed.

It wasn't a large mountain that killed Pike, however, but rather a stone. He died during the War of 1812 when a piece of rock fell on his back as the British garrison retreated after setting fire to an arsenal during the Battle of York (now Toronto), Canada.

In September 1819, his daughter Clarissa married John Symmes Harrison, the son of President William Henry Harrison.

In 1810, John Jacob Astor's Pacific Fur Company established Fort Astoria (in present-day Oregon) as its primary fur-trading post in the Northwest. It was the first permanent U.S. settlement on the Pacific coast.

When Astor died in 1848, according to his will he bequeathed $30,000 to former secretary of the treasury Alexander Hamilton. Unfortunately for the cabinet member, who could have used the cash, he had been killed in his famous duel with Aaron Burr forty-four years earlier and was in debt when he died. Thus the funds reverted to Astor's estate.

The luck of Astor's great grandson, John Jacob Astor IV, wasn't much better than Hamilton's. He was among those who perished aboard the *Titanic* in 1912.

James Madison was the fourth president of the United States. Although his writings made him a person of stature, the fact was that he was the shortest president at 5 feet 4 inches and weighing in at only one hundred pounds.

Madison invited Jefferson to ride with him in his carriage to the Capitol for his swearing-in. But the outgoing president declined, saying he did not want to be a distraction. Jefferson was present when Madison took the oath, but he sat with the citizens in the audience and not on stage.

Dolley Madison was the wife of the nation's fourth president. But few recall that the First Lady had a son from her previous marriage.

John Payne Todd earned a reputation in the capital city as a playboy. The problem became so serious that President Madison made an effort to rectify the source of his family's embarrassment by sending his stepson to St. Petersburg, Russia, as an attaché with the American diplomatic delegation. But the plan backfired as Todd continued to let the good times roll in Europe, running up huge bills on the president's tab.

James Madison died in 1836. After his death, Dolley was forced to sell off much of his property, including the estate at Montpelier, because of the debt incurred by her irresponsible offspring.

Todd's party came to an end in 1852 when he died of typhoid fever.

In 1808, an American who called himself Adolphus Arnot left for Europe and lived there for the next four years. On May 4, 1812, a transatlantic sailing ship, the *Aurora*, reached Boston harbor, bringing him back to his home country.

The man was known to everyone on board except for the captain of the ship as "Mr. Adolphus Arnot." The captain knew the truth that the individual was actually the famous—and infamous—Aaron Burr.

Following his return, for awhile Burr used the surname "Edwards," his mother's maiden name, to avoid creditors.

• 4 •

The War of 1812 . . . and 1813 . . . and 1814 . . . and 1815

I have given two cousins to war and I stand ready to sacrifice my wife's brother.

—Artemus Ward, American General and Congressman

$\mathcal{A}$ second conflict between the Americans and British became known as the War of 1812. But there was a chance that this action could have been stopped before it began.

After more than half a year of deliberations and debate, Congress declared war on June 18, 1812, and President James Madison officially signed the document the following day. Two days earlier and unknown to the members of Congress, the British Parliament had repealed the controversial Orders in Council.

The Orders were a centerpiece of the problem between the nations because they required neutral ships to call at British ports or be subject to search and possible seizure by authorities. By the time the news of the rescission reached the United States, it was too late, and the long-time enemies were once again eye to eye on the battlefield.

There were many famous battles during the War of 1812. One of the lesser-known conflicts was the Battle at Lacolle Mill in Canada in 1813.

It was the most embarrassing clash of the war for the United States as a force of two hundred British soldiers turned back four thousand Americans.

The "Star-Spangled Banner" was written during the War of 1812. There was also another famous American symbol that was born during that era. The

31

figure was dressed in brilliant red, white, and blue clothing that included a top hat, and he had a white beard that was based on that of a real person.

During the War of 1812, U.S. troops stationed in New York were supplied meat from a purveyor named Sam Wilson. Troops affectionately referred to Wilson by his nickname—Uncle Sam—and though the "U.S." stamp on all the meat stood for "United States," it was not long before all federal troops referred to the supplies as coming from Uncle Sam.

The homes of many historic figures have been preserved for viewing by future generations. There were plans to do the same with the residence of Francis Scott Key. But Key's house is lost and no one can find it.

Built in 1803, the structure was located at 3516–3518 M Street NW in Washington, D.C. Key was residing there in 1814 when he headed to Baltimore and was later inspired to write the poem that would one day become "The Star Spangled Banner."

The government purchased the Key home in 1930, but during the Depression era, no effort was made to restore it, and the house eventually fell victim to the growth-and-construction boom of the post–World War II era. Once the house had been dismantled, Congress passed a bill that would finance the reassembly of the residence and donate it to the D.C. Historical Society.

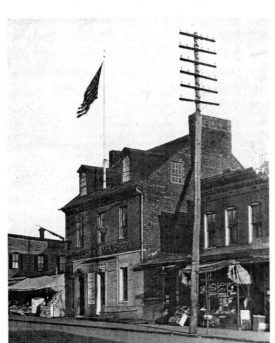

Figure 4.1 This picture was taken of Francis Scott Key's home in 1907. The dwelling disappeared forty years later. If you see it, call the U.S. government. *D.C. Public Library*

However, the bill was vetoed by President Harry Truman for budgetary reasons. Meanwhile the house, which was last seen in 1947, disappeared during roadway construction.

In 1814, British troops set fire to the White House and the Capitol Building. A little more than a year earlier, on April 27, 1813, American soldiers had set fire to the Parliament building in York (now Toronto) of Upper Canada. They also burned the governor's mansion. No doubt, the Brits believed that turnabout was fair play.

It also wasn't the last time that the executive mansion would be the victim of a fire. On Christmas Eve 1929, the Hoovers were hosting a gathering when smoke began filtering in from the West Wing. The cause was found to be an overheated flue in an open fireplace in Administrative Assistant Walter Newton's office in the northwest corner of the wing.

Fifteen firemen were injured fighting the blaze, but the White House was saved. Much of the West Wing had to be rebuilt.

Before British troops set fire to the White House during the War of 1812, First Lady Dolley Madison remained in the mansion after many of the government officials—including her own bodyguard—had already fled. She

Figure 4.2 Workers clean the West Wing after the White House fire of 1929. *White House Museum*

gathered valuables, documents, and other items of importance, including the famous full-length painting of George Washington by Gilbert Stuart, and was finally persuaded to leave just moments before invading soldiers entered the building.

Once inside, British troops found the dining hall set for a meal of forty people, so they elected to take a break. After eating all the food, they carried away souvenirs (e.g., one of the president's hats) and then set the building afire upon their departure.

A final note about the burning of the White House. The structure was once gray, the original color of its sandstone. After the War of 1812, the outside walls were painted white to hide the smoke stains.

The British occupied Washington, D.C., during the War of 1812. But it wasn't American troops who finally pushed out the redcoats; it was Mother Nature. Less than a day after the attack began, a hurricane which included a tornado passed through the nation's capital, killing more British soldiers than did American guns. The winds tossed the enemy cannons as if they were toys and the torrential rains acted as an extinguisher, putting out fires.

The storm forced the attackers to return to their ships, many of which were badly damaged by the elements, making their actual occupation of the nation's capital only a duration of about twenty-six hours. President Madison and the rest of the government quickly returned to the city.

The White House went through a major renovation following the War of 1812. But there were discussions about making some major changes to the location of the structure.

Among the proposals was one to rebuild the executive mansion away from inland waterways to prevent a repeat of the assault it had suffered during the war. There was a suggestion, which was turned down, to rebuild the White House in Cincinnati, Ohio.

Prior to moving into their own building in 1935, the Supreme Court has convened in the U.S. Capitol since 1819. One can still see that there are bullet holes near the old Supreme Court chamber made by the British during their attack on the Capitol in 1814.

During the War of 1812, James Madison became the first president to issue a formal declaration of war. When the fighting began, the U.S. Navy consisted of sixteen ships—nine of which were frigates, and about 5,000 seamen. The British boasted a fleet of eighty-five ships and more than 100,000 naval personnel.

Madison believed that instead of building up the navy's forces, the United States should simply rent Portugal's fleet and sailors. The idea was tabled in December 1812 when Congress voted funds for the building of ten more warships.

The Battle of New Orleans made Andrew Jackson a national hero. But it was fought two weeks after the War of 1812 had ended and more than a month before the news of the war's conclusion had reached the citizens of Louisiana.

The Senate conducts its business in a room of the U.S. Capitol Building known as the Old Senate Chamber. The oldest of the Senate desks, forty-eight of them, were made by New York cabinetmaker Thomas Constantine in 1819. All of them remain in use in the Old Senate Chamber to this day.

The original pre-1819 Senate desks were burned during the War of 1812, when most of Washington, D.C., was set on fire by the British Army.

The War of 1812 marked the final major conflict between the United State and Great Britain, and Hiram Cronk was the last surviving veteran of the hostility. He was born on April 29, 1800, in Frankfort, New York.

At the age of fourteen, Cronk enlisted along with his father and two brothers to serve with the New York Volunteers in the defense of Sackett's Harbor. He was honorably discharged after just three months of active duty.

For his service, Cronk received a pension of $12 per month. In 1903, the U.S. Congress increased his monthly stipend to $25. He also received a special pension of $72 per month from the State of New York.

Cronk spent most of his life working as a shoemaker. He died on May 13, 1905, at the age of 105. His body was displayed in the main lobby of New York City Hall, where an estimated 25,000 people paid their respects. He is buried in Brooklyn, New York.

· 5 ·

1815–1861: Growing Pains

Now, I know what a statesman is; he's a dead politician. We need more statesman.

—Bob Edwards

$\mathscr{B}$oston is a city that is steeped in history. But on June 6–7, 1816, a significant storm hit northern New York and New England, with several localities recording six inches of snow. It is believed that the June 7 flurries that occurred in Boston were likely the latest seasonal instance of snowfall in the area's history.

James Monroe was our fifth president, and as the nation's leader, he was expected to conduct himself with a certain decorum, but that wasn't always the case. As an example, he once became so angry with William Crawford, the secretary of the treasury, that he threatened the cabinet member in the White House by brandishing a pair of fire tongs.

The two men had been discussing possible appointees for customs officers—a desired political post for many prospective government employees. Monroe took offense at Crawford's list of candidates, and the two were soon arguing.

The sixty-seven-year-old treasury secretary waved his walking cane at the president, who grabbed the tongs from the fireplace to defend himself. The ruckus was quickly quelled and Crawford left the executive mansion of his own accord, but the two never spoke again.

Some people fight with their in-laws, but they rarely end up in a war against them. President James Monroe was a veteran of the Continental Army and was wounded at the Battle of Trenton. But his father-in-law Lawrence Kortright was a captain in the British army and remained loyal to the king.

There is no record that the two faced each other on the battlefield. Kortright had been a wealthy Tory merchant from New York who saw most of his fortune confiscated during the Revolution.

British troops burned and did serious damage to the White House during the War of 1812. The mansion was still being rebuilt when James Monroe became president in 1817. On New Year's Day 1818, the president and his wife held a public reception marking its reopening.

Monroe sold his own furniture to the government because the presidential residence was almost empty when he moved in. The charred remains of the mansion's interior were used to fill a pit on the grounds where Monroe planted his vegetable garden.

In 1975, archaeologists unearthed the old pit when a new swimming pool was being dug. Among the items that were discovered were Native American artifacts dating back 10,000 to 20,000 years.

James Monroe was a war hero and is rated high among America's presidents. He was also $75,000 in debt when he left office. His wife had died the previous year (1830) and Monroe was also in poor health, forcing him to live with his daughter's family in New York City.

On July 4, 1831, the author of the Monroe Doctrine died a virtual pauper.

John Quincy Adams won the election of 1824—which was decided by the House of Representatives—over Andrew Jackson and Henry Clay.

But there was another candidate who appeared to be the favorite that year. Secretary of the Treasury William Crawford had strong support on many fronts but suffered a massive stroke in 1823, thus ending his chances to win the White House.

In the election of 1824, since no candidate had the necessary number of electoral votes, it was up to the House of Representatives to determine the winner.

The deciding vote in the House was cast by Rep. Stephen Van Rensselaer of New York. He was originally uncertain between Andrew Jackson and William Crawford.

Each state was entitled to a single vote, and New York's delegation seemed deadlocked between John Quincy Adams and Crawford. Adams needed to claim New York to win the election, which made Van Rensselaer the deciding vote to capture the Empire State. But the sixty-year-old Congressman roomed at a boarding house with Crawford loyalists Martin Van Buren and Louis McLane, and he was believed to be leaning toward their candidate.

On the morning of the critical vote, February 9, 1825, Van Rensselaer assured his friends that he would never vote for Adams over Crawford. But when he arrived at the Capitol, the New York representative was intercepted by the powerful duo of Daniel Webster and Speaker of the House Henry Clay, who whisked him into the Speaker's office for an arm-twisting session in support of Adams.

The meeting made the Congressman indecisive and unnerved him to the point that he forgot to bring his ballot when he entered the House chambers. Still unsure, he bowed his head to pray and then opened his eyes to see an Adams ballot on the floor at his feet.

Van Rensselaer dropped it in the box, giving New York's vote and the presidency to John Quincy Adams. Clay, who was sure that he had swayed the deciding vote, was selected as the new secretary of state. No doubt, it was all part of divine guidance.

John Quincy Adams was the son of the second president and became the nation's sixth chief executive. He also owned a pet alligator which he kept in the East Room of the White House. In 1843, Adams became the first president to be photographed (see figure 5.1).

John Quincy Adams took the oath to become the nation's sixth president on March 4, 1825. He did not want to involve the Bible in politics so he was sworn in with his hand on a book of law along with the Constitution.

When John Quincy took the oath, his father

Figure 5.1 John Quincy Adams was the first president to be photographed and he looks pretty happy about it! *Philip Hass*

John Adams was still alive at age ninety but due to failing health he didn't attend the inauguration. John Quincy's wife Louisa was ill and was also absent. That night, he went to the inaugural ball without her.

John Quincy Adams and his family moved into the White House in March 1825. But the Adams presidency was almost over before it began.

On June 13, 1825, long before the creation of the Secret Service, Antoine Giusta, the White House steward, accompanied the president on what was to have been a pleasant excursion on Tiber Creek, a tributary of the Potomac River.

The two men had a long history together. Adams hired Giusta as his valet after they met in Belgium in 1814. Giusta was a deserter from Napoleon's army and later married Mrs. Adam's maid. The two men set out in a canoe which was not in good condition and was soon taking on water.

When the wind began to kick up, the pair jumped into the water, losing their hold on the boat. They swam to safety on the shore.

Adams and Giusta each lost several items of clothing, as well as the canoe, but they returned to the White House unharmed.

It is not unusual today for female journalists to conduct interviews with major political figures. However, during the early days of our nation's history, this was not done until one morning on the banks of the Potomac River.

President John Quincy Adams regularly enjoyed skinny dipping in the Potomac. The first American professional female journalist, Anne Royall, found out about his early morning aquatic sessions. After being refused interviews with Adams many times, she went to the river, gathered his clothes and sat on them until she had her interview. Before this, no female had ever interviewed a president.

Those who have traveled to Boston may have eaten at the Union Oyster House, which bills itself as the oldest restaurant in "Beantown" and the oldest eatery in continuous service in the United States. It has been serving hungry diners since 1826. But some customers may not have been aware that there was some history that took place on the building's upper floors.

In 1771, as the colonies moved closer to revolution, printer Isaiah Thomas was publishing the *Massachusetts Spy*, long known as one of the oldest newspapers in the United States. Thomas was spreading the seeds of revolt from a room above the restaurant, which served as a dry goods store during that era.

In 1796, a future king of France lived on the second floor. Exiled from his country, he earned his living by teaching French to many of Boston's fashionable young ladies. Later the upstairs tenant Louis Philippe returned to his home country to serve as king from 1830 to 1848.

Thomas Jefferson was a very famous man when he died but he was also deeply in debt. A series of financial mistakes led to his undesired plight. Only Jefferson's public stature prevented creditors from seizing Monticello and selling it out from under him during his lifetime.

On the day of his passing, July 4, 1826, friends were soliciting money for his relief at a ceremony in the House of Representatives marking the fiftieth anniversary of the Declaration of Independence. According to John Quincy Adams, only four or five people at the gathering contributed to assist the former president.

In his will, Jefferson left Monticello to the United States to be used as a school for orphans of naval officers. Today it is one of Virginia's largest tourist attractions.

Andrew Jackson won the election of 1828. But on December 22, 1828, his wife Rachel died of a heart attack just a few weeks after his victory. She was buried on Christmas Eve in the white dress which she had purchased for her husband's inaugural ceremonies. The Jackson's daughter Emily served as White House hostess until her death from tuberculosis in 1836. During the last months of the administration, Sarah Yorke Jackson, wife of Andrew Jackson Jr., presided at the mansion as First Lady.

Some of the most famous graduates of West Point include Robert E. Lee, Ulysses S. Grant, George Armstrong Custer, Douglas MacArthur, and Dwight Eisenhower. However, it is widely unknown that author Edgar Allan Poe was once an army cadet at West Point. He dropped out in 1831 after just one year.

The "Bank War" of the 1830s was led by Andrew Jackson's vetoing of the charter renewal of the Second Bank of the United States. He believed that "some of the powers and privileges possessed by the existing bank are unauthorized by the Constitution," and he referred to the bank as a monopoly.

What the president didn't know was that he wasn't the only one who was in the middle of a "Bank War."

In 1831, Edward Smith became the first person to be indicted for bank robbery. He stole $245,000 from the City Bank on Wall Street in New York City. Smith was sentenced to five years hard labor on the rock pile at New York's Sing Sing Prison.

Before becoming president, Andrew Jackson had been involved in several confrontations.

In 1832, he had surgery to remove a bullet from his arm resulting from one of those disputes. On September 4, 1813 (during the War of 1812), the Benton brothers (Jesse and Thomas) arrived in Nashville where they ended up in gun battle with Jackson, John Coffee, and Stockley Hays (Rachel Jackson's nephew). All of them were U.S. Army officers.

Remarkably no one was killed, but Jackson's wounds soaked two mattresses with blood at the Nashville Inn. He was nearly dead—his left shoulder shattered by a slug and a ball embedded against the upper bone of that arm, both from Jesse Benton's pistol. The doctors declared for the amputation of the arm. But Jackson said, "I'll keep my arm." And he did.

Thomas Benton could have been killed by the gunfire had he not fallen down a flight of stairs during the brawl.

In January 1832, Dr. Thomas Harris, chief of the Navy's Bureau of Medicine, was summoned to the White House to remove the bullet. Without anesthesia, Jackson remained conscious throughout the painful operation.

Thomas Benton went on to be elected to the U.S. Senate from Missouri and, in a stroke of political irony, became a major supporter of Jackson.

The money that is owed by the United States is called the "national debt." These are two words that elected officials dislike hearing when they are asked a question.

On January 8, 1835, for the first and only time in United States history, the national debt reached zero. That was under the presidency of Andrew Jackson. However, it only stayed there briefly as it quickly grew into the millions once again.

Abraham Lincoln was the first president to be assassinated. But the first attempt to murder the nation's chief executive was made against Andrew Jackson.

On January 30, 1835, Old Hickory attended the funeral of South Carolina Congressman Warren Davis at the Capitol Building. As he exited, Richard Lawrence, an unemployed house painter, pointed a pistol at him and fired. The percussion cap exploded but the bullet did not discharge.

The assault enraged the short-tempered Jackson, who raised his cane to strike his attacker as Lawrence fired again from a different pistol. The second weapon also misfired, and the sixty-seven-year-old president escaped unharmed.

The deranged Lawrence believed Jackson had conspired to keep him in poverty and without a job. The president was convinced that his assailant was hired by his political enemies, the Whigs, to stop his plan to destroy the Bank of the United States. The jury found Lawrence to be mentally incompetent, and he spent the rest of his life in jails and asylums.

The lawyer who prosecuted the case against the gunman was the attorney general for the District of Columbia and composer of "The Star-Spangled Banner," Francis Scott Key.

Following his election, Andrew Jackson moved swiftly to consolidate the power of the presidency. It was a tactic that didn't sit well with his political enemies. Among that group was a Congressman from Jackson's own state of Tennessee. The individual was an old friend who had even served with Old Hickory during the Creek War.

But he disagreed with the president's plan to bolster his power and spoke out against it. His most boisterous objection was aimed at Jackson's Indian Removal Act, which led to the infamous Trail of Tears that took thousands of tribal members away from their native soil.

The Congressman's outspokenness against the president made him a prime political target for the man who had been in his share of duels and wars and who now lived in the White House.

The popular incumbent lost his 1835 congressional re-election campaign by just 252 votes to Adam Huntsman, a peg-legged lawyer who was supported by Jackson and Tennessee governor William Carroll. Many believe that his challenging of the president's policies killed any chances of returning to his seat in Congress.

It was at that point that he decided, like so many others, to go west to a new locale where he might be able to restart his political career. So, having lost his re-election bid after angering the president of the United States, former Congressman Davy Crockett set off for Texas.

Before the Battle of the Alamo, Colonel William Barrett Travis drew a line in the sand with his sword and asked everyone inside the compound to cross it and join him in the upcoming fight for Texas freedom. Many believe that all of them stepped forward.

That is everyone except one individual. A Frenchman named Moses Rose crossed the line but kept on going. He fled the scene on the night before the famous battle.

Santa Anna ordered all of the bodies of the defenders of the Alamo to be burned. At one point, he had proclaimed himself "Napoleon of the West."

Ironically, it was the home country of his hero that started a downward spiral for the Mexican commander. Two years after the Alamo, Santa Anna's leg was amputated after he was hit by cannon fire during a melee with the

French in 1838. In typical grandiose fashion, he had the leg interred with full military honors.

In 1847 during the Mexican-American War, Santa Anna's artificial leg was captured by soldiers of the 4th Illinois Infantry and never returned.

He had been eating a lunch of roast chicken during the Battle of Cerro Gordo against the United States when the Americans surprised him. He quickly mounted his horse and galloped off without his man-made limb. The sergeant who grabbed the leg composed of wood and cork brought it home and exhibited it at county fairs charging a dime a peek. But since 1922, it's been in the care of the Illinois National Guard, which houses the prosthetic prisoner of war inside the Illinois State Military Museum in Springfield.

A second appendage, a common peg leg, was reportedly later used by Lieutenant Abner Doubleday, the creator of baseball, as a bat. It is on display at the Oglesby Mansion in Decatur, Illinois.

Following the Alamo, Sam Houston and his men defeated Santa Anna's army at the Battle of San Jacinto. But along with the conquest of the Mexicans, Houston is also known for a political distinction.

He is the only person in U.S. history to become the governor of two different states. Houston served as Tennessee's chief executive (1827–1828) and also as governor of Texas (1859–1861).

One of the duties of the vice president is to preside over the Senate. When Martin Van Buren was vice president, he oversaw the assembly while packing a pair of loaded pistols, claiming that it was a precaution against the frequent outbursts of violence.

Van Buren was elected president in 1836. But in 1831, when he was nominated minister to the United Kingdom, he was rejected by the Senate.

Many students are taught that the last conflict between the United States and Great Britain was during the War of 1812. That's because they are never told about the Aroostook War, which was also called the "Pork and Beans War."

It wasn't really a war but rather a border dispute that erupted between the two old rivals over the territory along the line of Maine and Canada. It began in the winter of 1838 and ended during the early spring of 1839.

A resolution was reached with the aid of U.S. senator Daniel Webster which avoided war, although there were thirty-eight deaths, most attributed to illness. The only two losses of life officially listed by gunfire were those of a pig and a cow which had been wandering aimlessly in the countryside.

There are many examples of political candidates who won elections by narrow margins. One of those took place in the 1839 Massachusetts gubernatorial election when Marcus Morton (Democrat) defeated Edward Everett (Whig) by just two votes—51,034 to 51,032.

Abraham Lincoln once said, "What has once happened, will invariably happen again, when the same circumstances which combined to produce it, shall again combine in the same way."

The ninth president, William Henry Harrison, delivered the longest inaugural address on March 4, 1841. It was an extremely cold day and the new chief executive did not wear a hat while giving the 105-minute speech. He contracted pneumonia and died in the White House thirty one days later. His month in office was the shortest term of any U.S. president.

Turn the clock ahead twelve years later.

On March 4, 1853, the inauguration of president Franklin Pierce took place on another cold and snowy day. Abigail Fillmore, First Lady to the outgoing president Millard Fillmore, caught a cold as she sat on the chilly, wet, exposed platform during the swearing-in ceremony. The cold developed into pneumonia and she died at the end of the month.

President William Henry Harrison died in 1841 after just one month in office. But his family had already seen its share of tragedy as by 1840, six of his ten children had died. The president's sixth child was a son, Benjamin, who was named after his grandfather, who had signed the Declaration of Independence.

Young Benjamin became a doctor but died just six months before his dad was elected president. He was thirty-four years old.

John Tyler was the first vice president to become president due to the death of a sitting commander in chief. He assumed the presidency when William Henry Harrison died in 1841. Tyler also has the dubious distinction of being the only president to later commit treason against the United States when he ran and was elected to the Confederate House of Representatives in 1861.

At age eleven, future president John Tyler led a revolt against his heavy-handed school master, William McMurdo. Tyler and his friends took over their small Greenway, Virginia, classroom subduing McMurdo and locking him inside.

When Tyler's father was confronted by the angry teacher, he supported his son by shouting, "Sic semper tyrannis"("Ever thus to tyrants"—yes, the same words used by John Wilkes Booth after he shot Lincoln).

Tyler's father, John Sr., was a friend of Thomas Jefferson.

In 1868, Andrew Johnson became the first president to be formally impeached by the U.S. Senate. But the first attempt to bring charges against a sitting chief executive had come years before on January 10, 1843, when attention was focused on the actions of John Tyler.

Tyler had vetoed a tariff bill in June 1842, at which point the House of Representatives began to look into possible proceedings. In a stroke of irony, the impeachment committee was headed by former president John Quincy Adams, who had become a member of Congress and who condemned Tyler's use of the veto.

The action went nowhere as the resolution was defeated, 83–127.

In 1842, nineteen-year-old Philip Spencer became the last U.S. Navy man hanged for mutiny. He had schemed along with two others to turn his ship, the USS *Somers*, to piracy. All three were hanged on the ship's yardarm.

This event didn't sit well with officials back in Washington, D.C., since the convicted sailor's father was John C. Spencer, who was the secretary of war.

John Tyler served out the remainder of the Harrison term but was unable to garner support for election in 1844. Five years after leaving office, the former president was so poor he was unable to pay a bill for $1.25 until he had sold his corn crop.

The Mexican-American War began in 1846. But on October 19, 1842, Commodore Thomas Catesby Jones mistakenly thought that the fighting had started between the United States and Mexico and seized Monterey, California. He held the area for one day before realizing his error and returned power to the governor.

Jones was only four years too early.

As with most other conflicts, there were members of Congress who were opposed to the Mexican-American War. One of them had a serious case of bad timing.

On January 12, 1848, with the war almost won, a freshman congressman stood inside the House chambers to deliver a blistering attack on President Polk and his "half-insane," aggressive militarism. The words came from Representative Abraham Lincoln of Illinois.

Thousands arrived in California during the gold rush seeking their fortune. In the throng was Domingo Ghirardelli, who was just one of the many that came west in 1849.

As a young teen, he had apprenticed under his father who was an expert Italian chocolatier. When gold prospecting didn't work out, he opened a store near Sacramento to supply chocolate and other goods to the miners. In 1852 he moved to San Francisco, which has been the home of the Ghirardelli Chocolate Company ever since.

Individuals such as Levi Strauss, Mark Hopkins, and Collis Huntington made their fortunes during the California Gold Rush by selling merchandise.

Another entrepreneur was San Francisco merchant Samuel Brannan, who in the first nine weeks of "gold fever" in California, made more than $36,000 selling supplies at inflated prices to miners. That's the equivalent of more than $750,000 today.

Among the items that Brannan was able to sell were mining pans (that he'd bought for 20¢) for $15 each. His store at Sutter's Fort began taking in $150,000 a month, eventually making him California's first millionaire.

Dolley Madison is remembered for her efforts to rescue artifacts when the British were on their way to set fire to the White House during the War of 1812. That wasn't the former First Lady's last brush with a house in flames.

In 1848, a would-be robber set fire to Dolley's Washington, D.C., home but she escaped to safety. There were no heroics this time as the eighty-year-old legend sent a servant to retrieve a trunk full of James Madison's papers. When the blaze subsided, the scrappy senior citizen returned to her upstairs bedroom in her bare feet and still clad in her black velvet nightgown.

Shortly afterward, Congress agreed to buy the rest of President Madison's papers for the sum of $25,000. Dolley, who was near poverty, died one year later.

While today's politicians spend millions of dollars campaigning and seeking maximum exposure, the story of Zachary Taylor's election isn't one that they would model their own campaign plan.

He was nominated for president by the Whig Party in 1848 and was later elected as the nation's twelfth president. But Taylor was a stubborn old soldier who refused all correspondence when required postage was due. Because of this, he didn't receive the official notification of his nomination for president until several days after the fact.

During his forty-year military career, Taylor was constantly moving from location to location. He never established an official place of residence, never registered to vote, and didn't even cast a ballot in his own election.

It wasn't until he was sixty-two that he voted for the first time. With all that, he still easily won the election of 1848 even though he had never previously run for public office.

Taylor was also James Madison's second cousin, keeping the presidency in the family.

Before becoming president, Zachary Taylor was one of the heroes of the Mexican-American War. When he moved into the White House, he not only brought his family with him but he also brought his old Army horse, Whitey, allowing him to spend his retirement grazing on the mansion's lawn.

Unfortunately for Whitey, visitors to the presidential palace would often pluck his hairs as souvenirs.

In 1849, Zachary Taylor succeeded James K. Polk as president. So, who was David Rice Atchison?

Polk's term ended at noon on March 4, 1849, but Taylor refused to be sworn in as president because the date fell on a Sunday. Thus he delayed the ceremony until the next day.

With no acting president or vice president, the president pro tempore of the Senate, per the Constitution, assumed the role of president. For one full day, from noon to noon, Atchison of Missouri was the president of the United States. He reportedly spent the day in bed after a few busy nights concluding Senate business. His family was proud of this accomplishment, and his tombstone was inscribed, "President of the United States for one day."

Prior to the second half of the nineteenth century, whale oil was the primary source of fuel used for lighting in the United States. What is not commonly known is that the substance is still used today to send man and machine into space. NASA uses whale oil as a lubricant in their space program, including their remotely operated vehicles (ROVs) for expeditions to the moon and Mars.

Whale oil is also an important lubricant for expensive spacecraft such as the Hubble space telescope and the Voyager space probe. The reason for its continued use is that whale oil doesn't freeze in subzero temperatures and scientists haven't found a suitable replacement.

President Taylor died suddenly on July 9, 1850, after just over a year in office. The official cause was listed as gastroenteritis but like most presidential deaths, conspiracy theories evolved over time. One of the primary stories that circulated was that Taylor had been poisoned.

On June 17, 1991, his remains were exhumed and examined, making him the first president to undergo such a procedure. The determination was made that he had not been poisoned.

The president is always solving problems or, as some like to say, "putting out fires."

On Christmas Eve 1851, President Millard Fillmore was busy putting out a real fire as he and members of his cabinet formed a "bucket brigade" to help fight a blaze that had broken out at the Library of Congress.

The fire destroyed 35,000 books including nearly 4,000 volumes purchased from Thomas Jefferson. It was the second major blaze at the facility as it had been burned by the British during the War of 1812.

Many pioneers went west in the 1800s along the Oregon Trail. One of them was Ezra Meeker. He became the top traveler of the Oregon Trail, having gone west for the first time in 1852.

The years progressed but time didn't slow him down. In 1906, at the age of seventy-six, Meeker, accompanied by two oxen, a driver, and a dog, went from Puyallup, Washington, to Washington, D.C., in a covered wagon. He wanted to bring the nation's attention to the Oregon Trail, which was being plowed under by civilization.

Meeker made three more journeys: once with an ox team, then by automobile in 1915, and his last by an airplane in 1924. In 1928, the king of the Oregon Trail died at the age of ninety-eight.

Franklin Pierce was elected as the nation's fourteenth president in 1852. On January 6, 1853 (two months before his inauguration), the Pierce family was returning by train to their home in Concord, New Hampshire, after spending the Christmas holidays with family. Along the route, the axle on their passenger car broke, hurling it down an embankment near North Andover, Massachusetts. The couple's son, eleven-year-old Benny, was thrown and instantly killed. The horrible accident was witnessed by his parents.

The family had already lost two children to typhus, and Jane Pierce believed the train accident was divine punishment for her husband's acceptance of the high office of the presidency. As a result, Pierce asked that the inaugural ball and all other celebrations be canceled. His wife was too deep in grief to attend the festivities, and she got as far as Baltimore before deciding not to go on to the nation's capital for her husband's inauguration.

Jane later moved into the White House but did not participate in social functions. She made her first formal appearance after her husband had been in office almost two years.

Some believe that Ulysses S. Grant was the first president who was an alcoholic. In reality, Franklin Pierce died in 1869, at sixty-four years old, from cirrhosis of the liver attributed to a heavy drinking problem that he carried throughout his life.

Even though he drank to excess, Pierce always insisted that grace be said before a meal. He was also the first president to have a Christmas tree in the White House.

In 1856 Pierce was denied renomination by the Democratic Party (the only elected president to have been rejected by his own party). After being given the political heave-ho, he has widely quoted as telling a friend, "There is nothing left to do but get drunk."

By the way, there is no solid evidence that Grant was an alcoholic, but he did smoke as many as twenty cigars a day.

Two U.S. presidents (Andrew Johnson and Bill Clinton) have been impeached. But Franklin Pierce was arrested while in office for running over an old woman with his horse. The case was dropped due to insufficient evidence.

James Buchanan was the fifteenth president of the United States and the only chief executive to remain a bachelor his entire life. Some speculated that he was gay, and his extremely close relationship with former vice president William Rufus King didn't do anything to dispel the rumors. The two were often referred to as "Mr. Buchanan and his wife." They shared a home in Washington, D.C., for fifteen years prior to King's death in 1853.

A century later, similar stories circulated about FBI director J. Edgar Hoover and Clyde Tolson, an associate director. The men not only worked closely together during the day, but also took meals, went to night clubs, and vacationed together.

Neither man ever married, and when Hoover died in 1972, he left his entire estate to Tolson, who passed away three years later. The former FBI directors are buried just a few yards from each other at the Congressional Cemetery in Washington, D.C.

Although there has been speculation that president James Buchanan was gay, in 1819, he almost married a woman.

Buchanan's fiancée, Anne Caroline Coleman, broke off the engagement and, a week later, committed suicide with an overdose of the narcotic laudanum. Buchanan never spoke publicly about the relationship throughout the rest of his life.

Most U.S. presidents have been college graduates. But at the age of seventeen, James Buchanan was dismissed from Dickinson College in 1808 for bad behavior.

Ironically, he stated that he found the school to be in "wretched condition" with "no efficient discipline." He later was re-admitted and graduated.

Arizona's Grand Canyon is one of the Seven Natural Wonders of the World. In 1857, Army Lieutenant Joseph Ives led a U.S. government mapping expedition up the Colorado River and into the Grand Canyon. Of the striking area he reported, "This was the first, and undoubtedly the last expedition that will see this useless place."

Ulysses S. Grant was among the soldiers who fought in both the Mexican-American War and the Civil War. Between the conflicts, he returned home to Illinois and the family farm. But things went so badly for the future president that in December 1857, he was forced to pawn his valuable gold pocket watch in order to buy Christmas gifts for his family.

In 1859 John Brown was captured during an unsuccessful raid of the federal arsenal at Harpers Ferry, Virginia. Among his captors were famed Civil War figures Robert E. Lee and J. E. B. Stuart.

During the standoff, Brown and his followers took hostages. Most prominent among the captives was Lewis W. Washington, a colonel on the staff of Governor Henry A. Wise of Virginia and the great-grandnephew of George Washington. The kidnappers forced their captive to hand over a sword given to the first president by Frederick the Great of Prussia and a pair of pistols that were once carried by General Lafayette.

One of Brown's objectives was to liberate the slaves from a member of the Washington family. Lewis was eventually rescued unharmed.

The San Juan Islands are part of the State of Washington. In 1859, they became the sector of a dispute about possession of the area between the United States and, who else but, Great Britain.

The latest conflict between the two nations was referred to as the "Pig War" due to the fact that the only casualty in the conflict was a giant black boar that belonged to a local farmer. The four-month otherwise bloodless showdown ended with the San Juan Islands being awarded to the United States through third-party arbitration.

No doubt the Founding Fathers would have been proud.

As president, James Buchanan lived in the White House during his term. When Britain's Prince of Wales visited the mansion in 1860, so many guests accompanied him that Buchanan had to sleep in the hall.

President James Buchanan was criticized severely by anti-slavery loyalists. What was unknown to most was that the commander in chief would quietly but consistently buy slaves in Washington, D.C., and then set them free in his home state of Pennsylvania.

Abraham Lincoln followed James Buchanan as the nation's sixteenth president. The outgoing chief executive left a note for his successor upon his departure. It read, "My dear sir, if you are as happy on entering the White House as I on leaving, you are a happy man indeed."

The Lincoln-Douglas debates are among the most notable in the nation's history. In the senatorial campaign of 1858, Douglas won the election and two years later, the two were running against each other for president.

Even though they competed hard in two major elections, the pair were actually good friends. During his inauguration, Lincoln took the oath beneath the unfinished Capitol Dome. As he read his speech, Senator Douglas assisted the new president by holding his signature stovepipe hat.

That evening, the Lincolns attended the Inaugural Ball where the new First Lady danced with Douglas, who died of typhoid fever three months later.

· 6 ·

There's Nothing Civil about War

They couldn't hit an elephant at this distance.

—The last words of Union General John Sedgwick,
who was shot and killed moments later by
Confederate troops at the Battle of Spotsylvania.

$\mathcal{T}$he song "Dixie" became the anthem of the Confederate states during the Civil War. It was written by Daniel Decatur Emmett in 1859. He was not a Southerner but hailed from Ohio and penned the tune in his flat in New York City.

Even though the Civil War had yet to begin, there was much tension in the South during the early days of the secessionist movement.

In the spring of 1861, U.S. senator and future president Andrew Johnson's denunciation of the breakup of the states made him rather unpopular in the southern region of the country. So much so that his life was often endangered by those in the opposition.

One day while Johnson was passing through Virginia on his way home to Greenville, Tennessee, several angry men dragged the pistol-packing senator from his train and were about to hang him when a quick-thinking crowd member intervened.

"His neighbors at Greenville have made arrangements to hang their senator on his arrival," the man declared. "Virginians have no right to deprive them of that privilege."

Johnson was released—and later became America's seventeenth president. The aptly named town from which Johnson narrowly escaped was Lynchburg.

When South Carolina seceded, other states followed its lead. Unknown to most Southerners was that they had a sympathetic neighbor in the North.

After South Carolina exited the Union on December 20, 1860, New York City mayor Fernando Wood proposed that his town should also secede to become an independent city-state. Wood cited the resources that were grown in the South were necessary for mills and businesses to prosper in his city, but his effort failed.

Nonetheless the issue was revisited in 1993 when Staten Island residents voted to secede from New York City but were unsuccessful because such a move would have required state approval.

The Southern states that seceded helped start the Civil War. That didn't sit well with Northerners. They were also not amused in 1861 when three U.S. Congressmen—John B. Clark (Missouri), John W. Reid (Missouri), and Henry C. Burnett (Kentucky)—were expelled from the U.S. House of Representatives after they enlisted in the Confederate army.

The trio were the last members of the House to suffer such a fate until 1980.

Robert E. Lee was made commander of the Confederate army. But before accepting the post, he took part in a meeting in an effort to avert a war.

Lee reached the capital on March 1, 1861, just three days before the inauguration of Lincoln. He met with Francis P. Blair, an influential D.C. insider and former editor of the *Washington Globe*, who asked him, "I come to you on the part of President Lincoln to ask whether any inducement that he can offer will prevail on you to take command of the Union army?"

This would have been a dream job for most military officers, but Lee could only reply that he "would take no part in the invasion of the Southern States." His resignation from the U.S. Army followed immediately, and a few days later he accepted the command of the Confederate military forces.

Following Lee's rejection of the Union's offer, Irvin McDowell was given control of the Army of Northeastern Virginia, despite never having commanded troops in combat.

Robert E. Lee was the only person to be offered the command of both armies which fought in the Civil War.

One of the states that seceded in 1861 was Tennessee. Even though major battles, which killed a number of civilians, were fought in the Volunteer State, more than one-fourth of the entire population of Memphis was wiped out by a yellow-fever epidemic in 1878.

The attack on South Carolina's Fort Sumter on April 12–13, 1861, is known as the official start of the Civil War. But there were already skirmishes taking place between the disgruntled factions.

On January 9, 1861, the U.S. steamer *Star of the West* attempted to reach Fort Sumter in Charleston Harbor and was fired upon by South Carolina troops.

On February 8, the arsenal at Little Rock, Arkansas, was seized by state troops.

And on February 12, U.S. stores were seized by state troops in Pine Bluff, Arkansas.

The South claimed victory in the battle at Fort Sumter. Although there were no battle casualties, one Union soldier was killed during the surrender ceremony when a cannon backfired.

At the conclusion of the fight, Union army major Robert Anderson was forced to surrender to General P. G. T. Beauregard. Anderson, the commanding officer at Fort Sumter, had been Beauregard's instructor while he was a student at West Point.

Prior to serving at Fort Sumter, Anderson was at Fort Moultrie in Charleston Harbor where his father had served during the American Revolution.

More than 600,000 Americans were killed during the Civil War. However, the first troops to die were not engaged on the battlefield.

On April 19, 1861, five days after Fort Sumter, Union soldiers were attacked by pro-Southern street rioters in Baltimore. Although located in the North, much of the city was sympathetic toward the Confederacy.

Four soldiers from the Union's 6th Massachusetts Regiment, in addition to twelve civilians, were killed in the riot, becoming the first official losses of the war.

There were many famous officers who fought in the Civil War, including, from the Union, Ulysses S. Grant, Don Carlos Buell, George McClellan, George Meade, and Winfield Scott; and from the Confederacy, Robert E. Lee, Richard Anderson, B. E. Bee, James Longstreet, Stonewall Jackson, Albert Johnston, and Joseph Johnston.

Thirteen years earlier during the Mexican-American War, all of them had fought together on the same side.

The Confederate States of America had their own flag, known as the "Stars and Bars." But it wasn't created by a native from the "Land of Cotton."

The national flag of the Confederacy was designed by a Prussian artist. Nicola Marschall had been born in Germany but lived in Marion, Alabama, when he produced the symbol for the South.

During the Civil War, some family members fought on opposing sides. Government officials were not exempt from that circumstance.

John J. Crittenden, author of the Crittenden Compromise and a U.S. senator from Kentucky, had two sons who served as generals in the Civil War but on contrasting sides: Thomas for the Union and George for the Confederacy. Both men survived the conflict.

Many forts saw action during the Civil War, but those did not include a pair of compounds that were built at Long Point, Massachusetts, on the tip of Cape Cod. Dubbed "Fort Useless" and "Fort Ridiculous" by the locals, the strongholds never fired a shot in battle.

Recycling is good for the environment, but who knew that the practice was taking place during the Civil War? No, not the recycling of glass or plastic items but the reuse of human teeth.

The chompers of dead soldiers were in high demand and used to make dentures—especially in England.

Maryland was one of the states that considered seceding from the Union. Two weeks after the attack on Fort Sumter, the state's legislature was scheduled to take up the matter.

The situation had become so serious that President Abraham Lincoln took the unprecedented step of filling Maryland's capital with federal troops and military authorities. They made several arrests, including those of the Baltimore marshal of police George P. Kane and Mayor William Brown.

Also included in the roundup was Francis Key Howard, the editor of the *Baltimore Exchange*, a local newspaper that was considered sympathetic to the Confederacy. He was the grandson of Francis Scott Key and, in an ironic twist, the men were imprisoned at Fort McHenry.

Four days later, on September 17, 1861, nine members of the Maryland legislature and the chief clerk of the Maryland Senate were also taken into custody. It was feared that, if they were allowed to attend the legislative session, they would vote for secession.

Maryland remained in the Union for the duration of the war.

Some soldiers deserted during the Civil War. Among those was Samuel Langhorne Clemens, aka Mark Twain. In 1861, he and his friends had been

Confederate volunteers for two weeks before disbanding their company. At that point, Twain decided that he had seen enough and went west to Nevada.

Many of the early battles of the war took place in Virginia, including the Battle of Ball's Bluff in Loudon County on October 21, 1861.

Among the Union's approximately one thousand casualties on that day was Colonel Edward Baker, who was killed in action. At the time of his death, Baker was a United States senator for the state of Oregon, and he was a former member of the House of Representatives.

To this day, he is the only United States senator to die in a military conflict.

The Medal of Honor was created in 1862 by the Army to recognize soldiers who distinguished themselves in action. Mary Walker was the first woman to receive the award. She was, in fact, the only woman so awarded for her work as a surgeon during the Civil War. Her award was rescinded in a "purge" of medals in 1917 but reinstated in 1976.

Arlington National Cemetery is located on property that was once the home of General Robert E. Lee and his family. But the U.S. government had their sights set on the expansive property, so in 1862 Congress passed an Act for the Collection of Taxes in Insurrectionary Districts. It was the Union's method of confiscating land that was owned by citizens who had become members of the Confederacy.

That law levied property taxes on Confederate lands, including Arlington House which was assessed a rate of $92.07.

The general's wife, Mary Lee, sent representatives to Washington, D.C., to pay the fee but the U.S. federal government would not accept the money, arguing that the property owner must pay the levy in person. Because of the delay, Mrs. Lee defaulted on the taxes and the land was confiscated by the government.

Early burials were done in the vicinity of Mrs. Lee's rose garden to prevent the family from returning to their home. Many of the deceased were Union soldiers who had been killed by her husband's army. The plan worked. In 1873, when Mary Lee arrived at Arlington House, she was distraught by its condition and retreated to the confines of her other home in Lexington, Virginia, where she died five months later.

The Lees may have originally lost the battle for their Arlington estate, but years afterward they gained a legal victory. In 1882, the Supreme Court declared that the U.S. federal government had trespassed on the Arlington grounds and ordered the lands returned to the Lee family. In 1883, with over ten thousand grave sites already there, George Washington Custis Lee (George Washington's step-grandson and Robert E. Lee's oldest son) sold the land (over one thousand acres) to the U.S. government for $150,000.

The U.S. federal income tax was first enacted in 1862 to support the Union's Civil War effort. It was eliminated in 1872, revived in 1894, and then declared unconstitutional by the Supreme Court the following year. In 1913, the Sixteenth Amendment to the Constitution made the income tax a permanent fixture in the U.S. tax system and the lives of Americans.

But it all began with the Civil War.

The Battle of Pea Ridge took place in Arkansas in March 1862. It was a Union victory that was fought near Bentonville (the future home of Walmart).

The fighting included the personal story of Sergeant Henderson Virden of the 2nd Arkansas Volunteer Infantry. A local resident, at one point during the battle, he found himself fighting on his own farm.

Virden was wounded and carried into his house where his wife tended to him until he could return to his regiment. He not only survived but lived to be ninety-three years old with a Yankee Minié ball under the skin of his back and a huge white scar on his chest that he received during the fighting that had taken place on his farm.

Sergeant Virden died in 1912—fifty years before the first Walmart opened.

It's common knowledge that the Battle of Yorktown ended the Revolutionary War. But it isn't as well known that the Civil War had its own Battle of Yorktown.

It occurred from April 5 to May 4, 1862, as part of the Peninsula Campaign. Neither side was able to score a decisive victory as the conflict took place near the site of the 1781 siege against the British, the final major battle of the American Revolution.

Thousands of soldiers on both sides were held as prisoners of war. But there was one event known as the Great Hanging where justice was harsh and swift.

Forty suspected Unionists in Confederate Texas were hanged at Gainesville in October 1862. Two others were shot as they tried to escape. Although the affair reached its climax in Cooke County, men were killed in neighboring Grayson, Wise, and Denton counties. While most were accused of treason or insurrection, few had actually conspired against the

Confederacy, and many were innocent of the abolitionist sentiments for which they were tried.

The lynchings made it the largest vigilante-style mass killing in American history.

The military draft was ongoing during the Civil War. One of the requirements for the new soldiers was at least two opposing front teeth so they could open a gunpowder pouch. In a ploy to avoid service, some draftees had their front teeth removed.

Fighting was heavy at the Battle of Pittsburgh Landing (also known as the Battle of Shiloh), in Tennessee, and a large number of soldiers were taken as prisoners of war. One was a Confederate private named Henry Stanley who was captured by Union troops during the battle. After the barrage, he was sent to Camp Douglas, Illinois, as a prisoner but later was allowed to leave the lockup by volunteering to fight for the Union.

Stanley went on to have an amazing career as a journalist and African explorer. In 1872, the reporter made international news by finding the lost missionary, Dr. David Livingstone, in the Congo.

Thomas "Stonewall" Jackson was one of Lee's top generals. Experts consider him to be one of the best military strategists of all time.

But his younger sister Laura was a Union sympathizer who was devoted to the North. She was known for nursing wounded troops in her West Virginia home and she once sent a message via a Yankee soldier which said that she could "take care of the wounded Federals as fast as brother Thomas would wound them."

The two had been close while growing up, but in 1863 a Pennsylvania Cavalry officer recorded her reaction to her brother's death in a letter home stating that she "seemed much depressed, but said she would rather know that he was dead than to have him a leader in the rebel army."

Laura's wartime views were so devout that it led to problems with her husband, who divorced her in 1870.

Paul Revere had a significant role in the American Revolution. He also had three grandsons who fought in the Civil War.

Colonel Paul Joseph Revere was killed at Gettysburg and Edward H. R. Revere died at Antietam. Joseph Warren Revere rose to the rank of brigadier general and fought at the Battle of the Seven Days; the Second Battle at Bull Run; and Chancellorsville. But he was such a poor commander that the Union officer was eventually court-martialed and sentenced to be dishonorably discharged before President Lincoln finally allowed him to resign.

One of the casualties of Antietam was Confederate brigadier general John Brown Gordon. A fearless leader, prior to Antietam he had been wounded in the eyes at the Battle of Malvern Hill, but that was just the beginning.

At Antietam he was helping defend the rebel's center, but as the fighting progressed, a Minié ball passed through his calf. A second ball hit him higher in the same leg. A third went through his left arm as he continued to lead his men despite the fact that the muscles and tendons in his limb were mangled and a small artery had been severed. Another ball hit him in his shoulder. Despite pleas that he go to the rear, Gordon continued to lead his men.

The Georgia native was finally stopped by a ball that hit him in the face, passing through his left cheek and out his jaw. He pitched forward and fell face-first into his hat, which started to fill with blood. Fortunately for the officer, there was a bullet hole in the hat big enough to act as a drain. Otherwise, he would have drowned in his own fluid.

John Brown Gordon may have been on the losing side of the war but he had proven that he was the ultimate survivor. He had better luck as a politician after the conflict, serving as governor of Georgia and two terms as a U.S. senator.

Figure 6.1 John Brown Gordon was relentless in battle. *National Archives*

In terms of casualties, the Battle of Antietam brought the bloodiest day of fighting during the Civil War. On September 17, 1862, Union and Confederate forces fought alongside Antietam Creek near Sharpsburg, Maryland. In that single day, the battle produced nearly 23,000 casualties (killed or wounded). What makes the statistic even more incredible is that this was before the introduction of automatic weapons.

Amazingly, the number of casualties at Antietam is roughly nine times higher than the total from D-Day in World War II.

It was a colossal battle with no declared winner even though each side squandered an opportunity for victory. General Lee's battle plans were known in advance. Two Union soldiers (Corporal Barton W. Mitchell and First Sergeant John M. Bloss of the 27th Indiana Volunteer Infantry) discovered a mislaid copy of the Confederate commander's detailed battle strategy—Special Order 191—wrapped around three cigars.

They passed on the information, but Union general George McClellan delayed acting on this knowledge for eighteen hours, thus wasting an opportunity for a major victory. After Antietam, McClellan was removed from command by Lincoln, first as general in chief, then from the Army of the Potomac. The president was once accused of treating horses better than he did his generals. He was famously quoted as saying, "I can make more generals, but horses cost money."

The resentful McClellan didn't take the news sitting down, and two years later (1864), he ran for president against Lincoln. He didn't win that one either.

Today's soldiers wear a form of identification known as dog tags. But during the Civil War, some troops going into combat improvised their own identification, pinning slips of paper with their name and home address to the backs of their coats, stenciling identification on their knapsacks, or scratching it in the soft lead backing of their Army belt buckle. Over half of the Union soldiers who were killed in battle still remain unidentified.

Former U.S. senator Jefferson F. Davis of Mississippi became the Confederate president. But the North had their own Jefferson Davis.

Jefferson C. Davis was a Union general who was born in Indiana and fought in the Mexican-American War. He not only battled the enemy but was known to take on members of his own army.

On September 29, 1862, in the lobby of the Galt House Hotel in Louisville, Kentucky, a quarrel developed between Davis and another Union general, William "Bull" Nelson.

The argument began over the recruiting of troops. Davis tossed a wad of paper at Nelson's face, and he countered with a slap. Nelson then turned to go upstairs with Davis trailing him.

Davis called to his fellow Union officer and pointed a borrowed pistol at him. He fired the weapon from about three feet away, striking his commander in the chest. Nelson died about an hour later, but the shooter was never prosecuted as the incident was ruled "a matter of honor." Among those who witnessed the confrontation was Indiana governor Oliver P. Morton, who happened to be at the scene.

Many children have heard the well-known line from the nursery rhyme "Mary Had a Little Lamb": "Everywhere that Mary went, the lamb was sure to go."

There was actually a situation in the Civil War where battles followed Jefferson Davis wherever he would go. In one of the strangest coincidences of the conflict, the Confederate president was visiting various camps from November to December 1862. He toured several commands, including those stationed at Fredericksburg, Virginia; Greensboro, Tennessee; and Vicksburg, Mississippi.

Northern and Southern troops clashed shortly after Davis left each place: December 13 at Fredericksburg; December 28 at Vicksburg (Chickasaw Bluffs); and December 31–January 2 at Greensboro.

One might believe that everywhere that Davis went, the fighting was sure to follow.

General Lee's troops were victorious at the Battle of Fredericksburg in December 1862. One of the lesser-known individuals in that conflict was Dr. William T. Passmore, an Englishman, who was used as a spy by the commander.

The British physician dressed in rags and pretended to have mental problems. He wandered through the camps of Union general Ambrose Burnside, selling produce from an old cart. His charade was so effective that Burnside gave him a pass for daily entry into the federal lines and felt at ease enough to talk freely in front of him at headquarters.

Passmore was credited with discoveries which enabled Lee to make plans leading to his victory at Fredericksburg.

Thousands of Irish citizens immigrated to the United States because of the Potato Famine during the 1840s. On December 13, 1862, at the Battle of Fredericksburg, some of these men met in battle. The Union's Irish Brigade (literally all-Irish) during the final stages of the assault fought a Confederate regiment comprised mainly of Irish immigrants, with terrible results. After cutting down their countrymen, the Irish rebels tearfully saluted their courageous compatriots.

The South was successful during the first two years of the Civil War. So much so that on December 20, 1862, during the Battle of Holly Springs, Mississippi, members of Ulysses S. Grant's family were on the move.

The general's wife Julia and their son Jesse had been visiting him at the battle site. But when the Confederate troops began their raid, Mrs. Grant and her son escaped by train before they could be taken as prisoners of war.

The Southern victory at Holly Springs was the highlight of Confederate general Earl Van Dorn's career. However, the low point came five months later when he was murdered by the husband (a Tennessee doctor) of a woman with whom he was having an affair.

It was Abraham Lincoln who issued the Emancipation Proclamation. He, along with Secretary of State William Seward and his private secretary John Nicolay, signed forty-eight copies of the historic document in 1864. The prints were sold to support sick and wounded Union soldiers and to improve military camps.

Confederate general Thomas "Stonewall" Jackson was accidentally shot by one of his own men at the Battle of Chancellorsville on May 3, 1863. He died from his wounds a week later.

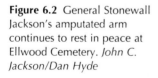

Figure 6.2 General Stonewall Jackson's amputated arm continues to rest in peace at Ellwood Cemetery. *John C. Jackson/Dan Hyde*

Jackson had been shot through the left arm, which had to be amputated. The limb was buried, complete with headstone, at the Ellwood Cemetery near the battle site. The remainder of Jackson's body was laid to rest in Lexington, Virginia, about 130 miles away.

Sometimes history repeats itself. Nearly one year to the day after Stonewall Jackson was shot by one of his own men, Confederate lieutenant general James Longstreet was riding with his staff on Plank Road just four miles from where Jackson had been mistakenly struck down during the Battle of the Wilderness.

Suddenly Confederate soldiers opened fire, shooting at Longstreet and his party, believing that they were the enemy. Longstreet took a bullet in the neck, but unlike Jackson he survived and rejoined the army in November.

One of Ulysses S. Grant's biggest victories came at the siege of Vicksburg. The general also suffered a loss during that period.

One day, while aboard a gunboat on the Mississippi River, Grant removed his false teeth and placed them in a glass of water. A servant who was cleaning up the area grabbed the glass and mistakenly tossed the water overboard including the dentures.

Over the next few days, Grant dined on soft foods until his dentist, Dr. S. L. Hamlin, was able to cast another set of teeth.

There were several minor skirmishes leading up to the Battle of Gettysburg. One of those was at the Battle of Hanover, which took place on June 30, 1863, the day before Gettysburg began.

There was no decisive victor but the fighting kept J. E. B. Stuart's troops from linking up with Robert E. Lee until July 2. Although insignificant by comparison with other battles, the Hanover conflict had a major impact on the outcome at Gettysburg.

It has been said that Gettysburg was the northernmost battle site of the Civil War. But take another look at the map.

There was a short skirmish that took place on June 30, 1863, at Sporting Hill, just two miles west of Harrisburg, Pennsylvania. At least sixteen Confederates from the 16th and 36th Virginia Cavalry were killed during the fighting, and an additional twenty to thirty were wounded. Union casualties were listed at eleven men wounded.

From the standpoint of Pennsylvania geography, Harrisburg is about forty miles north of Gettysburg, making Sporting Hill the northernmost battle of the Civil War.

For those who think that the raid at St. Albans, Vermont, was the site of the northernmost fighting, most historians consider it more of a bank robbery than a battle.

The Union army was constantly trying to capture the Confederate capital at Richmond, Virginia. Meanwhile, the town of Winchester, Virginia, changed hands seventy-six times during the war, as the armies surged in and out of the Northern Shenandoah Valley. It was indefensible and was the site of three major battles.

The Confederates were successful during the Battle of Cold Harbor in Virginia. It is estimated that on June 3, 1864, nearly seven thousand men died in a span of twenty minutes.

The extreme number of casualties was the result of an ill-advised Union assault on heavily fortified Confederate positions, and attack that quickly became a slaughter. General Ulysses S. Grant would later say, "I have always regretted that the last assault at Cold Harbor was ever made."

Figure 6.3 Workers bury the dead following the Battle at Cold Harbor. *John Reekie*

Many families lost several members during the Civil War. A young Confederate officer, Captain Isadore Guillet, was fatally shot on the same horse on which three of his brothers had been previously killed. He willed the animal to a nephew as he died.

Guillet's death took place during the Battle of Columbus, the last major encounter of the war in Georgia.

Andersonville Prison Camp in Georgia was one of the worst lockup facilities of any war. It was built to hold 9,000 captives but Confederate officials packed more than 30,000 Union soldiers into the 16.5-acre space.

The Stockade Branch, which provided the only water for the inmates, was polluted with grease from a cookhouse, laundry waste water, and human excrement. Those who drank it in trying to quench their thirst were likely to die from dysentery and diarrhea.

On the night of August 9, 1864, a downpour caused the area to overflow, washing away much of the camp's foul waste. A bolt of lightning struck a pine stump near the camp, and a spring of fresh water emerged. The source had been covered over during the construction of the camp, and it now became known as Providence Spring. Andersonville was only operational for fourteen months, but more than thirteen thousand soldiers died there during that period.

Stonewall Jackson's death was an accident but the same cannot be said for the passing of another Confederate officer.

On April 6, 1865, with the surrender just three days away, Confederate colonel George Wythe Baylor was meeting with Major General John Austin Wharton about the reorganization of the Trans-Mississippi Department of the Confederate States. The gathering was taking place at the headquarters of General John B. Magruder in the Fannin Hotel in Galveston, Texas.

At some point, the meeting became heated and the duo quarreled. Wharton reportedly slapped Baylor's face and called him a liar, whereupon the former Texas Ranger lawman drew his revolver and then shot and killed the unarmed Confederate officer. Baylor stated that he regretted the incident, and he was never prosecuted.

Every conflict has a beginning and a conclusion. In a strange concurrence, the Civil War started in Wilmer McLean's backyard in 1861 and ended in his parlor in 1865.

The First Battle of Bull Run, fought on July 21, 1861, took place on the McLean farm.

Wilmer was a successful grocer and a retired major in the Virginia militia, but he was too old to reenlist at the outbreak of the Civil War. In 1863, he decided to move to the community of Appomattox Court House in order to get his family away from the fighting.

On April 9, 1865, the war came back to McLean when General Robert E. Lee surrendered to General Ulysses S. Grant inside the family home. After Lee and Grant rode away, mass confusion overtook the premises as the McLeans were besieged by offers to buy "souvenirs." Other items such as chairs and tables were looted by federal troops who attended the ceremony.

There was one clause in the surrender terms that puzzled some people. It stated that every Confederate cavalryman was entitled to take his horse home with him. This provision, insisted on by Lee, was accepted by Grant when he was told that once they returned to civilian life, former soldiers wouldn't be able to plant spring crops without their horses.

The surrender took place on April 9, 1865, at Appomattox Court House, Virginia. But the actual last battle of the war was fought on May 12–13, 1865, at the Palmito Ranch near Brownsville, Texas. It was a Confederate victory.

Only one man was killed, Private John Jefferson Williams, of Jay County, Indiana. The number of wounded totaled 9, and 103 officers and men captured, most of them from the 34th Indiana. Confederate casualties were listed as "five or six, wounded."

The prisoners from the 34th Indiana carried their comrade's body to the outskirts of Brownsville, where they buried him.

Among the legendary names from the Civil War are Lee, Grant, and Jackson. But if the War between the States had a champion soldier, it would have to be Confederate George Barnhart Zimpleman of Terry's Texas Rangers.

He was a private by choice who survived more than four hundred battles and skirmishes. Zimpleman, a native German, lead his regiment in the number of horses shot from under him, and he suffered two wounds, one that maimed him for life.

On December 17, 1861, at the Battle of Woodsonville in Kentucky, he ran out of ammunition but proceeded to chase down and rope a federal soldier. Two years later, Zimpleman ran along with a bugler and an ensign as they forced General Rosecrans's regiment to retreat during a charge.

After the war, most soldiers returned home to resume their lives. One of those was a Georgia pharmacist named John Stith Pemberton. He had served with distinction as a lieutenant colonel in the 3rd Georgia Cavalry Battalion during the Civil War, and in April 1865, he was almost killed in the fighting at Columbus, Georgia.

But his heroics were forgotten following the end of hostilities because in 1886 he became better known as the inventor of Coca-Cola.

Ulysses S. Grant went on to become president of the United States following the war. But whatever became of Robert E. Lee?

In August 1865, General Lee was offered and accepted the presidency of Washington College in Lexington, Virginia (now Washington and Lee University), a post which he occupied until his death on October 12, 1870. He is buried on the college grounds.

Even though Lee's side lost the war, most experts agree that he was a great general. That could be because of his bloodline. Lee was George Washington's third cousin, twice removed.

Before he took command in the War between the States, Ulysses S. Grant had been an officer in the Mexican-American War and had then resigned. Having served fifteen years in the regular military, he offered to return and serve when conflict broke out between the North and South.

But his original letter of reinstatement was overlooked by the War Department and remained lost until after the war was over.

Horses played a major role in the Civil War. According to late-nineteenth-century newspaper reports from Aiken, South Carolina, the oldest surviving four-footed veteran of the conflict was living there in 1894.

Old Jim had been sired in Sevierville, Tennessee. He had seen action at Gettysburg where his rider, Union brigadier general Strong Vincent, was killed.

A year later in the summer of 1864, Lieutenant McMahon rode him to the Battle of Atlanta, then to Savannah, and into South Carolina.

It was in the Palmetto State where the steed once again lost his rider. He wandered to the plantation of W. T. Williams and was later identified by his brands and saddle markings. Old Jim spent his postwar years as an attraction in parades for veterans of the War for Southern Independence.

It is estimated that four hundred women disguised themselves as men in order to enlist for military service during the Civil War.

Over 600,000 soldiers died during the Civil War, but twice as many men died of disease. Dysentery, measles, small pox, pneumonia, and malaria were the soldier's greatest enemies.

The overall poor hygiene in camps, the lack of adequate sanitation facilities, the cold and damp weather, the lack of shelter and suitable clothing, and the poor quality of food and water, along with the crowded conditions, made the typical encampment a breeding ground for disease. Resulting illnesses and deaths were even worse for Civil War prisoners, who were held in the most miserable of conditions.

As the Civil War continued, the Confederate states began to fall, one after the other. However, there were two Southern state capitals that were never captured by the Union. They were Austin, Texas, and Tallahassee, Florida.

The Civil War ended in 1865. Lemuel Cook died on May 20, 1866, but he never fought in the War between the States. He was one of the last surviving veterans of the American Revolution.

Cook enlisted in the Continental Army at the age of sixteen and fought at Brandywine and in the Virginia campaign. He was present at Lord Charles Cornwallis's surrender and received an honorable discharge signed by George Washington on June 12, 1784. He died at the age of 107 (he was born September 10, 1759) and was buried with full military and masonic honors. Cook was also one of seven Revolutionary War veterans who survived into the age of photography.

The Civil War was fought between the Northern and Southern states. But following the surrender, the United States sued Great Britain for damages that were caused by ships that the Brits had built for the Confederacy.

In 1872, the United States was awarded $15.5 million by an international tribunal of five members in Geneva, Switzerland. In addition, the former mother country apologized for the destruction caused by the British-built Confederate ships, but like most who are accused in today's courtrooms, they admitted no guilt.

The North defeated the South in the Civil War and also won the battle for oldest surviving soldier. On August 2, 1956, Union veteran Albert Woolson, died at the age of 109.

There were several Confederate veterans who claimed to be older, but none was proven to be so.

In 2008 there were students who were studying the Civil War. What wasn't mentioned in those lessons was that in that same year, Maudie Hopkins died. She was believed to be the last known surviving widow of a Civil War veteran.

On February 2, 1934, then nineteen-year-old Maudie married former Confederate soldier William M. Cantrell, who was eighty-six when they wed. He died in 1937 and was collecting a bimonthly military pension of $25 until his death.

· 7 ·

Abraham Lincoln:
Days of Dreams and Nightmares

If I were two-faced, would I be wearing this one?

—Abraham Lincoln

There is the well-known story that Abraham Lincoln was born in a log cabin. That part is true but, as usual, there are a few missing details.

The log cabin on display for tourists in Hodgenville, Kentucky, which is officially registered as the "Abraham Lincoln Birthplace Historical Site," is not the original Lincoln home even though it was confirmed by Lincoln's son Robert as well as a member of a family who later lived in the cabin. According to that family member, the original Lincoln cabin was destroyed by fire before 1840 and the logs that remained were used as firewood.

The structure that sightseers view today is made from the salvaged parts of another log cabin in the area that has been disassembled, moved, and reassembled so many times that it may not look anything like the original cabin. But Kentucky didn't corner the market on the house of Lincoln.

If you're in Illinois, stop by the town of Lerna where you can visit the Lincoln Log Cabin State Historic Site. That one is also a reproduction.

Abraham Lincoln is considered to be one of our greatest presidents. But it was a long and rugged road for him to get to the White House.

When the Kentuckian was twenty-two years old, his business failed. At age twenty-three, he lost his first bid for U.S. Congress. When he was twenty-four, he failed in business again.

The following year he could finally claim a victory as he was elected to the state legislature, but when he was twenty-six, his sweetheart died. At age

71

twenty-seven, he suffered a nervous breakdown. When he was twenty-nine, the Illinois lawmaker was defeated for the post of Speaker of the House in the state legislature.

When Lincoln was thirty-four, he ran for Congress again and, just like before, he lost. At the age of thirty-seven, he ran for Congress yet again and finally won, but his joy was short-lived as two years later he was defeated in his re-election campaign.

At the age of forty-six, Abe ran for a U.S. Senate seat and lost that one too. The following year he ran for the job that most politicians never want—vice president. It didn't matter if he really wanted it or not because he didn't get the nomination.

Finally, at the age of fifty-one, he was elected president of the United States. It could be argued that Lincoln is the ultimate symbol of perseverance.

As a young man, Abraham Lincoln was a hard worker who was mainly self-educated. But young Abe was a pretty fair wrestler who would travel from town to town taking on challengers. It is estimated that he lost only one match in twelve years. Today, Lincoln is enshrined among the greatest grapplers of all-time at the National Wrestling Hall of Fame in Stillwater, Oklahoma.

Abraham Lincoln wrote the Gettysburg Address, which is considered to be one of America's great speeches. What many readers don't know was that he was a pretty fair crime writer who knew how to tell a good story.

Back in Illinois in 1841, attorney Lincoln defended William Trailor, one of three brothers on trial for murder. A few years later, using the circumstances of the case, Lincoln published a short story, "A Remarkable Case of Arrest for Murder." While he dramatized the actual event, readers who were familiar with the trial recognized the proceedings.

Trailor was not convicted as it was later proven that no murder had occurred. However, some historical accounts allege that he never paid Lincoln for his legal services, which may have been the real motive behind the book.

Lincoln's law practice and home were located in Springfield, Illinois. But his only arguments weren't restricted to the courtroom.

His wife, Mary Todd, was a high-strung individual who could become very loud during a verbal exchange, so much so that a disagreement would often end up on the couple's front porch in view of the neighbors.

In one such instance, the former wrestler toted his turbulent spouse back into their home and pulled down the shades to avoid the eyes and ears of nosy neighbors.

Abraham Lincoln was known as the president who freed the slaves, but he was also concerned about the rights of women. In 1836, twelve years before the Seneca Falls Convention (the first public assembly in America for the promotion of women's rights), the first-term state legislator gave an Illinois newspaper, the *Sangamon Journal*, a statement endorsing "female suffrage."

Andrew Jackson is known as the president who fought several duels, most notably the one where he killed his friend Charlie Dickinson. But there was also a time when young Abraham Lincoln almost joined the dueler's roster.

On September 22, 1842, Lincoln had an inflammatory letter published in a Springfield, Illinois, newspaper (once again the *Sangamon Journal*) that was critical of James Shields, who was the Illinois state auditor. As it was a customary form of retaliation for the era, Shields challenged Lincoln to a duel to take place on "Bloody Island," which was actually a Mississippi River sandbar that was a popular location for those wishing to settle disputes by dueling since it was not under the jurisdiction of officials from either Missouri or Illinois.

As the challenged party, Lincoln decided that the weapon of choice would be swords instead of the traditional pistols. Shields immediately realized that he was at an overwhelming disadvantage against his taller and long-armed foe.

Friends of the would-be combatants, who had gathered to watch the showdown, began encouraging the pair to forego the spectacle and settle their differences in a more peaceful manner. The two men agreed and elected to surrender their blades.

As the two men headed back to Alton, they realized that their supporters were right, and so they remained friends and political allies for the rest of their careers.

There are many pictures of Abraham Lincoln and his famous beard, including the one on the $5 bill. But how did he get the idea to grow that famous facial hair?

It was the fall of 1860. Lincoln was the Republican nominee for president of the United States. Election Day was less than a month away and the candidate, a lifelong clean shaven man, received a letter written by Grace Bedell, an eleven-year-old girl from Westfield, New York, who had seen a photo of the GOP's nominee. Written October 15, 1860, the letter urged him to grow a beard and further explained that it would help his facial appearance due to his thin features. Lincoln wrote her back four days later, thanking her for the suggestion.

Following his victory, the president-elect left Springfield on February 11, 1861, bound for the White House and was fully bearded. On February

16, the train stopped in Westfield, New York. Lincoln appeared on the station's platform and he called out for Grace. The little girl was in the crowd with her two sisters, Alice and Helen. She came forth, the president-elect kissed her, and told her that he had taken her advice.

Lincoln went on to Washington, D.C., to command a war while the little girl remained in her hometown and grew into a young woman. On Tuesday April 25, 1865, Grace, who was now sixteen years old, stood with other mourners along the tracks as Lincoln's funeral train made its way from New York City to Albany. In her pocket was the famous letter of October 19, 1860, that she had received from the presidential hopeful.

Today, the original of Grace's letter to Lincoln is in the Burton Historical Collection of the Detroit Public Library. In the early 1990s it was offered for sale at a price of $1 million.

The Gettysburg Address was a very short speech. So much so that most of the audience didn't realize that Lincoln had finished speaking until he put on his hat to leave.

It is not common knowledge that the president was ill with varoloid, a mild form of smallpox, when he delivered the famous composition and spent three weeks in quarantine when he returned to the White House.

Figure 7.1   **Figure 7.2**

Grace Bedell (L) in the 1870s. As an eleven-year-old, she advised Lincoln (R) shown here in 1860, to grow a beard and so he did. *Grace Bedell Foundation / Matthew Brady*

The Battle of Fort Stevens was fought July 11–12, 1864, in northwest Washington, D.C. The fort was one of the links in the ring of strongholds that defended the nation's capital during the Civil War.

President Lincoln came out from the city to visit the post and watch the 6th Army Corps repulse the Confederates, who were under the command of Lieutenant General Jubal A. Early. This fight was as close as the "graybacks" got to the White House during the War between the States. The commander in chief also came under fire from rebel sharpshooters during the attack.

That day the president escaped unharmed, but ten months later he was assassinated. Today, the area where Fort Stevens once stood is adjacent to the Walter Reed Army Medical Center.

The Lincolns lived at the White House as all First Families have since John Adams. But in order to escape the humidity of Washington's summers, they began to use a cottage of the Soldiers' Home on a hill northeast of the White House. From there, President Lincoln commuted to his official residence on horseback.

From 1862 to 1864, Lincoln spent June through November living in the cottage while he commanded the war. He enjoyed the change of scenery, which meant slightly cooler temperatures, and a chance to ride his horse each morning.

One night in August 1864, a shot fired from the bushes caused the president's horse to bolt, and he lost his hat. When soldiers retrieved the stovepipe headpiece, they found a bullet hole in it. The assassination attempt was made as the unaccompanied Lincoln neared the Soldiers' Home on his return from the White House aboard his trusted steed, Old Abe. The president was fortunate on that occasion, but unfortunately the next shot taken at him, nine months later, did not miss.

Lincoln was reelected in 1864 even though his wife had become a negative issue during the campaign. At times, Mary could be a political asset to her husband, but she was often a liability, testing the president's energy and patience. Her frivolous expenditures for French wallpaper and fine china irritated the frontier-raised chief executive, who referred to the extravagance as "flub-adubs."

Little did he know that by 1864, his wife's shopaholic ways had placed them $27,000 in debt. The First Lady was not only spending freely but also sharing political secrets with officials whom she then pressured for personal loans.

Most inaugurations usually go according to plan without any unexpected excitement. But that wasn't the case when Abraham Lincoln was sworn in for his second term on March 4, 1865.

While Honest Abe reaffirmed the oath of office, the new vice president, Andrew Johnson, was drunk. As Lincoln's running mate in the election of 1864, the governor of Tennessee had campaigned incessantly across the country, until he became exhausted and contracted malaria. When he awoke on the day of the ceremony, he could barely get out of bed. Johnson was not a hard drinker, even though his two sons were alcoholics, but he consumed some "medicinal" whiskey to help with the malady.

To complicate his condition, he had not eaten and thus he quickly became intoxicated from the drink. It was apparent to spectators during his inauguration address that he was drunk. With a light rain falling, the muddled vice president was eventually led away from the podium by a Supreme Court justice following his speech.

U.S. senator Zachariah Chandler described Johnson's actions in a letter to his wife: "The inauguration went off very well except that the Vice President Elect was too drunk to perform his duties and disgraced himself and the Senate by making a drunken foolish speech. I was never so mortified in my life, had I been able to find a hole I would have dropped through it out of sight."

However, a report by a *New York Times* journalist made it sound like everything went well when the correspondent wrote, "Mr. Johnson is in fine health and has an earnest sense of the important trust that has been confided in him."

Meanwhile, also attending the swearing-in was John Wilkes Booth and five of his coconspirators, who were standing directly below the president— Lewis Powell (alias Paine or Payne), George Atzerodt, David Herold, John Surratt, and Ned Spangler.

Booth's original plan was to assassinate Lincoln on the Capitol steps, which would serve as a massive stage for the actor's sinister plot. But he couldn't get a clear sight of his target and eventually departed the area.

To conclude the festivities, at the White House reception following the inauguration, the president had to intervene with a guard to allow Frederick Douglass to be admitted because he had been detained at the door of the mansion.

Other than that, it was just a normal day in Washington, D.C.

Abraham Lincoln made several trips to military hospitals to visit with wounded soldiers. On April 8, 1865, the president was at a Union army field hospital in Virginia where he spent hours shaking hands with thousands of wounded soldiers and others.

At some point, the commander in chief decided to show his troops that he was still a formidable specimen. Holding his arm straight out, Lincoln picked up an ax by the butt with the handle parallel to the ground and held the seven-pound tool motionless. At the time of the exercise, he was fifty-six years old and one week away from assassination.

The much younger soldiers looked on in amazement, with some attempting to duplicate the feat but failing. Lincoln then displayed further gusto as he went to work chopping a log just as he had in prior decades. Some of the troops collected the chips as souvenirs of the day.

Whatever happened to the ax? It is now part of a display at the Abraham Lincoln Presidential Library and Museum in Springfield, Illinois.

Abraham Lincoln was shot on the evening of April 14, 1865. That tragic event followed a meeting that he had held at the White House that same afternoon.

His visitors were Congressman Thaddeus Stevens and Senator Benjamin Wade who had come to inform the president that if he didn't support their plans for Reconstruction, they would push for his impeachment. A few hours later, Lincoln was dead and his successor would eventually be impeached (but not for those reasons).

The actor John Wilkes Booth assassinated Abraham Lincoln. In an odd coincidence, the president's son Robert was once saved from possible serious injury or death by Edwin T. Booth, the brother of the assassin.

Edwin was also an actor, and he was held in higher esteem by many theater-goers than his gun-toting younger sibling. He also developed the elaborate Booth's Theater in New York City, which he owned for twelve years (1869–1881).

The incident happened on a platform at the train station in Jersey City, New Jersey. The exact date is uncertain, but it is believed to have taken place in late 1864 or early 1865, while Edwin's brother was plotting the murder of the president.

Robert Lincoln recalled the episode in a 1909 letter to Richard Watson Gilder, editor of *The Century Magazine.*

> There was some crowding, and I happened to be pressed by it against the car body while waiting my turn. In this situation the train began to move, and by the motion I was twisted off my feet, and had dropped somewhat, with feet downward, into the open space, and was personally helpless, when my coat collar was vigorously seized and I was quickly pulled up and out to a secure footing on the platform.

Upon turning to thank my rescuer I saw it was Edwin Booth, whose face was of course well known to me, and I expressed my gratitude to him, and in doing so, called him by name.

In the latter days of the Civil War, Robert served as a captain on General Grant's staff. He relayed the story of Booth's heroics to another staff officer, Colonel Adam Bardeau, who happened to be a friend of Edwin.

Bardeau sent a letter to the heroic Booth, complimenting the actor for his act of bravery. Until he received his friend's correspondence, Edwin had no idea that the life he had saved was that of the president's son. That information provided him some degree of inner peace following his brother's murderous act.

Abraham Lincoln was a person who was known to have vivid dreams that he would often recall and talk about to others. Here is the recollection of one of the president's dreams.

"There seemed to be a deathlike stillness about me," Lincoln said. "Then I heard subdued sobs, as if a number of people were weeping. I thought I left my bed and wandered downstairs."

Finding no one, Lincoln roamed from room to room seeking the source of the sorrowing sounds. "I kept on," he continued,

until I arrived in the East Room, which I entered. There I met with a sickening surprise. Before me was a catafalque, on which rested a corpse in funeral vestments. Around it were stationed soldiers who were acting as guards; and there was a throng of people, some gazing mournfully upon the corpse, whose face was covered, others weeping pitifully.

"Who is dead in the White House?" I demanded of one of the soldiers.

"The President," was his answer. "He was killed by an assassin."

Lincoln told this story to a group of his friends who were visiting the White House, three days prior to his assassination.

Abraham Lincoln was assassinated on Friday evening April 14, 1865. On that same afternoon, he had a conversation with his bodyguard William Crook as they walked to the War Department.

The president said, "I believe there are men who want to take my life. And I have no doubt they will do it. I know no one could do it and escape alive. But if it is to be done, it is impossible to prevent it."

John Wilkes Booth was an actor who was familiar with the layout of Ford's Theatre. Almost one and a half years before the assassination, on November 9, 1863, Booth was performing at that venue in the role of Raphael in the play *The Marble Heart*. Among those in the audience that evening, seated in the presidential box, was Abraham Lincoln.

At one point during the performance, the Confederate-sympathizing actor wagged his finger in Lincoln's direction as he delivered a line of dialogue. Lincoln's sister-in-law, sitting with him in the same presidential box where he would later be slain, turned to him and said, "Mr. Lincoln, he looks as if he meant that for you." The president replied, "He does look pretty sharp at me, doesn't he?"

Following the performance, Lincoln sent word backstage that he would like to meet with Booth to congratulate him. The actor did not respond to the request.

There was another couple sitting next to the Lincolns in the presidential box at Ford's Theatre on the night the president was assassinated. They were U.S. Army Major Henry Rathbone and his date for the evening Clara Harris. She was the daughter of U.S. senator Ira Harris of New York.

As John Wilkes Booth made his escape from the box, he slashed Major Rathbone across the arm with the knife that he was carrying.

Figure 7.3 Clara Harris and Major Henry Rathbone—not so happily ever after. *Matthew Brady*

The couple was part of the presidential outing as last-minute replacements for Ulysses S. Grant and his wife Julia who were originally scheduled to accompany the Lincolns. The Grants had elected to return home rather than go to the theater.

The romance blossomed as Rathbone and Harris were married in 1867 and lived happily—until he murdered her in 1883.

Abraham Lincoln was shot at Ford's Theatre and died the following morning. However, the president wasn't the only individual to meet his demise at the famous show palace.

On June 9, 1893 (twenty-eight years after Lincoln's death), a structural failure of the top floor caused a collapse of the interior of the building which killed twenty-two and injured sixty-eight.

Lincoln had an elaborate funeral that lasted three weeks as his casket traveled by train through several cities. He was finally laid to rest at Oak Ridge Cemetery in Springfield, Illinois. His remains were buried six times before being permanently entombed.

In 1876 two counterfeiters, Jack Hughes and James "Big Jim" Kennally, made a failed attempt to steal Lincoln's body and hold it for ransom. His remains were ultimately placed in concrete to prevent further efforts to abduct the corpse.

In the funeral procession, in addition to Lincoln, was the casket of his son Willie, who had originally been buried in Washington, D.C.

Mary Surratt was convicted as coconspirator in the Lincoln assassination. The boarding-house matron was sentenced to death and on July 7, 1865, became the first female hanged for a crime by the United States federal government.

As officials prepared the woman for her moment on the gallows, they held an umbrella over her head to shield her from the sun. Then she was executed.

Surratt was a cousin of F. Scott Fitzgerald, author of *The Great Gatsby*.

Abraham Lincoln's funeral procession traveled through several municipalities including New York City. That meant that it was a busy time for the cops in the Big Apple, and their activities had to be coordinated with officials from Washington, D.C., and the military.

That job fell on the shoulders of the city's police superintendent. His name? John Kennedy.

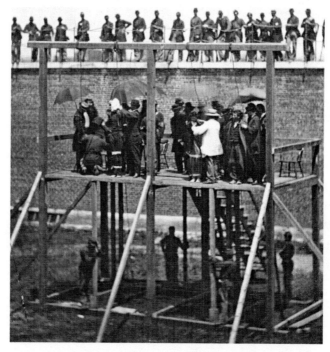

Figure 7.4 Members of the execution party prepare Mary Surratt to be hanged along with the other conspirators. She's standing on the left under the umbrella to prevent her from getting sunburned before being put to death. *Alexander Gardner*

The first two presidents to be assassinated were Abraham Lincoln and James Garfield. Army doctor D. W. Bliss attended to both fallen leaders after they had been shot by their assassins. In 1865, Bliss was one of the sixteen doctors who tried to save Lincoln. In 1881, he supervised the care of Garfield.

Before There Was Law and Order, There Was the Wild West!

I never hanged a man who came back to have the job done over.

—George Maledon, who officiated at the hangings of eighty-six men for Judge Isaac Parker at Fort Smith, Arkansas.

Eli Whitney's cotton gin was one of the most significant inventions in American history. Eli Sr. and his wife Henrietta had four children: Frances was born in 1817, Elizabeth in 1819, Eli Jr. in 1820, and Susan in 1821. But it was Eli Jr. who made a name for himself as an innovator.

After graduating from Princeton University in 1841, Eli Jr. returned home to New Haven, Connecticut, to take over the family's arms production business.

Six years later, he accepted a contract from Samuel Colt to produce one of the legendary weapons of the Old West and the Texas Rangers—the Walker Colt. The Whitneyville Armory produced 1,100 of the famed pistols, which are cherished by today's gun collectors. One was sold at an auction in 2008 for $800,000 plus a $120,000 commission fee.

Whitney's plant also produced about eleven thousand rifles for the Union army during the Civil War. He eventually sold the Armory to the Winchester Repeating Arms Company in 1888.

Back in the 1800s, it was commonplace to form a posse to hunt down outlaws. The California State Rangers were created on May 11, 1853, when Governor John Bigler signed a legislative act establishing the new law enforcement group, which was led by Captain Harry Love, a former Texas Ranger.

The California Rangers were paid $150 a month and had an opportunity to share in a $1,000 reward pool. Their primary objective was to hunt down an outlaw gang known as the "Five Joaquins." They were led by Joaquin Murrieta and composed of Joaquin Botellier, Joaquin Carrillo, Joaquin Ocomorenia, and Joaquin Valenzuela, along with Jack "Three Finger" Garcia.

On July 25, 1853, a group of Rangers encountered the band of armed Mexican desperados near Pacheco Pass in San Benito County, fifty miles from Monterey. A confrontation took place, and two of the outlaws were killed. They were believed to be Murrieta and Garcia.

In order to claim the reward, the Rangers needed to return with proof. Rather than lug two dead bodies back to the then-state capital of Benicia (located near Vallejo), they simply severed Garcia's hand and Murrieta's head as evidence of their deaths and preserved them in a jar of alcohol. Garcia's hand decayed and was eventually buried.

After a period of time, Murietta's head, which was still in the jar, was taken on tour and displayed in Mariposa County, Stockton, and San Francisco. The container was later exhibited throughout California, with

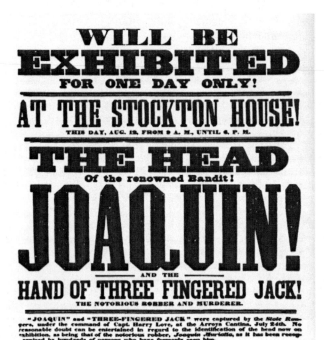

Figure 8.1 Joaquin Murrieta may have lost his head but he gained a following. *California Historical Society*

spectators paying $1 to see the bandit's soggy cranium. Although there were doubts about the actual identity of the remains, seventeen people, including a Catholic priest, signed affidavits confirming that the floating head in the glass container was once attached to the rest of Joaquin Murrieta's body. That enabled Love and his Rangers to receive the reward money.

The question as to the actual identity of the noggin will never be answered because on April 18, 1906, the jar that held the preserved head was destroyed in the San Francisco Earthquake.

The duel in 1842 between Abraham Lincoln and James Shields that was supposed to take place on the Mississippi River's Bloody Island never went forward. Nonetheless, there was no shortage of disputes that were settled on the sandbar. The location hosted at least five duels involving lawyers, politicians, and businessmen.

The last major showdown took place on August 26, 1856, between Benjamin Gratz Brown and Thomas C. Reynolds. It became known as the "Duel of the Governors."

Brown was, at the time, the abolitionist editor of the *St. Louis Democrat* and Reynolds a pro-slavery district attorney from St. Louis. Their opposing views on slavery led to a dispute which eventually landed them on Bloody Island.

When the combatants fired their weapons, the newspaperman was shot in the leg, causing him to limp for the rest of his life, while his adversary was unscathed. Reynolds, a Democrat, had been the governor of Missouri from 1840 to 1844, while Republican Brown held the office from 1871 to 1873.

Oakland is a major California city that was founded in 1853 and sits across the bay from San Francisco. One of the community's founding fathers was the legendary Texas Ranger lawman Jack Hays. In the years following Oakland's establishment, Hays amassed a considerable fortune in real estate and ranching enterprises.

Tombstone, Arizona, was nicknamed the "Town That Was Too Tough to Die." The same might have been said about an Old West gunman named Jack Slade.

In the spring of 1860, Slade rode into a little town on the border of the Nebraska Territory that was run by a French Canadian immigrant named Jules Beni. The two men were in a dispute over some horses that Slade had confiscated which had belonged to the Overland Stage Company.

On the day of his arrival, the unarmed Slade was entering a local dry goods store and saloon when Beni emerged firing a pistol. After hitting him with all six shots, the assailant followed up that attack with two blasts from his double-barreled shotgun, announcing to the townspeople, "When he is dead, you can put him in one of those dry goods boxes and bury him."

Slade looked up from the ground and replied, "I'll live long enough to wear your ears on my watch chain."

Amazingly the wounded man recovered and made good on his word. The following year, he killed Beni by tying him to a fence post and shooting him several times. Then, as he had previously warned, Slade proceeded to remove his victim's ears, attaching them to his watch chain. The two rotting pieces of flesh became items of conversation among the locals, who would gawk as the ears dangled from Jack Slade's watch chain.

Slade made his way to Virginia City, Montana, where he constantly drank and fought too much. In 1864, a vigilante group decided to put an end to his behavior and hang him even though he hadn't committed a major offense in their town.

Slade pleaded for an opportunity to say a final goodbye to his wife Virginia but the execution was carried out before she arrived.

Train robberies were a common occurrence during the era of the Old West. To the surprise of many, it wasn't Frank and Jesse James but the Reno Gang that conducted the first known train robbery in the United States.

On October 6, 1866, the outlaws boarded an Ohio & Mississippi Railway train near Seymour, Indiana, and stole about $16,000 from a safe.

In the summer of 1868, while pursuing a horse thief, the legendary Western figure Wild Bill Hickok rode into Atchison, Kansas. There he met a twelve-year-old boy whose name was also Bill.

Young Bill recalled of Hickok, "He spoke in a slow assured manner."

"Good morning boys and young ladies," Hickok said to the group of children. He then asked them some questions concerning the man he was tracking.

This incident had a profound impact on the boy. Hickok became his hero, and he strove to emulate him in many ways during his life. Eventually Bill Tillman, who had met Wild Bill Hickok as a child, became one of the premier law enforcement officers in the West.

Today's society lives in a world of twenty-four-hours-a-day news reporting. That was not the case for the citizens of the Old West back in 1876.

As an example, it took twelve days for the news of Custer's defeat at the Battle of the Little Bighorn to be delivered to the American public. A scout had to ride three hundred miles from the battlefield to Stillwater, Montana, and then on to Salt Lake City, which had the nearest telegraph office. The dispatch arrived in New York, was transcribed in longhand, and then delivered on foot to the *New York Times.* On Friday, July 7, the public read the account of the front page story with the headline "The Little Horn Massacre."

One of the primary means of transportation in the days of the Old West was the stagecoach. There was a stagecoach driver named Charley Parkhurst who had a secret—he was a woman who had disguised herself as a man and drove a prairie coach for twenty years.

In 1868, before suffrage for females, Charley voted in the presidential election. Many believe that she was probably the first woman to vote in a California election, casting her ballot in the town of Soquel in Santa Cruz County. Charley died of cancer on December 18, 1879, without ever revealing her true identity to her longtime neighbors and friends.

There is an old aphorism that says, "He shot himself in the foot." It means that a person made a mistake against himself. But the Old West actually had a true "He-shot-himself-in-the-foot" story.

On April 30, 1871, gunfighter Clay Allison and two others were said to have stolen twelve government mules belonging to the Fort Union (Texas) commander, General Gordon Granger.

Figure 8.2 Gunfighter Clay Allison proudly poses for a photo after shooting himself in the foot. *Socorro Public Library*

In the fall, Allison tried the same stunt again in Colfax County, New Mexico, but when military men came running to the corral, Allison accidentally shot himself in the foot during the confusion. The would-be rustlers escaped to a hideout along the Red River, where Allison sent his friend Davy Crockett (a nephew of the American frontiersman) to fetch a Dr. Longwell from Cimarron. Though Clay was treated, he spent the rest of his life with a permanent limp.

Wyatt Earp was one of the most famous lawmen of the Old West and well-noted for his participation in the Gunfight at the O.K. Corral.

On May 15, 1871, before he was a peace officer, Earp was indicted for horse theft in Indian Territory. He avoided trial by escaping custody and jumping bail. Following his escape, a warrant was issued for his arrest. But it was returned unserved on November 21, 1871.

President Grover Cleveland lived most of his life in New York City and Washington, D.C. But judging from his actions, he would have been a good fit in the Old West.

On January 1, 1871, some fourteen years before he was the nation's commander in chief, Cleveland was elected sheriff of Erie County, New York.

During his term as the county's top cop, he personally hanged two convicted murderers. The future president carried out the execution of Patrick Morrisey on September 6, 1872. He then strung up another killer, John Gaffney, on February 14, 1873. Although Cleveland had personal qualms about the method of execution, he opted to carry out the duty himself.

Stories that the Old West consisted of hundreds of shootouts with bodies piled up in heaps are exaggerated. In fact, most towns had no shootings at all. The infamous Dodge City's worst year for killings was 1878, when only five people were sent to Boot Hill.

Gun control and regular police forces were, by and large, successful in curtailing violence. There were never more than five murders in any given cattle town during a single year despite the presence, on both sides of the law, of gunfighters. During the peak years of the cattle towns, the average number of homicides was less than two a year for each community.

In many cases, towns required visitors to turn in their guns at the sheriff's office for safekeeping until they departed. But that's not to say that there weren't those who were trigger happy.

While many books and movies have been done about the O.K. Corral, one of the worst gunfights of all time took place on August 20, 1871, in

Newton, Kansas. It was known as the Hyde Park Shootout, where eighteen-year-old Jim Riley killed four men and wounded three others. That amounted to greater casualties than those of the more famous shootouts at Coffeyville, Kansas, or Tombstone, Arizona.

Little is known about Riley, who may have killed more men than his legendary counterpart Billy the Kid received a great deal less publicity. At the time of the shootout, he was dying of tuberculosis and he left the area after the smoke had cleared, never to be heard from again.

In the Old West, William "Buffalo Bill" Cody was best remembered for his spectacular Wild West Show. The town of Cody, Wyoming, is named after the master showman.

All of the troops that were under the command of George Armstrong Custer were killed at the Battle of the Little Bighorn. But another young commander had met a similar fate two decades earlier.

A lesser-known encounter was the Grattan Massacre of 1854 near Fort Laramie, Wyoming, which started when a cow belonging to an Oregon Trail immigrant wandered into a Lakota Sioux Indian camp and was killed and eaten. Lieutenant John L. Grattan of the 6th U.S. Infantry, a recent West Point graduate who lacked real battlefield experience, was dispatched with twenty-nine soldiers to capture the cow killer. The outcome left Grattan and all but one of his men dead.

George Armstrong Custer was promoted to brigadier general during the Civil War but held the rank of lieutenant colonel at the time of his death at the Battle of the Little Bighorn. So why was the youngest general in the Union army demoted?

Custer was court martialed in 1867 and suspended from the U.S. Army for one year with no pay. While stationed at Fort Wallace, Kansas, he had ordered his troops to abandon the post and march to Fort Harker, which meant that he was absent without leave from his station.

Custer also ordered his men to take horses and mules belonging to the U.S. government (this was theft of government property).

While marching, he suspected three members of his column of deserting and ordered them shot. They initially survived their wounds, but the twenty-seven-year-old general ordered the doctor not to tend to them, and one died on the way back.

It was Custer's old friend General Phil Sheridan who helped get him returned to active duty and an eventual assignment against the Sioux Nation in Montana.

The James Gang, headed by brothers Jesse and Frank, became notorious due to a series of robberies that included banks, trains, and stagecoaches in Missouri, Kentucky, Iowa, Texas, Arkansas, Kansas, and West Virginia.

In 1875, the gang pulled off their biggest heist, consisting of $1 million in gold bullion near the border town of Calera, Mexico. They attacked a detail of Mexican guardsmen driving eighteen burros transporting the wealth, which was believed to belong to Mexico's insurgent general Porfirio Díaz.

Following the theft they headed north, crossing Texas toward the Wichita Mountains of Indian Territory (modern-day Oklahoma) where they buried the stash.

Jesse never returned to the area, having been killed in 1882. Frank built a house near Fletcher, Oklahoma, not far from the gold's burial site, and lived there from 1907 to 1911. He made a number of journeys into the mountains in search of the riches that had been hidden three decades earlier but was never able to remember the exact location.

To this day, it is unknown if anyone has ever found the lost treasure of the James Gang.

Wyatt Earp might be best remembered for the Gunfight at the O.K. Corral, but he almost became his own victim.

In 1875, Earp was hired as a deputy marshal in Wichita, Kansas. On January 9, 1876, he was sitting with others in the back room of the Custom House Saloon. Suddenly his revolver, with the hammer resting on the cap, slipped from its holster and fell to the floor, causing a discharge of one of the chambers. The shot passed through Earp's coat before striking the wall and exiting through the ceiling. Patrons quickly cleared the room, fearing that a shootout had begun. It was a close call for the marshal who, five years later, would go on to play a part in the best-known gunfight in the history of the Old West.

Wyatt Earp was neither the town marshal nor the sheriff of Tombstone, Arizona, at the time of the famous shoot-out. His brother Virgil was the town marshal and he had temporarily deputized Wyatt, his brother Morgan, and sidekick Doc Holliday prior to the gunfight.

Also, the showdown did not occur at the O.K. Corral. It took place in a vacant lot between Fly's Photograph Gallery and the Harwood House on Tombstone's Fremont Street. The O.K. Corral was actually located nearby.

Sometimes a victim has a long memory. In 1868, a young man was involved when Custer's troops attacked a Cheyenne village in the Washita Valley. The attack surprised the tribe's leader, Chief Black Kettle. Many

Plains Indians were captured or killed, including their chief, during this battle.

Chief Magpie, a teenager at the time who lived in Black Kettle's village, shot a soldier and then took his horse, riding away to safety.

The young chief survived and lived on to fight Custer another day. Their next meeting was eight years later at the Little Bighorn.

Every one of Custer's men was wiped out at the Battle of the Little Bighorn. However, there was one survivor.

It was Captain Myles Keogh's horse, Comanche, who was discovered badly wounded two days following the battle. After being transported to Fort Lincoln, he was slowly nursed back to health and then retired.

Comanche died in 1890. He is one of only two horses in U.S. history to be buried with full military honors, the other being Black Jack (the famous riderless horse of John F. Kennedy's funeral). His remains were sent to the University of Kansas and preserved, where they can still be seen today in the university's natural history museum.

Lieutenant Colonel George Armstrong Custer and all of his troops from the 7th Cavalry were wiped out at the Battle of the Little Bighorn.

It was also a bad day for several other members of the Custer family. Along with the former Civil War hero, the roster of the dead included his brother Captain Tom Custer, 31; another brother, civilian guide Boston Custer, 27; their sister Margaret's husband, 1st Lieutenant James Calhoun, 31; and their nephew Autie Reed, 18.

It might be more appropriate to refer to the massacre as the "Custer Family's Last Stand."

Under the provisions of the U.S. Constitution, a person cannot be tried twice for the same crime when a verdict has been rendered. This is known as *double jeopardy*.

But there was a well-known event that might fall into the double-jeopardy category.

On August 2, 1876, Jack McCall shot and killed the famous Western figure "Wild" Bill Hickok in Deadwood, South Dakota. The act became a part of Old West folklore because Hickok, who was playing poker at the time, was superstitious about sitting with his back toward the entrance of a room, exposing him to a potential gunmen.

On this day, he had taken a seat with his back facing the saloon doors. After McCall entered the establishment, he shot Bill in the head and then said, "Take that." The bloody gunman dropped his cards on the table as he slumped over, having held two aces and two eights, which has since become known as the "Dead Man's Hand."

During a trial that was hastily put together, McCall claimed that Hickok had killed his brother in Abilene, Kansas. Subsequently, a jury of local miners and businessmen found him not guilty.

McCall then fled from Deadwood and headed to Wyoming, where he bragged, at length, about the details of how he had killed Hickok in a fair gunfight. But the Wyoming authorities refused to recognize the result of McCall's first trial on the grounds that Deadwood was part of Indian Territory and contended that McCall could legally be tried again.

Because Deadwood was an illegal settlement with no constituted law enforcement or court system, the federal court in Yankton, Dakota Territory, declared that double jeopardy did not apply.

That was bad news for twenty-four-year-old McCall, who was retried in Yankton for Hickok's murder, found guilty, and hanged on March 1, 1877. He was the first person to be executed by U.S. officials in the Dakota Territory.

In regard to his testimony, after his execution it was determined that Jack McCall had never had a brother.

In the autumn of 1878, former Union army general Lew Wallace became governor of the New Mexico Territory. In an effort to restore peace in Lincoln County, he proclaimed an amnesty for any man involved in the Lincoln County War who was not already under indictment.

William Henry McCarty, aka Billy the Kid, had fled to Texas after the uprising in Lincoln County. He was under indictment, but Wallace was intrigued by rumors that the young man would be willing to surrender himself and testify against other combatants if amnesty could be extended to him.

In March 1879, Wallace and Billy met in Lincoln County to discuss the possibility of a deal. True to form, the outlaw greeted the governor with a revolver in one hand and a Winchester rifle in the other. After taking several days to consider Wallace's offer, McCarty agreed to testify in return for amnesty.

Wallace was not only a negotiating politician but was also a well-known author who went on to write *Ben-Hur* while living in the "Palace of the Governors" in Santa Fe. The book, published in 1880, was made into a play and three movies.

It is said that Buffalo Bill Cody killed over four thousand of the roaming beasts to feed the railroad workers of the Great Plains. In truth, he never killed a single buffalo because there were none where he hunted.

There are two main species of buffalo: the Domesticated Asian Water Buffalo and the Cape Buffalo. The water buffalo has a range that extends across Asia into North Africa and southern Europe. Small populations can also be found in Australia and South America. The Cape Buffalo is found on the sub-Saharan plains of Africa.

The animal killed by Buffalo Bill was the bison. While bison and buffalo are members of the same family (*Bovidae*), they do not share the same genus or species.

Also, the tag name "Bison Bill" just doesn't have the same ring to it.

Native American tribes would pray to the spirits for healing. In addition, the seeds of the pumpkin were used medicinally in Native American medicine, primarily for the treatment of kidney, bladder, and digestive problems.

From 1863 to 1936, the U.S. Pharmacopoeia listed pumpkin seeds as a treatment for intestinal parasites.

Chief Sitting Bull returned to the United States from Canada in 1881. Because of his involvement in the Battle of the Little Bighorn, he had attained celebrity status but was still confined by the U.S. military.

When the Northern Pacific Railroad opened in September 1884, Sitting Bull was sent to Bismarck to participate in the ceremonies along with former president Ulysses S. Grant. En route, the Sioux chief sold his autograph to souvenir hunters from the back of the wagon that was transporting him.

In the nineteenth century, the Sioux Indians of the Great Plains became addicted to coffee, which they called *kazuta sapa*—"black medicine." For a time, white traders were able to obtain a buffalo robe in exchange for a single cup of java.

And you thought that you were paying too much for your morning cup.

On April 3, 1882, Jesse James was shot dead in his St. Joseph, Missouri, home by his friend Bob Ford who wanted to collect the state's $10,000 reward. The outlaw was then buried—not just once but three times.

Shortly after his murder, Jesse's mother Zerelda had him laid to rest in her yard at the family cabin in Kearney, Missouri, so she could watch over the grave and protect it from thieves. The cabin had been his birthplace.

In 1902, Jesse was exhumed for the first time when his body was moved to Kearney's Mt. Olivet Cemetery. He was reburied beside his wife, who had died on November 13, 1900.

Rumors of Jesse James's survival began almost as soon as the newspapers announced his death. Those speculations grew over the decades, and his body was once again exhumed in 1995, this time for DNA testing. The report stated the remains were consistent with the DNA of Jesse's relatives. After the test, the outlaw was returned to the ground for his third, and perhaps final, burial.

One of the more interesting claims of James's survival came from J. Frank Dalton, who died in 1951 at the age of 102 in Granbury, Texas. A few years earlier while living in Oklahoma, Dalton had professed to being the famous outlaw and had many believing it.

Dalton was so convincing that in May 2000 his body was exhumed to determine if his story was true. But that didn't work out so well.

When the coffin was opened, it was not Dalton resting inside but another Granbury resident named Henry Holland who had died in 1973. It was discovered that Dalton's tombstone had been placed incorrectly, and to this day, his body (wherever it is) has yet to be tested.

The story of the Alamo is probably the most famous American tale about an individual or group that made a heroic last stand against insurmountable odds. Another that can be added to that list is the Frisco Shootout. But unlike the freedom fighters in San Antonio, this story had a much different ending.

On December 1, 1884, at Lower San Francisco Plaza, New Mexico, self-appointed town sheriff Elfego Baca arrested a cowboy who had shot at him. Baca was attacked by about eighty of the cowhand's friends and took refuge in an adobe house.

Over the course of a thirty-six-hour standoff, the mob put four hundred bullet holes in the dwelling without touching Baca. The lawman, in turn, killed four of his adversaries and wounded eight. The shooting ended when the attackers ran out of ammunition.

The uninjured Baca went on to a distinguished career as a New Mexico lawyer and legislator. In 1945, at the age of eighty, he died quietly in his own bed without any bullets flying around him.

Race riots have occurred at various times in the nation's history. Most of the better-known uprisings have taken place at inner-city locations with large numbers of protesters.

But there was one that took place on September 2, 1885, in the unlikely locale of Rock Springs, Wyoming. It was a clash between Chinese and white immigrant miners over the Union Pacific Coal Department's policy of paying workers from the Far East lower wages than whites.

The practice meant that the company could hire more miners from the Far East for less money, making a racially tense situation even worse. At the time, Rock Springs had a population of 763, of which 497 were Chinese.

When the rioting ended, at least twenty-eight Chinese miners were dead and fifteen were injured. Agitators burned seventy-five Chinese homes, resulting in approximately $150,000 in property damage as immigrants fled to safety away from town.

One week following the riot, U.S. Army troops escorted Chinese families, who had escaped the destruction, back to Rock Springs, where many returned to work. As a result, the Union Pacific fired forty-five of the white miners for their roles in the disturbance, although no legal action was ever taken against them. The episode lead to passage of the Geary Act of 1892, which placed further restrictions on Chinese immigration to the United States.

The famous gunfighter Doc Holliday was not killed at the O.K. Corral but was a victim of tuberculosis. The affliction was the number-one killer disease during the Gilded Age with about one-third of the people in the United States succumbing to the illness.

Along with Holliday, other famous people who were claimed by the scourge included Vice President Rufus King, along with First Ladies Hannah Van Buren and Eleanor Roosevelt.

Quanah Parker is remembered as the last chief of the Comanche. During his lifetime he was never defeated in battle.

Even though U.S. soldiers and the Texas Rangers couldn't kill him, the great warrior was almost done in by a freak accident. In December 1885, he visited his father-in-law, Yellow Bear, in Fort Worth, Texas. They were staying at the Pickwick Hotel, which had rooms equipped with gas lighting.

One evening they extinguished the flame before going to bed but did not turn off the gas. A short while later, Yellow Bear died of asphyxiation. Quanah was discovered the following afternoon by a hotel employee and barely survived. It was his good fortune that he had passed out on the floor near an air draft. While many hotels had already switched over to electric lighting, the Pickwick had yet to do so.

In 1892, the Dalton Gang was unsuccessful in their attempt to rob two banks at once in Coffeyville, Kansas. Four members of the outfit including two of the Dalton brothers were killed in the fracas.

But the family had their share of bad luck while they were on either side of the law. Five years earlier, the Daltons' older brother, Frank, had been killed in a gunfight with outlaws in Indian Territory. He had been a deputy marshal.

Annie Oakley was the most famous female sharpshooter in American history. In the spring of 1898, the star of Buffalo Bill's Wild West show wrote to President William McKinley offering to lead a contingent of fifty female sharpshooters into the Spanish-American War. The president did not act upon Oakley's offer, but she made a similar proposal when World War I started almost twenty years later.

Teddy Roosevelt and the Rough Riders became well known for their heroics during the Spanish-American War. Surprisingly, their feats were accomplished by a group with virtually no military experience.

Roosevelt had been serving as assistant secretary of the Navy when he resigned to go fight in Cuba. Most of the Rough Riders were from Arizona, New Mexico, and Indian Territory (Oklahoma).

Captain William H. H. Llewellyn of New Mexico was one of the most noted peace officers of the frontier, having already been shot four times in battles with outlaws. Lieutenant Charles Ballard was another former lawman who had gained Western fame for breaking up the dreaded Black Jack Gang. Benjamin Franklin Daniels, who had one ear partially bitten off in a fight, had been the marshal of Dodge City in its heyday before joining the unit along with the deputy marshal of Cripple Creek, Colorado, Sherman Bell.

The new recruits included characters with such names as Cherokee Bill, Happy Jack of Arizona, Smoky Moore, the Dude, Hell Roarer, Tough Ike, and Rattlesnake Pete. Among the ranks were at least four former or current ministers and several former members of the famed Texas Rangers.

The Goodnight-Loving Trail was one of the Southwest's most heavily used pathways for moving cattle. Charles Goodnight also created the first chuck wagon by taking an old Army wagon and adding extra axles.

Maybe you've purchased a meal from a food truck in recent years. The concept for the modern-day mobile restaurant is derived from the chuck wagon of the Wild West era, proving once more that what was once old is new again.

The major cattle trails of the Old West were the Chisholm, Goodnight-Loving, Santa Fe, and Shawnee. But they were almost empty during a period known as the "Winter of Death."

During the brutal winter of 1886–1887, more than half the cattle in the west froze to death, unable to move in the large snow drifts. At the conclusion of 1887, the rugged weather had wiped out more than half of the United States' western cattle and severely impacted the nation's economy. Most cattle investors went bankrupt; there were shortages of meat for restaurants; cattle rustling increased; and thousands of cowboys were left unemployed.

Federal judge Isaac Parker of Fort Smith, Arkansas, was known as the "Hanging Judge." While his reputation said one thing, his numbers tell a different story.

Parker tried 13,490 cases, of which 9,454 resulted in guilty pleas or convictions. Over the years, he sentenced 160 men to death by hanging, although only 79 of them were actually executed. The rest died in jail, successfully appealed, or were pardoned.

Cattle ranching is most closely identified with life in the west. But the oldest working cattle facility in the United States is the Deep Hollow Ranch in—of all places—Montauk on the tip of Long Island, New York. It was established in 1658.

In 2010, the ranch was purchased for $11.4 million.

In the 1920s, during the Teapot Dome Scandal of the Harding administration, the only member of the group to go to jail was Secretary of the Interior Albert Fall, who spent ten months in a New Mexico prison.

Before entering politics, Fall had worked as a defense attorney. Among his better-known clients was Jesse Wayne Brazel, who confessed to the shooting of Sheriff Pat Garrett and was tried for first-degree murder. Garrett gained fame as the man who killed Western legend Billy the Kid.

Brazel claimed self defense, saying that Garrett was armed with a shotgun and was threatening him. A witness backed up the story. The jury took less than a half hour to return a not-guilty verdict and a victory for Albert Fall.

Like that of the James brothers, there might be another buried treasure waiting for someone to find. The cache is said to be hidden in Beaver Canyon, near Spencer, Idaho, and was placed there by a Montana sheriff turned outlaw, Henry Plummer.

In 1864, Plummer was taken by a group of Montana vigilantes in Bannack but promised to tell them where $100,000 in gold was hidden if they would let him live. The offer was ignored as they gradually hoisted him up by the neck.

Although there have been a number of efforts, as of yet no one has retrieved Plummer's fortune.

Prior to becoming president, Theodore Roosevelt was a hero during the Spanish-American War. But a few years before he and his troops were chasing the enemy, Roosevelt was a deputy sheriff in Medora, North Dakota. He hunted down outlaws and cattle rustlers but was personally opposed to hanging.

Many outlaws were hanged in the days of the Old West. But Thomas "Black Jack" Ketchum became the only person ever hanged under a territorial law that imposed the death penalty on train robbers.

Ketchum attempted a train heist on August 16, 1899, and was eventually captured. He was first taken to Trinidad, Colorado, to face justice but was later transferred for trial to the town of Clayton in the New Mexico Territory, which is where things began to go badly for him.

Ketchum pleaded innocent, but the judge found him guilty and sentenced him to death by hanging. The ultimate punishment was scheduled for April 26, 1901, at 8:00 am. It turned into the town's biggest attraction ever as local lawmen sold tickets to view the event.

As he awaited the noose, Black Jack allegedly told his executioners, "Better hurry up boys, because I'm due in Hell for dinner."

But it was a bad day to be a convicted robber because when the trap was opened and Ketchum hit the end of the rope, his head popped off, which stunned the large throng of spectators. However, the local mortician was able to sew it back on before the burial. Thus Black Jack Ketchum became the only outlaw ever hanged in the New Mexico Territory for a botched train robbery.

· 9 ·

The Inventors: Lots of New Stuff

Put your hand on a hot stove for a minute, and it seems like an hour. Sit with a pretty girl for an hour, and it seems like a minute. That's relativity.

—Albert Einstein

The accomplishments and discoveries of Benjamin Franklin are well documented. But here's one that they may have left out of some biographies.

In 1751, Pennsylvania Hospital—the nation's first—was founded by Franklin and Dr. Thomas Bond. The care facility is very much in business today, with over 25,000 admissions each year, including over 4,200 births. Ben's hospital is part of the University of Pennsylvania Health System.

Samuel Morse was the person who developed the Morse Code that was used over telegraphs. But what got lost in the history books was that Morse's first love was painting.

In 1811 he traveled to Europe to train at London's Royal Academy of Arts. One of his most famous works is his 1825 portrait of the Revolutionary War hero, the Marquis de Lafayette.

It was in 1832 during his voyage home to New York on the ship *Sully* that Morse first conceived the idea of an electromagnetic telegraph as part of his conversations with another passenger, Dr. Charles T. Jackson of Boston. Jackson discussed European experiments using electromagnetism with the would-be artist.

Morse took the information and wrote down in his sketchbook some ideas for a prototype of an electromagnetic recording telegraph and a dot-and-dash code system.

After the creation of his historic invention, he attempted to parlay his fame into the political arena when, in 1836, he ran for mayor of New York City. Although he didn't win the election, among the paintings that hang in the metropolis's city hall is Morse's portrait of Lafayette.

Samuel Colt gained fame for improvements and patents related to various firearms. But he also developed underwater mines and the waterproof telegraph cable. At the time of his death in 1862, his estate was valued at $15 million. But before he became famous, Colt had his share of problems. He was expelled from school at the age of sixteen.

Why, you might ask? For experimenting with explosives.

The famous portrait *Whistler's Mother* was painted by the artist James Abbott McNeil Whistler. His father George Washington Whistler was an early railroad pioneer who invented contour lines for mapping, which are still used today. They are lines drawn on a map connecting points of equal elevation. He also invented the whistle for the railroad train, which, judging by the family name, is logical.

Abraham Lincoln was a lawyer and a politician, but not an inventor by trade. However, he is the only U.S. president to hold a patent (no. 6469 granted on May 22, 1849). It was for a device to lift riverboats over shoals.

He also had ideas for other inventions, such as an agricultural steam plow and a naval steam ram, but he failed to get around to them as there were other matters that claimed his attention.

The safety pin was invented by Walter Hunt in 1849. Unfortunately for Hunt, he sold the patent rights for $400. Hunt is the same person who invented the sewing machine in 1834, although, once again, he failed to file a patent.

But the New York native learned his lesson. He invented several more items, like the fountain pen and a nail-making machine, all of which he got patented. Even though he didn't die a wealthy man, after his death his family was able to prosper from his inventions.

Most elementary schoolchildren have heard the story of the mythological lumberjack Paul Bunyan and his blue ox, Babe. Although the tales are enjoyable, they are works of fiction.

However, there is the true story of Mark Carr. In 1851, he drove two ox-pulled sleds loaded with pine trees from the Catskill Mountains and sold the trees in Manhattan, about one hundred miles away, making New York City the site of the country's very first retail Christmas tree lot.

Investor information is constantly flowing at the stock exchanges on Wall Street. However, one of the more important people in the history of investing is usually omitted during lessons on economics.

His name was Edward A. Calahan, and he invented the stock ticker in 1863, enabling quotes for stocks, bonds, and commodities to be transmitted directly from exchange floors to brokers and investors across the country.

At age eleven, he became a telegrapher for the firm that later became Western Union.

While he was working as chief telegrapher in the company's New York office, he had a chance encounter with a group of messenger boys near one of the exchanges that inspired him to improve business communications. That led to the creation of the ticker.

Calahan, working with George B. Field, also invented the pneumatic telegraph system, the first telecommunications system that allowed transmission from a central station to multiple points within a district.

Birdsill Holly, a native of Auburn, New York, received the patent for the fire hydrant in 1869. He passed away on April 27, 1894, at 7:00 pm. At 1:30 am, six and a half hours after his death, almost the entire city of nearby Gasport, New York, burned to the ground.

There were only two cities that did not incorporate his fire hydrant system in those days; one was Gasport and the other was Chicago, Illinois, and both experienced major fires.

Joseph Glidden created barbed wire in order to keep cattle from roaming away in far-reaching areas such as the Great Plains. This is somewhat notable because Glidden's roots were a long way from cattle country. He grew up in New Hampshire and New York.

Listerine has sold a lot of mouthwash but what does that have to do with history? Listerine Antiseptic mouthwash wasn't born in the bathroom but in the operating room.

Back in 1865, Dr. Joseph Lister, the son of a well-known physicist, first demonstrated the use of an antiseptic in surgery, which was considered a major medical breakthrough in saving lives. In 1879, Dr. Joseph Lawrence and J. W. Lambert refined his product and named it "Listerine," after Dr. Lister.

Levi Strauss and the denim pants that he created revolutionized the clothing industry. That's not new information, but who was Jacob Davis?

In the 1870s, Davis, a tailor from Reno, Nevada, began using rivets to repair pockets on pants. Soon after, he departed Reno for San Francisco, where he went to work for his denim supplier, the Levi Strauss Company.

In 1873, a joint patent was issued to both Davis and the Levi Strauss Company for the process of using rivets on denim pants. Davis remained with Levi Strauss the rest of his career until his death in 1908 when he was succeeded at the job by his son Simon, who ended up running the business. It was Simon who was instrumental in rebuilding the company following the 1906 San Francisco Earthquake.

Thomas Edison is credited with inventing the electric light bulb. But there are some Canadians who might take issue with that statement.

Henry Woodward was a Toronto medical student who, along with help from Matthew Evans, a Toronto innkeeper, invented a glass bulb that housed a carbon filament and nitrogen gas. They patented their creation in 1874.

But like many inventors, they didn't have enough money to mass produce and market the product. A year later they sold the patent. Who bought it? Thomas Edison.

In most states, lethal injection has replaced the electric chair as a state's chosen method of execution. While it may be gone for the most part, the hot seat has not been forgotten.

The electric chair was invented in 1889 by Alfred P. Southwick of Buffalo, New York. He was not an electrician—he was a dentist. Ouch!

The first official underground transportation system in the United States opened in downtown Boston in 1897. That's seven years before the famous New York City subway line made its debut.

However, their predecessor came in February 1870, when Alfred Ely Beach, the publisher of *Scientific American* magazine, opened a below-ground transportation system in New York City that began the trend of subterranean travel.

The worsening situation of New York's streets had prompted searches for an alternative mode of transportation. Beach's "Pneumatic Transit" system consisted of a 312-foot wind tunnel and a 22-passenger car propelled over the tracks by a 100-horsepower fan. While this curious solution to urban transport was not the wave of the future, it helped pave the way for the American subway.

Henry Ford was an innovator in many aspects of automobile production. But there is one facet that the Ford family cannot claim—the car dealership. It is believed that Normandin Chrysler Jeep of San Jose, California, can lay claim to being the nation's first automobile dealer.

Figure 9.1 Here's a look at Beach's "Pneumatic Transit," system in New York City. *Scientific American*

The dealership's roots date back to 1875, when Henry Ford was twelve years old, two decades before the advent of the American auto industry and during the horse-and-buggy days. The company's founder Amable Normandin was a blacksmith and sleigh maker from Montreal who opened his business as a buggy-making shop.

In 1906, the enterprise expanded to include the sale of horseless carriages. The first franchise, the Franklin automobile, came along in 1915. An original Franklin car purchased from Normandin is in the showroom today. An authentic Normandin buggy, built in 1882, graces the roof of the modern building.

Over the years, the dealership sold—and outlasted—a number of car makes, including Hupmobiles, Saxons, and Hillmans. Second-generation owner Louis Normandin sold all his stock before the stock market crash of 1929 and reinvested it elsewhere, such as in real estate.

In 1933, the family obtained a DeSoto-Plymouth franchise from Chrysler Corporation. The Chrysler line replaced ill-fated DeSoto in 1958. A fifth generation of Normandins now runs the dealership, which is on a ten-acre spread that's part of the Capitol Expressway Auto Mall.

Alexander Graham Bell invented the telephone . . . or did he? His primary rival was a scientist named Elisha Gray. On the morning of Monday February 14, 1876, Gray signed and notarized a document which described a telephone that used a liquid microphone. His lawyer then submitted the document to the U.S. Patent Office. That same morning, the attorney for Alexander Graham Bell filed his patent application.

Bell was awarded the patent but Gray challenged it, and after two years of litigation, Bell was awarded rights to the invention. As a result, Alexander Graham Bell is credited as the inventor.

But there were others who claimed that they had actually created the telephone. Before Bell and Gray were locked in their patent scuffle, there was Philipp Reis.

In 1860, the German scientist constructed the first prototype of a telephone, which could cover a distance of just over one hundred yards. Reis had difficulty generating interest in his invention among the German populace, despite demonstrating it in 1862 to (among others) Wilhelm von Legat, inspector of the Royal Prussian Telegraph Corps. A decade later, the invention aroused more attention in the United States when Dr. T. H. Vanderwyde exhibited it in New York.

Reis never enjoyed the fruits of his labor, as he died in 1874 of a lung ailment. He was just forty years old.

Alexander Graham Bell is credited as the inventor of the telephone, but before that, when he was twelve years old, young Alexander was sensitive to disabilities. Over the years, he was constantly seeking a way to cure them through technology.

Like Edison, Bell had dyslexia, which would cause him problems at school, but he always kept his interest in science, especially biology.

Not only was he the inventor of the telephone, but the one-time poor student Alexander Graham Bell is also well known as one of the founders of the National Geographic Society.

Alexander Graham Bell's first successful telephone call in 1876 went to his assistant Thomas Watson, who was in the next room of their Boston laboratory.

What many do not know is that Bell, the inventor of the telephone, never called his wife or his mother because they were both deaf. He was actually trying to invent an improved hearing aid, but his creation became the phone.

The first telephones did not have a dialing mechanism, so all callers had to be connected by operators. The first phone operators were boys, but many of them were rowdy, shooting spit wads and rubber bands, wrestling, and sometimes being rude to the customers. It wasn't long before they were replaced with young women, who were friendlier and less troublesome.

Usually the first people in town to have a phone were the doctor and the pharmacist because their calls were important to a person's well-being. Many pharmacists let their customers make free phone calls, which made their drugstore a community gathering place and resulted in increased sales.

Thomas Edison patented over one thousand different inventions. When he was a young man, Thomas saved a station-master's son from being hit by a train, and out of gratitude, the boy's father taught Edison how to use the telegraph.

That talent came in handy a few years later when the inventor proposed to his girlfriend Mina by Morse Code with the use of a telegraph. Mina replied, -.-- . . . . (which is Morse Code for "yes").

In 1876, at the age of twenty-nine, Alexander Graham Bell invented his telephone. Five years later, he was summoned to the White House, but not to make a phone call.

While boarding a train in Washington, D.C., on July 2, 1881, President James A. Garfield was shot twice. During the nearly three months that Garfield lay ill, his case became one of national interest, and it caught the attention of the prominent inventor.

Bell reasoned that the technology used in his telephone could actually be used in the construction of a device that would be able to detect metal and thus find the assassin's bullet lodged in Garfield's chest. It was a mechanism that was first proposed by astronomer Simon Newcomb.

Bell had previously used it to find bullets lodged in the bodies of Civil War veterans, and he thought the noninvasive technique would also work on the president.

But when he tried to use the machine on Garfield, it was unsuccessful because, unbeknownst to Bell, the commander in chief was lying on a coil-spring mattress.

That type of bedding had only been recently invented. In fact, they were so new that the general public had little knowledge of them, and the White House was one of the few places at the time that was able to get one. Bell's invention detected metal, but unfortunately, instead of the bullet, it was the coil springs. If Garfield had been moved off his new mattress and onto the floor or a table, the apparatus would have stood a greater chance of detecting the small projectile and could have possibly saved the president's life.

Nikola Tesla was a Serbian immigrant who is best known for his many revolutionary developments in the field of electromagnetism in the late nineteenth and early twentieth centuries. But for all of his genius, Tesla suffered from obsessive-compulsive disorder coupled with many unusual quirks and phobias.

He did things in threes and was adamant about staying in a hotel room with a number divisible by 3.

Henry Ford is often credited with creating the assembly line. But contrary to many history textbooks, Ransom Olds was actually the first person to use the assembly line in the automotive industry. The new approach of putting together automobiles enabled him to more than quintuple his factory's output, from 425 cars in 1901 to 2,500 in 1902. Ford's assembly line came about in 1913.

Ford and Dodge are two major auto makers. But the first Fords that were produced had Dodge engines.

In 1903, Henry Ford needed a large sum of money in order to get his new car company off the ground. The parties reached an agreement in which the Dodge brothers (Horace and John) agreed to give Ford $7,000 worth of their automobile parts and $3,000 in cash in return for a 10 percent stake in the Ford Motor Company.

In order to protect themselves, the brothers included a clause in the contract that they would receive all of Ford's assets if he went bankrupt, as he had with another car company in 1901. They never had to enforce the codicil as the brothers eventually made a fortune from that initial investment.

Orville and Wilbur Wright made the first successful plane flight on December 17, 1903, at Kitty Hawk, North Carolina. Forgotten by many is that the first person killed in an airplane accident was U.S. Army lieutenant Thomas E. Selfridge.

On September 17, 1908, Selfridge was a passenger on a demonstration flight at Fort Myer, Virginia, when the crash occurred. The pilot had luck on his side and survived the accident. Who was the pilot? Orville Wright.

The Wright Brothers' famous flight was photographed, which provided the evidence that they had successfully accomplished their goal. Fortunately for the pair, Orville had brought his camera with him.

However, there was an earlier flight, but someone forgot the camera.

It was reported that on August 14, 1901, near Bridgeport, Connecticut, Bavarian immigrant Gustave Whitehead made a successful flight.

Two years, four months, and three days before the historic jaunt of the Wright brothers at Kitty Hawk, a birdlike monoplane took to the air in the early dawn. The craft carried its inventor and builder a distance of approximately one-half mile. Unfortunately for Whitehead, and unlike the flight of the Wright Brothers, his journey into the sky was not recorded on film.

Wilbur Wright was part of the tandem that made the first successfully recorded airplane flight on December 17, 1903. He was also the first person to fly an airplane around the Statue of Liberty performing the feat on September 29, 1909.

Figure 9.2 Wilbur Wright gets an up close and personal look at Liberty. *Smithsonian Air and Space Museum*

In 1903, Mary Anderson, a young woman from Alabama, was touring New York City on a streetcar whose driver had to keep stopping to wipe snow and ice off of the windshield. She made a quick drawing in her sketchbook, and later patented a device which is now standard on all vehicles—the windshield wiper.

Anderson received a patent for her creation, and in 1905 she attempted to sell the rights to a Canadian auto manufacturer. They turned down her invention, stating that it had no "commercial value."

It was a missed opportunity for the company as Mary's invention eventually became essential equipment on all automobiles.

Albert Einstein arrived at his famous Theory of Relativity in 1905. He defected to the United States from Germany in 1933 and alerted President Franklin Roosevelt that the Nazis had begun work on nuclear weaponry.

But for all of his brilliance, Einstein didn't speak until he was four years old. Like Edison and Bell, he suffered from dyslexia and had problems memorizing simple tasks.

The scientific genius could not remember the months in the year or how to properly tie his shoelaces. But that didn't stop him from playing detailed works by Mozart and Bach on the violin and the piano.

Albert Einstein and Charles Darwin were men of science. They also married their first cousins.

Alexander Graham Bell made that historic first phone call to his pal Thomas Watson when the two men were just one room away from each other at Bell's lab in Boston. But they expanded the distance on January 25, 1915 (thirty-nine years after the first telephone call) when Bell, at New York City's Telephone Building, called his old partner, who was on Grand Avenue in San Francisco.

It took more than a few able bodies to pull off the first transcontinental telephone call. There were 15,000 telephone repair men, 5 for every mile of wire—that wire supported by 130,000 newly erected poles—to thwart potential problems. Making the connection through a series of operators, the two men were able to place the call after twenty-three minutes, and the project went as planned as the two famous inventors talked to each other from their locations on opposite sides of the country.

Henry Ford's contributions to the automobile industry are well known. What isn't common knowledge is the part that he played in the world of barbeque.

That's because Ford created the charcoal briquette from the wood scraps and sawdust of his car factory. He found that he could use the charcoal for a clean, smoke-free source of heat. When he discovered a new heat supply for his workers, the automaker didn't realize that he had also discovered a unique way of cooking food.

In 1921, Ford and his good friend Thomas Edison designed and opened a charcoal manufacturing plant in Iron Mountain, Michigan, about five hundred miles north of Detroit. For every ton of scrap wood, the facility produced 610 pounds of a product known as "Ford Charcoal."

By the end of 1924, the plant was churning out fifty-five tons of briquettes each day under the watchful eye of E. G. Kingsford, the husband of Ford's cousin. The product's name was later changed from "Ford" to "Kingsford," and in 1923, the part of Iron Mountain where the plant was located was also renamed for the master of hot coals.

Along with vehicles, Ford dealerships sold the bagged briquettes, which carried the Ford logo, for 25¢. As the company never turned down an opportunity to make a sale, customers who didn't have a grill could also purchase one for just $2.

Today, under ownership of the Clorox Company, Kingsford charcoal uses plants in five states to convert millions of tons of waste wood into the top-selling charcoal briquettes in the world.

Henry Ford's use of the assembly-line process completely revolutionized manufacturing. But in 1938 he was awarded Adolf Hitler's Grand Cross of the Supreme Order of the German Eagle. Taking a page from the automaker's business practice, Hitler used the assembly line to speed up production of weapons in order to create better quality and interchangeable products.

Among others who were presented with similar awards from the Nazi leader were aviator Charles Lindbergh and Thomas J. Watson, chairman of IBM.

The first cigarette-vending machine was created in 1926 by American inventor William Rowe. The device dispensed packs of cigarettes during an era when the economy was flourishing and smoking was popular across the country.

But during the Great Depression, vendors began dispensing individual cigarettes because many smokers could not afford a whole pack due to the economic downturn. Consumers began paying a penny for a single smoke from the machines.

In 1926, Dr. Robert Goddard was the creator of the world's first liquid-fueled rocket, which paved the way for future space travel.

Back in 1920, the *New York Times* had chastised Professor Goddard, the father of space exploration, for his claim that rockets could function in a vacuum. "He seems only to lack the knowledge ladled out daily in high schools," the editorial stated in its January 13 issue.

However, some forty-nine years later, on July 17, 1969, just before Apollo 11 landed men on the moon, the *Times* published the following statement: "It is now definitely established that a rocket can function in a vacuum. The *Times* regrets its error."

The retraction was a bit late. Dr. Goddard died in 1945.

There are many famous stories about various automakers. But there was another guy, not known as a car designer, who had a role in the creation of another well-known vehicle.

While dictator Adolf Hitler was recognized for his treachery and evil, he was also behind the concept of the popular Volkswagen. As post–World War I Germany tried to dig its way out of its economic depression, many of its citizens couldn't afford a car.

After Hitler assumed power as chancellor of Germany in 1933, he met with automotive designer Ferdinand Porsche and charged him with the task of creating an affordable new vehicle. The dictator required that the vehicle carry two adults and three children, go up to 60 miles per hour, get at least 33 miles per gallon, and cost only 1,000 reichsmarks (about $300 in 1933).

It was a pretty tall order, but by 1938 a factory at Wolfsburg was ready to mass-produce Porsche's cars known as "Beetles." Unfortunately for the public, the idea was then pushed to the background as the plant was needed to build war machinery for the Nazis.

After the war, the British military re-opened the factory for its original purpose. They named it Volkswagen, and gave control of the company to the West German government.

Over the decades, Volkswagen introduced new models across Europe. By 1955, over one million cars had been built. The VW Beetle started selling in the United States, and by 1972 it had become the most popular car ever made.

Perhaps the Führer should have stuck to the car business.

Thomas Edison and Henry Ford were two of history's most noted inventors. They were also close friends.

On Edison's deathbed, Ford demanded that Edison's son Charles catch Edison's final breath in a test tube. Charles did as instructed and quickly sealed it. Today that test tube can still be found in the Henry Ford Museum.

The Ford Edsel, named after Henry Ford's son, was one of the biggest automotive failures of all time. It was only around for the 1958, 1959, and 1960 model years.

The car was so unpopular that during that period, the brain trust at Ford was scrambling to save their floundering project. The company went as far as to run a promotion giving Edsel buyers the opportunity to win a pony.

The end of the line mercifully arrived in November 1959, which dropped the *Kelly Blue Book* value of the car by $400. In an effort to retain their customer base, the company issued $400 vouchers on other Ford autos. The vehicle had been a total disaster.

But the model's owners have gotten the last laugh. Today, fewer than six thousand Edsels survive, and they are considered collectors' items. A mint 1958 Citation convertible sometimes sells for over $100,000, while rare models, like a 1960 convertible, may bring up to $200,000.

In science class, students learn about the planets along with the famous rings of Saturn. But how many students know that Uranus also has rings? In 1977 the rings of Uranus were discovered by accident by astronomers James L. Elliot, Edward W. Dunham, and Douglas J. Mink of NASA's Kuiper Airborne Observatory.

On March 10, 1977, Dunham and Mink were studying Uranus and found that a star that they had been following briefly vanished from view five times before and after it was eclipsed by the planet. They began to believe that, like Saturn, Uranus was surrounded by rings. In 1986, their theory was confirmed by the Voyager 2 spacecraft. Over the years, the Hubble Space Telescope has validated the finding and set the planet's number of rings at thirteen.

But just to prove that what was once old can be new again, Sir William Herschel, who discovered Uranus in 1781, stated in a paper that he presented in 1797 that there might be rings around Uranus. However, his colleagues dismissed the theory because the rings were too difficult to observe.

Bill Gates was one of the founders of Microsoft, and he created a number of computer programs. He went on to become the world's richest person.

So what does someone buy when they have billions to spend? In 1994, Gates purchased the Codex Leicester—a seventy-two-page collection of Leonardo da Vinci's scientific writings. They are a mixture of observations on water's properties, astronomy, rocks, and fossils.

Gates paid nearly $31 million for the document, making it the most expensive book ever sold. Today, he puts the codex on public display once a year in a different city around the world.

And you thought that your books were expensive.

· *10* ·

1900–1916:
Don't Get Stuck in the Bathtub!

One of the lessons of history is that nothing is often a good thing to do and always a clever thing to say.

—Will Durant, American Historian

On March 4, 1901, William McKinley was sworn in for his second term as president. In that same year, a lightbulb was installed in the firehouse in Livermore, California. The switch was turned on and the beam began to shine. It continued to do so, to the point that in 1972, that lightbulb was declared by the *Guinness Book of World Records* as the oldest known working lightbulb ever.

Today, it is known as the "Centennial Light Bulb" and it continues to run with no problems. If you don't live in Livermore but want to see it for yourself, travel on your computer and go to www.centennialbulb.org/photos.htm.

It has been suggested that the first U.S. president to ride in an automobile was Theodore Roosevelt. But his predecessor, William McKinley, had previously ridden in a Stanley Steemer and was also transported to the hospital in a 1901 Columbia electric ambulance after being shot by anarchist Leon Czolgosz.

However, the quick attention to the president's condition was in vain as he died eight days later.

When William McKinley was assassinated, his vice president Theodore Roosevelt became the nation's new chief executive.

But that was not TR's first experience with a presidential assassination. On Monday April 24, 1865, nine days after Abraham Lincoln's death, his body arrived in New York City as part of the three-week farewell tour that concluded in Springfield, Illinois.

Six-year-old Teddy's grandfather, a powerful NYC businessman, greatly admired Lincoln. The Roosevelt home was located at the end of Broadway, and the funeral procession passed directly by the front of the house.

There is a picture of the moment when the procession passes the Roosevelt home, and if you look closely at the second-story window of the dwelling, you can see two small children observing the cortege. One of them is Teddy Roosevelt who, thirty six years later, would become president when William McKinley was killed by an assassin.

The other boy is his younger brother Elliot.

In 1901, William McKinley was shot at the Pan-American Exposition in Buffalo, New York. He was superstitious and made a habit of wearing a red carnation in his lapel for luck. Occasionally, when he wanted to share his good fortune with others, he would give away the flower.

Figure 10.1 If you look closely at the second story window, you can see a future president. *New York Historical Society*

At the gathering, McKinley gave his lucky red carnation to a young girl in the receiving line. A short time later, the president was approached by assassin Leon Czolgosz who was in the same line and wearing a fraudulent bandage over his right hand which concealed a gun.

At that point, and without his lucky red carnation, McKinley's luck had just run out.

Leon Czolgosz died in the electric chair on October 29, 1901, six weeks after he shot President McKinley. But in those days, electrocutions weren't limited to humans.

In 1902, a performing circus elephant named Topsy who resided at Coney Island's Luna Park went berserk and killed a drunk circus employee who tried to feed her a lighted cigarette. There was also a rumor that Topsy had previously killed two other workers. The owners of the pachyderm decided that their jungle beast needed to be put down, which raised the ire of animal advocates when it was suggested that the behemoth offender be hanged.

Inventor Thomas Edison entered the controversy with an alternative method of execution. He recommended using electricity to kill the elephant just like it had been done for the presidential assassin.

As one might imagine, the execution of a huge circus animal was an immense public spectacle. It took place on January 4, 1903, at Coney Island, with about 1,500 people in attendance and Edison filming the event.

To subdue her, Topsy was fed carrots laced with cyanide, which was then followed by the coup de grâce when she was struck with a charge of 6,000 volts AC. The animal died within seconds.

In 1916, another elephant was tried and, this time, hanged for the murder of a circus worker in Erwin, Tennessee. The execution was performed by using a heavy-duty chain and a lifting crane before a crowd of 2,500.

There were four American presidents (Lincoln, Garfield, McKinley, and Kennedy) who were assassinated, and there is a common link to the first three.

Lincoln's son Robert was invited to accompany his parents to Ford's Theatre on the evening that his father was shot by John Wilkes Booth, April 14, 1865. But he was tired after arriving in the nation's capital from the scene of the Confederate surrender at Appomattox Court House.

Robert remained at the White House and went to bed. He was later awakened and notified that his father had been shot.

When James Garfield was elected president in 1880, he tapped the younger Lincoln as his secretary of war. On July 2, 1881, Robert Lincoln was with his commander in chief at the 6th Street train station in Washington, D.C., where he was about to depart for Massachusetts when Garfield was shot by Charles J. Guiteau. He succumbed to his wounds several weeks afterward.

Twenty years later, president William McKinley invited Robert, who was then president of the Pullman Car Association, to the Pan-American Exposition in Buffalo, New York.

On September 6, 1901, Lincoln was running late and wasn't inside the building when the president was shot by Leon Czolgosz, although he quite possibly heard the gunfire. Robert was aware of the tragedies that seemed to follow him. He once said after turning down an invitation to a presidential function, "No, I'm not going, and they'd better not ask me, because there is a certain fatality about presidential functions when I am present."

He did make an exception and attend the dedication of the Lincoln Memorial in 1922 in the presence of President Warren G. Harding and former president William Howard Taft. Harding died suddenly just a little more than a year after the ceremony.

Robert Todd Lincoln died in 1926, thirty-seven years before President Kennedy's murder.

Theodore Roosevelt enjoyed hunting and had spent time in the west working as a cowboy. Following William McKinley's assassination in 1901, he became justifiably concerned about his personal security, so he began carrying a concealed handgun.

When Roosevelt visited his alma mater Harvard University, the school's president Charles W. Eliot was taken aback when he saw Roosevelt strapping on a holster in his room, ignoring the Massachusetts law restricting concealed handguns.

The president is protected by the Secret Service whenever he's traveling. But sometimes the nation's chief executive can't be protected.

An example of that took place when President Theodore Roosevelt, touring New England, was slightly injured when his carriage collided with an electric trolley on September 3, 1902, in Pittsfield, Massachusetts. During the accident, Secret Service agent William Craig lost his life, making him the first from the agency to be killed in the line of duty.

The president, a veteran of the Spanish-American War, emerged with a swollen face and injured leg, but he continued the tour for the day, stopping in Bridgeport, Connecticut, to speak to a crowd of thirty thousand.

There have been several White House weddings during the history of the country. Eight of them were the daughters of presidents.

What a number of historians believe was the most bizarre executive mansion nuptial took place on February 17, 1906, when Theodore Roosevelt's oldest child, Alice, married Congressman Nicholas Longworth of Ohio. Her mother, Alice Lee Roosevelt, had died hours after giving birth to her in 1884.

Two years later, when Roosevelt decided to marry Edith Kermit, his new bride insisted that she be permitted to raise Alice as her daughter, but the association of the two women was like mixing oil and water. As an adult, the presidential offspring reveled in the publicity that she garnered from her unladylike public displays. She carried a live snake in her purse, smoked in public, drove fast cars, and once jumped into a swimming pool fully dressed.

Her exasperated father stated, "I can either run the country or attend to Alice. . . . I cannot possibly do both."

She and the president argued during his inauguration as Alice waved from the viewing stand at the crowd. Roosevelt ordered her to stop and remarked, "This is my inauguration!"

Family friend Ruth Lee called her "a young wild animal . . . put into good clothes."

As one might expect, her wedding turned into the hottest ticket in town as journalists scrambled to get a seat inside the White House. And for those who made it to a chair, they weren't disappointed.

What began being planned as a small ceremony ended up with more than seven hundred guests with gifts from almost every world leader, including a box of slithering reptiles from a snake collector.

Alice had no bridesmaids, and she used a military sword to cut the wedding cake. As the bride left the White House, her stepmother pulled her close and told her, "I want you to know that I'm glad to see you go. You've never been anything but trouble."

The marriage lasted until Congressman Longworth's death in 1931.

In 1906, a mighty earthquake nearly destroyed San Francisco. And when the 1915 Panama-Pacific Exposition was held in the city, much of the site was built on a landfill that partly consisted of debris from the massive disaster.

In 1908, William Howard Taft was elected the nation's twenty-seventh president.

Almost everyone who has ever heard his name also knows the famous story about the 350-pound commander in chief getting stuck in the White House bathtub and needing the help of aids to get him back on dry land.

But unlike most who have held the office, becoming president wasn't Taft's idea of his "dream job." The position that he deeply wanted, and secured in 1921, was that of chief justice of the U.S. Supreme Court.

As such, he became the only president to serve as chief justice, and thus is also the only former president to swear in subsequent presidents, giving the oath of office to both Calvin Coolidge (in 1925) and Herbert Hoover (in 1929).

Taft remains the only person to have led both the executive and judicial branches of the U.S. government. He considered his time as chief justice to be the high point of his career and once remarked, "I do not remember that I was ever president."

He served as chief justice until 1930.

Cincinnati, Ohio, was the birthplace of William Howard Taft. On April 1, 1853, four years before Taft was born, the Queen City became the first in the United States to have a full-time paid fire department. It was also the first city in the world to use steam fire engines.

On April 6, 1909, American explorer Admiral Robert Peary claimed to have reached the geographic North Pole. That announcement followed a similar one by Dr. Frederick A. Cook, who had been a surgeon on an 1891–1892 Peary expedition, and who claimed to have reached the pole the previous year.

In January 1911, the U.S. government attempted to find the truth when Peary appeared before the Naval Affairs Subcommittee of the U.S. House of Representatives. His diary of the journey was entered into proceedings as evidence.

Some of the congressmen noted that the journal looked clean rather than like one that had traveled on a mission to a polar icecap. Also, Peary's report of his group traveling an average of 26.7 miles per day as compared to Cook's more acceptable 15 miles a day raised some eyebrows in the committee chambers.

The panel barely approved a bill by a vote of 4 to 3 confirming Peary had been first to reach the pole. It was then passed by the full House and Senate and was signed by President William Howard Taft.

Although his achievement had been validated by Congress, Peary was bitter. He felt demeaned and never showed his polar diary or any of the other data in public again. He died in 1920, and his family consented to an examination of the records in 1988 by *National Geographic.* The examiners concluded that Peary probably never made it to the North Pole.

If Peary's story had a sad ending, Cook's tale was even worse. In November 1923, he was found guilty on charges of mail fraud and sentenced to serve fourteen years and nine months imprisonment at Leavenworth Penitentiary in addition to a $12,000 fine. He was pardoned by President

Franklin Roosevelt in 1940, shortly before his death. To this day the debate continues: Who discovered the North Pole?

The Chicago Fire is the most famous blaze in the nation's history. But it wasn't the largest.

The Great Fire of 1910, also known as the Big Burn, charred about three million acres in northeast Washington, northern Idaho (the Panhandle), and western Montana. The area that burned included parts of ten national forests. The firestorm lasted over two days (August 20–21, 1910) and killed eighty-seven people, including seventy-eight firefighters.

The president travels thousands of miles each year aboard the official plane, Air Force One.

On October 11, 1910, before the first luxury jet was ever produced, Theodore Roosevelt climbed into the passenger seat of a plane during an airshow at Aviation Field in St. Louis, Missouri. The pilot was Arch Hoxsey, who had just completed a record flight from Springfield, Illinois.

The plane, which was built by the Wright Brothers, reached an altitude of about fifty feet and stayed airborne for about four minutes. The brief excursion made TR the first president to fly in an aircraft.

The adventurous former chief executive said he wished they could have stayed in the air for an hour. That may have been so at the moment, but just a few weeks later, on December 31, 1910, Arch Hoxsey was killed in a plane crash.

In 1911, the Supreme Court ruled that John D. Rockefeller's Standard Oil Company had become a monopoly and must be dissolved. It was eventually split into thirty-four different companies.

Two of the companies that emerged from that order were Jersey Standard and Socony. In 1963, Socony became Mobil, and in 1972, Jersey Standard became Exxon.

In 1999, Exxon and Mobil merged. Eighty-eight years after the nation's highest court ordered its breakup, two of the descendants of the Rockefeller empire were rejoined to form the largest, non–state owned energy company in the world and one of the largest publicly traded companies on earth.

When citizens are unsatisfied with the job that their political leaders are doing, they have the right to vote them out of office.

But most residents are unaware that there was once a move to get rid of the entire U.S. Senate. In 1911, freshman congressman Victor Berger of

Wisconsin introduced a resolution that called for abolishing the Senate along with eliminating the presidential veto.

Berger was neither a Democrat nor a Republican but rather a Socialist. The following year Congress began work on the Seventeenth Amendment (direct election of U.S. senators by popular vote), but Berger wasn't around for the debate. He was defeated in his bid for re-election.

The official presidential retreat is Camp David, Maryland. In addition to that getaway site, many chief executives have also spent parts of summers at their own private residences in order to catch up on a little rest and relaxation. But at one time, there were plans to construct a western White House on a hill above the town of Morrison in Jefferson County, Colorado.

In the early 1900s, millionaire land speculator and magazine publisher John Brisben Walker bought over four thousand acres, and in 1909, he constructed a magnificent stone castle atop Mt. Falcon.

Walker then decided to build a retreat for U.S. presidents on a ridge near his own home. A fund-raising drive got underway with children across Colorado each donating 10¢ to the project. A cornerstone with the words "Summer Home for the Presidents of the United States, gift from the People of Colorado, 1911" was laid out as construction began.

But luck was not on Walker's side as funding dried up when America became involved in World War I. After that, his wife died, and in 1918, his own estate caught fire and burned when it was struck by lightning. Although he had made vast fortunes at various times in his life, Walker died penniless in 1931 at the age of eighty-three.

Today, the spot on Mt. Falcon where Walker once envisioned a western White House is a favorite destination of hikers who can view the building's cornerstone, which stands as a reminder of one man's unfinished vision.

Arizona became the nation's forty-eighth state on February 14, 1912, but it also can claim some Civil War history.

In 1855, Secretary of War Jefferson Davis (yes, that Jefferson Davis) was told of an innovative plan for importing camels to help build and supply a western wagon route from Texas to California. The idea seemed plausible as it was a hot and desolate region like the animal's natural habitat in the Middle East.

Davis thought so much of the concept that he proposed a Camel Military Corps to Congress. He stated his belief that "the camel, it is believed, would remove an obstacle which now serves greatly to diminish the value and efficiency of our troops on the western frontier."

Congress agreed and appropriated $30,000 for Davis's concept. But with the first shots of the Civil War, the plans for the Camel Military Corps became a combat casualty. Most of the animals were auctioned off, although a few escaped into the desert, where they were shot by prospectors and hunters.

HMS *Titanic* sank in 1912, which was William Howard Taft's last full year as president. During his single term in the White House, one of Taft's top military aides was Major Archie Butt, who had served during the Spanish-American War in 1898.

Through the years, Butt had never taken a vacation, but in the spring of 1912 the soldier's health took a turn for the worse. Taft urged him to rest and to get away from his job for awhile, so the officer booked a six-week vacation to Europe. Butt's only official duty during his journey was an audience with Pope Pius X, during which he delivered a personal message from the president.

Butt sailed for Europe aboard the steamship *Berlin*, of the North German Lloyd Line. However, he booked passage on the new British ship *Titanic* for his return crossing to the United States. During that homebound voyage, the major was playing cards on the night of April 14, 1912, in the first-class smoking room when the ill-fated vessel struck an iceberg.

According to some accounts, Butt immediately began acting as another ship's officer, herding women and children into the lifeboats. At one point, he drew his pistol to prevent mobs from trying to storm their way onto one of the small rescue crafts.

Some survivors claimed that he gave up both his lifeboat seat and life vest to a young woman, choosing instead to go down with the ship as a hero. His remains, if found, were never identified.

Taft had made it an annual ritual of throwing out the first ball at the Washington Nationals' opening home game of the baseball season. However in 1912, just a few days after the sinking, the nation's leader declined to attend the event due to the loss of his close friend.

Somebody once said, "Don't believe everything that you read in the newspapers." On the morning following the sinking of the *Titanic*, this headline appeared on the front page of the *Baltimore Sun*, "All Titanic Passengers Are Safe; Transferred in Lifeboats at Sea."

The *Titanic* was advertised to the public as a ship that was "unsinkable," but it went down on its maiden voyage. This marked perhaps the second major event where that type of claim turned out to be untrue.

The majestic Iroquois Theater in Chicago was advertised as "Absolutely Fireproof" on its playbills. But on December 30, 1903, the Iroquois was the site of the deadliest single-building fire in U.S. history. The blaze took 571 lives within twenty minutes, and including those who died in the hospital, the death count climbed to a total of 602.

The theater had been open for only thirty-seven days.

There have been numerous books written and movies made about the sinking of the *Titanic*. But many have never read an account or seen a motion picture about the sinking of the SS *Sultana*.

The vessel was a Mississippi River steamboat paddle-wheeler de-stroyed in an explosion on April 27, 1865. She was one of the many ships being used by the U.S. government to transport former Union prisoners of war who had been released at the conclusion of the Civil War. The men, most of whom had spent time at the appalling Andersonville Prison Camp, were gathered at Vicksburg to be shipped up the Mississippi River to Cairo, Illinois.

Designed to legally carry 376 people, the *Sultana* left Vicksburg carrying 2,300 ex-POWs, plus its crew and other civilian passengers. The boat that had been built in Cincinnati was so overloaded that the upper decks sagged from the excess weight.

At 2:00 am on April 27, 1865, approximately seven miles north of Memphis, Tennessee, one of the *Sultana's* boilers, that had been improp-erly repaired in Vicksburg, exploded. The blast and resulting fire that raged through the wooden steamboat quickly sent it to the bottom of the Mississippi.

This resulted in the greatest maritime disaster in U.S. history. An esti-mated 1,547 passengers (more than died on the *Titanic*) were killed, as the *Sultana* sank near Memphis.

However, due to this happening so soon after the end of the Civil War together with the assassination and funeral of Abraham Lincoln, the story, then as now, received little attention.

Former president Theodore Roosevelt once attempted a political come-back, running for his old office as a third-party candidate. One night during the campaign, his life was saved by one of his speeches.

During a stop in Milwaukee on October 14, 1912, in the course of his third party "Bull Moose" campaign for the presidency, Roosevelt was shot at close range by John Schrank, a psychotic New York saloonkeeper. Schrank had his .38 caliber pistol aimed at Roosevelt's head, but a bystander saw the weapon and deflected the gunman's arm just as the trigger was pulled.

The ex-chief executive did not realize he was hit until someone noticed a hole in his overcoat. When he reached inside, the former president found blood on his fingers.

The one-time Spanish-American War combatant insisted on delivering his speech even though he had been shot. As Roosevelt spoke, still wearing the blood-stained shirt, audience members cheered the address but encouraged the ex-leader of the Rough Riders to get medical attention. He lost a great deal of blood and spent a week in a Chicago hospital after completing his speech.

Roosevelt was extremely lucky. He had the manuscript of his long, fifty-page speech in his coat pocket, folded in two, and this slowed the bullet as it passed through. He also had a steel spectacle case in his pocket that the bullet traversed before entering Roosevelt's chest. The bullet's passing through these two items is what doctors believed saved his life.

However, the bullet was never removed, and when Roosevelt died seven years later, he did so with the reminder of that close call still lodged inside him. Like his predecessor Andrew Jackson, Roosevelt lived for a period carrying the evidence of his shooting inside his body.

On March 4, 1913, Woodrow Wilson was sworn in for his first term as president. About 250,000 spectators lined the streets of Washington, D.C., where they watched an inaugural parade which included Annapolis midshipmen and West Point cadets. Among the marching group of future servicemen was a twenty-two-year-old who one day would be enjoying the festivities from the presidential viewing stand—Dwight D. Eisenhower.

July 10, 1913, was the hottest day ever recorded in the history of the United States as the temperature hit 135 degrees Fahrenheit in Death Valley, California. A perfect name for that location.

The Panama Canal was completed in 1914. It is considered one of the engineering wonders of the world.

The waterway was originally started by the French in 1880, but they gave up after twenty years and an estimated twenty thousand deaths. The United States took over the task in 1903 and poured hundreds of millions of dollars into the project.

Most of the work on the canal took place during the Theodore Roosevelt administration. One of the biggest challenges was keeping workers from contracting malaria. But there was one sufferer of the disease who was better known than the others.

In 1914, long after he had left the presidency and just two years after the assassination attempt, Roosevelt was stricken with malaria while in the jungles of Brazil. He lost fifty-seven pounds and nearly died.

The massive Panama Canal undertaking cost Americans around $375 million. In October 2007, Norwegian Cruise Lines paid a toll fee of $313,000 to get the *Norwegian Pearl* through the fifty-mile waterway between the Atlantic and Pacific oceans. It was the highest amount ever paid to go through the canal.

The lowest toll came in 1928 when American adventurer Richard Halliburton paid 36¢ to swim the inlet. Today, an average passage through the man-made fjord takes about nine hours.

In 1914, President Woodrow Wilson's main objective was keeping his country out of the Great War in Europe. During that same year, Wilson denounced the automobile as a symbol of "the arrogance of wealth," even though motoring around the nation's capital was one of the president's favorite activities during his years in the White House (1913–1921).

He reportedly spent an average of two hours a day cruising Washington, D.C., by car to relax. On December 28, 1923, Wilson's sixty-seventh birthday, the former president found an extraordinary present outside his house on S Street: a brand new Rolls-Royce Silver Ghost Touring Car. The car was a gift from four of his dearest Princeton friends: Cleveland Dodge (no relation to the auto family), Bernard Baruch, Jesse Jones, and Tom Jones.

The Liberty Bell is located at its permanent home in Philadelphia. But at one time, 500,000 California schoolchildren signed a petition asking Philadelphians to send the nation's bell of freedom to the Panama-Pacific Exposition in San Francisco in 1915.

It was decided to dispatch the revolutionary artifact on a national tour rather than just shipping it directly to the west coast. It was taken by train, making brief stops in Chicago, Denver, Salt Lake City, Ogden, Boise, and Portland before traveling down the California coast to San Francisco. Thousands of onlookers were on hand just to catch a glimpse. It was the bell's farewell tour as this was the last time that it left Philadelphia.

It gets very cold in Montana in January, and the citizens from the town of Browning can testify to that fact. On January 23, 1916, they witnessed the world's greatest temperature change in a twenty-four-hour period—a whopping 100 degrees when the mercury fell from 44 degrees Fahrenheit to minus 56 degrees.

One of the duties of the president is the appointment of federal judges. On March 13, 1916, Judge Joseph W. Woodrough was nominated by

President Woodrow Wilson to a seat on the United States District Court for the District of Nebraska.

Woodrough served on that court from 1916 to 1933 and then went on to the U.S. Court of Appeals for the Eighth Circuit from 1933 until 1977. He never retired and was still on the bench when he died at the age of 104 on October 2, 1977.

Judge Woodrough served a record sixty-one years on the federal bench. His tenure lasted through a dozen presidential administrations, both world wars, Korea, and Vietnam.

In 1916, President Wilson sent General John "Blackjack" Pershing and U.S. troops into Mexico to capture the bandit Pancho Villa. But the Americans had almost invaded their neighbor to the south a few years earlier.

On March 6, 1911, President William Howard Taft ordered twenty thousand U.S. troops under the command of Major General William Harding Carter to the border as the Mexican Revolution began to intensify. The fighting was so close to the United States that citizens would gather on the banks of the Rio Grande to watch.

World War I: From Pancho to Paris

You can't say that civilization don't advance, however, for in
every war they kill you in a new way.

—Will Rogers

*W*orld War I was touched off by the assassination of Archduke Franz
Ferdinand, the heir to the Austro-Hungarian throne, and his wife Sophie.
But was it actually started over a wrong turn?

On Sunday June 28, 1914, the royal couple were on their way to a hospital where they were going to be visiting people who had been injured during a
previous assassination attempt earlier that day when a grenade was thrown at
their car. The explosive was deflected and detonated far behind them, causing
injury to others.

On the way to the hospital, the driver made a wrong turn. Nineteen-
year-old Gavrilo Princip, a coconspirator in the earlier attempt, had gone
into a cafe for a sandwich, having given up on the plot. Suddenly, he spotted
Ferdinand's car as it drove past after taking that wrong route. The car's driver,
realizing the mistake, put his foot on the brake and then began to back up.
In doing so, the engine of the car stalled and the gears locked, giving Princip
his opportunity at redemption.

The Bosnian Serb approached the vehicle and fired his weapon, killing
the royal couple. It was a wrong turn that had a profound effect on history. If
only they'd had GPS in those days.

When troops arrive for battle, they usually do so in planes or tanks. But
taxi cabs?

The story of the Marne Taxis began on September 6, 1914, when the military governor of Paris, General Joseph-Simon Gallieni, was attempting to bring troops through France's congested rail system. Most were arriving from the outskirts to defend Paris. In order to counter the rail problem, Gallieni proposed using taxi cabs.

In an unorthodox move, taxis and their drivers were immediately assembled at the Esplanade des Invalides. Contrary to their regular fares, the government agreed to pay them a war rate of 27 percent of their meter reading. A convoy of 150 empty taxis left Paris that night and went to Tremblay-les-Gonesses to assume their new roles as troop transporters.

Each cab brought five soldiers to the front, and after just two days, four thousand French troops had been moved to the battle site near Nanteuil.

The tale of the Taxi Cabs of the Marne has become legendary in French history. The strategy was repeated during the battle at Verdun's Voie Sacre.

Carrier pigeons have been used in combat for centuries. But it was a bird of another feather that shared the stage with them during World War I.

Many of the biggest battles of World War I were fought in France. During the war, parrots were kept in the Eiffel Tower to warn of approaching aircraft. They could detect planes long before human lookouts due to their sensitive hearing.

One of the events that brought the United States into World War I was the sinking of the British liner *Lusitania* by the German submarine, U-20. Of the 1,195 who lost their lives, 124 were Americans.

At 2:10 pm on May 7, 1915, the ship suffered a direct hit and went down in just twenty minutes after she was torpedoed twelve miles off the south coast of Ireland. Lifeboats were jammed due to the position of the vessel, and several were smashed as people spilled into the sea.

Of the ship's forty-eight lifeboats, only six made it to land, and most of the other survivors were rescued by small boats that had come out from Kinsale and Queenstown. Some survivors who were plucked out of the water had been forced to leave loved ones on the sinking ship.

Just as with another famous British vessel (HMS *Titanic*) that sank three years earlier, many died because of a problem with the lifeboats.

The United States did not enter World War I until three years after it began. But as the fighting was raging in Europe, President Woodrow Wilson was dealing with his own set of problems that were taking place in the United States.

Among those was a public-relations disaster in his home state of New Jersey in July 1916. Four people were killed and another seriously injured in separate attacks. The deaths were not committed by the Central Powers or Pancho Villa but by another well-known predator—sharks.

The subsequent panic cost seaside merchants millions of dollars in lost summer revenue. It also didn't help that German U-boats were spotted cruising off the eastern shores.

However, the shark attacks of that summer did eventually produce a profit. They inspired author Peter Benchley to write his best-selling novel *JAWS*, which later became a hit movie.

When American troops returned home after World War I, they were welcomed back as heroes with parades. That's because they had more luck in Europe than they did in Mexico.

On March 9, 1916, the Mexican revolutionary Pancho Villa led 1,500 raiders in an attack on Columbus, New Mexico, in response to the U.S. government's official recognition of the Carranza regime. They swarmed a U.S. cavalry detachment, seized one hundred horses and mules, burned the town, and killed seventeen of its residents.

On March 15, President Woodrow Wilson responded by sending twelve thousand troops, under General John "Blackjack" Pershing, into Mexico to pursue Pancho Villa. The United States used air support for the first time ever in its efforts to capture the vaunted outlaw. But the situation continued to worsen. A series of tragic events began on May 15 when Villa attacked Glen Springs, Texas, where a civilian was killed and three American soldiers were wounded; then a June 15 raid saw four soldiers killed at San Ygnacio, Texas; and finally on July 31, one American soldier and a customs inspector were killed at a Rio Grande border crossing.

The situation had become an embarrassment for the administration and the military as they were unable to capture the bandit. Wilson called off the Villa expedition on January 28, 1917, as the general and his troops were sent to Europe.

General John "Blackjack" Pershing led the United States' effort to capture Pancho Villa, but during his pursuit of the outlaw, the army officer was dealing with his own personal grief.

His family resided in San Francisco where Pershing commanded the 8th Infantry Brigade at the Presidio. When the problems arose in Mexico, the general was transferred to Fort Bliss in El Paso, Texas.

While her husband was away, Mrs. Frances Pershing and the four children remained in the family's two-story Victorian house at the Presidio. But tragedy struck on Friday August 27, 1915, when a fire broke out at the Pershing home.

The house was quickly consumed by flames; Frances and her three daughters—ages eight, seven, and three—perished in the blaze. Only the couple's five-year-old son Warren survived, after being rescued by Pershing's long-time orderly. Visiting the site, Pershing could only comment, "They had no chance."

Mrs. Pershing and the children were scheduled to leave the following week to join her husband in El Paso.

The First Battle of Ypres in Belgium took place just after the war began in the fall of 1914.

British private Henry Tandey led a bayonet charge even though his unit was outnumbered, and he helped capture the French village at Marcoing. As the fighting concluded, German troops surrendered while others retreated.

At the battle site, a wounded German soldier limped into Private Tandey's line of fire. It appeared that the defenseless man knew that he was about to step into history.

Tandey recalled, "I took aim but couldn't shoot a wounded man. So I let him go."

Figure 11.1 General John Pershing posing with his wife Frances and three of their children Helen, Ann, and Warren. Another daughter, Mary, is not in the picture. The soldier dealt with the loss of his family as he chased Pancho Villa. *Library of Congress*

The two men went their separate ways and never saw each other again. Tandey was awarded the Victoria Cross, the highest military decoration of the British Empire. He left the military in 1926 and went on to live his life in relative obscurity.

The German soldier to whom Tandey had given a second chance won the Iron Cross during the battle. After the war, he went on to a career in politics but never forgot about his near-death experience.

In 1938, he met with Neville Chamberlain in Munich. The former soldier asked the British prime minister to pass along his best regards and gratitude to Tandey. The British leader fulfilled the request with a telephone call upon his return to London.

The name of that German soldier whom Tandey allowed to walk away? Adolf Hitler.

Over the years, Tandey expressed his regret, "If only I had known what he [Hitler] would turn out to be. When I saw all the people, women and children he had killed and wounded I was sorry to God I let him go."

Adolf Hitler was actually a pretty good soldier who was wounded in the leg in 1916 and gassed in 1918.

Significantly enough, he was never promoted to a leadership position, but he was awarded unusually high decorations for bravery in action.

Hitler, who was an Austrian, was fighting in the German Army because his dream had been to go to Vienna to study art. But he twice failed to get admitted to the Academy of Fine Arts, once in 1907 and again in 1908. In 1913, Hitler had moved to Munich in the hope of evading Austria's mandatory military service.

Perhaps it was a case of payback in 1938 when he chose Austria as the first country to be invaded by the Nazis.

A number of presidents owned pets and other animals while living at the White House. Woodrow Wilson kept a flock of sheep on the mansion's lawn. The wool was used to raise money for the Red Cross during World War I.

There were famous names who fought in World War I like Pershing, York, and von Richthofen. But they weren't the only ones as others who (or would later) became well known served on the battlefields.

Some of those individuals included Humphrey Bogart, Walt Disney, Charles de Gaulle, Ernest Hemingway, Lawrence of Arabia, Winston Churchill, Bela Lugosi, Fritz Kreisler, Benito Mussolini, Fiorello LaGuardia, Harry Truman, King Edward VIII, Guglielmo Marconi, F. Scott Fitzgerald, and Walter Brennan.

There was also a group of young officers who were around during World War I but who would make their way into the history books for their exploits in the next big conflict. Included in that elite group were Eisenhower, MacArthur, Patton, Marshall, Rommel, and Montgomery.

Soldiers can often be seen traveling in military vehicles known as Jeeps. But Lawrence of Arabia, otherwise known as Colonel T. E. Lawrence, added some style to his ride even though he was in the middle of a war.

Lawrence entered Damascus in a custom-made wood-body Rolls-Royce Blue Mist. During World War I, he used a fleet of nine Rolls-Royce armored cars and tenders specially adapted for desert warfare. He claimed, "A Rolls in the desert is above rubies."

The final year of World War I was 1918. On July 14, Quentin Roosevelt, the youngest and favorite son of former president Theodore Roosevelt, was shot down behind enemy lines. He was a fighter pilot for the U.S. Army Air Corps.

The news of Quentin's death hit his father especially hard, and he died six months later. New York's Roosevelt Field was named after the fallen pilot. This field was the takeoff point for Charles Lindbergh's historic New York to Paris flight.

Harry Truman is the only president who saw action during World War I. After reenlisting in the Missouri National Guard in 1917 at age thirty-three, he was elected an officer, and in 1918 was shipped to the front with other American troops.

Truman was on horseback on August 29 when his artillery battery came under German fire. His steed was hit by shrapnel and fell into a shell hole, trapping the man from Missouri under his mount. Other soldiers helped pull him from beneath the fallen animal.

About that time, several troops ran away from an enemy attack. Truman rallied the remaining men with some salty language that he had learned while working on the Santa Fe railroad. They were so shocked to hear such vulgar utterances coming from the future president that they swung into action immediately.

Without horses there was chaos, but Captain Truman calmly marched his unit back to base camp.

On January 20, 1949, 79 of the original 138 members of Battery D gathered in Washington, D.C., for Truman's inauguration. During a reunion breakfast that morning, one of his former soldiers walked up to him and appropriately addressed him as "Mr. President."

Truman countered, "We'll have none of that now. When I put on those striped pants and that top hat, you can call me 'Mr. President,' but here and all such reunion occasions you can make it just 'Captain Harry.'"

During World War I, Dwight Eisenhower was a lieutenant colonel stationed at Camp Colt, the Army's tank corps training center located near the Civil War battlefield at Gettysburg, Pennsylvania. The young officer stated that not being involved in the fighting in Europe was one of the biggest disappointments of his military career.

Thousands of soldiers died during the four years of fighting of World War I. But the influenza pandemic of 1918–1919 killed more people than all of the battles of the Great War combined. It is estimated that between 20 million and 40 million people worldwide died due to the "Spanish Flu," or "La Grippe," making it a true global disaster.

The outbreak has been cited as the most devastating epidemic in recorded world history. More people succumbed to influenza in a single year than in the four years (1347–1351) of the Black Death.

An estimated 675,000 Americans fell victim to influenza during the pandemic, ten times as many as in World War I. Of the U.S. soldiers who died in Europe, half of them fell to the flu and not to the enemy.

The homecoming of the troops wasn't all joy and celebration as large masses of Americans died from the virus after being exposed to the disease that was carried back from the battlefields by the returning soldiers.

The armistice of World War I went into effect on November 11, 1918, at 11:00 am. It was said that peace came at the eleventh hour of the eleventh day of the eleventh month.

The conflict began with the assassination of the Archduke Ferdinand and his wife Sophie on June 29, 1914, in Sarajevo while riding in an automobile.

The license plate of the car that Ferdinand and Sophie were in when they were killed was "A 11 11 18". . . . as in Armistice 11/11/18.

World War I ended at 11:00 am on November 11, 1918. The last American soldier to die in action was U.S. Army private Henry Gunther of Baltimore, Maryland, near Metz, Germany. He was shot twice and died at 11:01 am.

Gunther posthumously received the Distinguished Service Cross and is buried in his hometown of Baltimore.

The Versailles Treaty ended World War I. But because of concern about some of the items in the document, the U.S. Senate twice voted against ratifying the treaty (on November 19, 1919, and again on March 19, 1920).

In late June 1921, the House and Senate reconciled their differences and on July 1, 1921, the Knox-Porter Resolution passed Congress. The only thing required to finalize the agreement was the signature of the president. Woodrow Wilson was out of office and had been replaced by fun-loving Warren Harding. But there was one small problem with getting Harding's signature—he was out of town.

During the Fourth of July holiday, the chief executive was relaxing at the home of his friend Senator Joseph S. Frelinghuysen in Raritan, New Jersey, and enjoying one of his favorite past-times, playing golf.

The duo was playing a round on July 2, 1921, when a messenger from Washington, D.C., arrived with an important document requiring the president's signature. The game was halted as everyone returned to the Frelinghuysen mansion. The Knox-Porter Resolution, also known as the Treaty of Raritan, was signed by President Harding in the library of Frelinghuysen's home on that day. The resolution officially ended World War I.

Today the estate is long gone, but a marker is displayed at the spot where Harding signed the law. It's in a patch of grass near a Burger King restaurant.

Figure 11.2 Almost two years after the shooting had stopped, President Harding took time away from his golf game to officially end World War I. *History of Raritan*

Between the Wars, 1918–1941: Other than the Great Depression, the Dust Bowl, and Hitler, Things Were Pretty Good

A doctor can bury his mistakes but an architect can only advise his clients to plant vines.

—Frank Lloyd Wright, architect

*F*rank Lloyd Wright became America's best-known architect. But for all of his famous buildings, Wright designed only one skyscraper. It was the nineteen-story Price Tower in Bartlesville, Oklahoma.

Not to be outdone, his son John invented the popular toy Lincoln Logs in 1918. John based the well-known design on his father's earthquake-proof interlocking foundation for the Imperial Hotel in Tokyo.

Many major historical events have taken place in Boston, like the Boston Tea Party and the Battle of Bunker Hill.

One that the local residents still talk about is the Boston Molasses Disaster that occurred on January 15, 1919. A large molasses tank burst at a distilling company site, and a wave of molasses rushed through the streets at an estimated 35 miles per hour, killing 21 and injuring 150. The event has entered the realm of New England folklore, and residents claim that on hot summer days, the area still smells of molasses.

Prior to becoming governor of New York, Franklin Roosevelt was assistant to the secretary of the Navy. On the night of June 2, 1919, FDR had a close call. He was leaving the home of U.S. attorney general Mitchell Palmer when an explosion destroyed the front of the house.

Figure 12.1 The headline told the story of Boston's sticky dilemma. *Boston Globe*

Palmer was a controversial figure, and the blast came from a bomb that had been left in a package on the porch. Had the device detonated a few moments earlier, there is a likelihood that both men would have been killed.

It wasn't FDR's last brush with the grim reaper. In 1933, he survived another assassination attempt just weeks before his inauguration.

The United States has never had a female president . . . or has it?

At one time, a woman was running the government. Woodrow Wilson suffered a stroke with three months remaining in his second term. His wife Edith kept the truth about his condition from the public by taking over the presidential duties herself. All communication with the chief executive, including that of the vice president, went through the First Lady.

Leprechauns are Irish characters who wear green hats. But at one time, Congress had their own leprechaun who would roam the halls bearing gifts.

In 1919, the nation's lawmakers passed the Volstead Act, which marked the beginning of Prohibition. It meant that the country was supposed to go dry. But that was before George Cassiday arrived.

He was a World War I veteran who had trouble finding a job after returning from Europe. One day, he did a favor for a friend by securing liquor for two House members who had voted in favor of Prohibition. Like any congressional perk, word spread quickly through the chambers that the cocktail hour had returned to the nation's capital.

It wasn't long before Cassiday's new business was thriving. He averaged twenty-five deliveries a day that were made using a large leather briefcase. The booze supplier was easily recognized by his trademark emerald hat, which allowed him undisturbed access at all hours. The Capitol Police were instructed that when the "Man in the Green Hat" arrived at the offices, they were to look the other way.

Business was brisk from 1920 to 1930 until federal authorities stepped in and arrested Cassiday. Three years later, the great experiment of Prohibition was brought to an end.

But Cassiday was not forgotten. In the late 1970s, decades after the repeal of Prohibition, his exploits were memorialized on the Senate side of Capitol Hill when a popular new restaurant opened. It was named "The Man in the Green Hat."

New York City suffered terrorist attacks in 1993 and 2001. But on September 16, 1920, thirty-eight people were killed and another four hundred were injured by a blast in the financial district of New York City.

The FBI has theorized that a small group of Italian anarchists orchestrated the bombing that took place five days after Nicola Sacco and Bartolomeo Vanzetti were indicted on charges of first-degree murder. Officially, the case is still unsolved.

KDKA in Pittsburgh has always billed itself as the nation's first radio station. There is some degree of truth in that statement.

The world's first broadcast by a commercially licensed radio station was done on November 2, 1920, by KDKA. They presented the Harding-Cox presidential election results, starting at 6:00 pm local time.

But Detroit's WWJ had gone on the air three months earlier, on August 20, 1920.

Mobster Al Capone made a fortune selling bootleg liquor during Prohibition. His most trusted associate was his brother Ralph.

But "Scarface" also had an older brother named Jim. During World War I, Jim enlisted in the infantry and served in the American Expeditionary Force of General John "Blackjack" Pershing.

While the rest of the Capone brothers drifted into lives of crime, Jim became a Prohibition agent in 1920 even though he would spend the holidays with his criminal family members in Chicago.

During the summer of 1927, Jim Capone served as a bodyguard for President Calvin Coolidge when the First Family vacationed in the Black Hills. The president had not known his protector was the brother of the most infamous gangster of all time.

When Prohibition ended in December of 1933, Jim accepted a position as justice of the peace of Homer, Nebraska, while his headline-making brother languished in federal prison.

President Warren Harding was well known for his weekly poker parties at the White House. There were two cabinet members who chose not to take a seat at Harding's gaming table, which included an ample supply of Prohibition-era whiskey—Secretary of State Charles Evans Hughes and Secretary of Commerce (and future president) Herbert Hoover. The gambling and drinking gatherings went against the beliefs of the two straight-laced officials.

But Harding wasn't the only chief executive who enjoyed cards. Harry Truman was an avid poker player who regularly held games aboard the USS *Sequoia,* the 104-foot presidential yacht.

Not to be overworked, Harding also set aside two afternoons a week to play golf.

Just prior to being elected president, Warren Harding fathered a daughter with a woman named Nan Britton. In fact, one of Nan's teachers back in her days as a student in Ohio was Harding's sister Abigail.

Until his inauguration in 1921, Harding made child-care payments to Britton in person, but always refused to meet his daughter Elizabeth Ann. After he entered the White House, Secret Service agents took over the delivery of the payments.

But Britton wasn't a lone interest as there was a long line of women from the nation's capital and New York City who shared time with the president, many of whom were procured by Harding's close friend *Washington Post* publisher and owner Ned McLean. The commander in chief had assorted other flings, including one who was said to have conceived his only illegitimate son and another whose pregnancy was terminated. In 1921, he publicly ogled sixteen-year-old Margaret Gorman in Atlantic City, days after she was crowned the first Miss America.

But Harding isn't the only chief executive to have been linked with Miss America. In 1982 Elizabeth Ward Gracen, who won the pageant that year, claims to have had a one-night stand with future president Bill Clinton.

Members of the cabinet meet with the president at the White House. Back in the early 1920s, sitting among the decision makers was Warren Harding's dog, Laddie Boy (an Airedale terrier), who was given his own hand-carved seat at the cabinet table.

Laddie Boy was so famous, newsboys collected 19,134 pennies to be melted and sculpted into a statue of the dog. Harding's widow died before the statue was completed in 1927, and the likeness was presented to the Smithsonian Institution, where it currently resides.

Laddie Boy outlived the president by six years. That's human years.

The term of a United States senator is six years. In 1922, Georgia governor Thomas W. Hardwick, who was a former senator, was a candidate for the office when incumbent Thomas E. Watson died prematurely.

Hardwick sought an appointee who would not be a competitor in the special election but could attract new female voters. On October 3, he chose writer and reformer Rebecca Felton to serve as a temporary U.S. senator.

At the time, the lawmakers were in recess so Felton's appointment was put on hold. But in early November, Hardwick's plan backfired when he was defeated in the special election by State Supreme Court Justice Walter F. George.

Although Hardwick had lost, Felton's appointment went forward. On November 21, 1922, she was officially sworn in, thus becoming the first woman seated in the Senate and at age 87, the oldest freshman senator. A leader of the Georgia suffrage movement, she served just one day until George, proving he was a good sport, took office the following morning. It was the shortest term ever served by a U.S. senator.

President Harding died at the conclusion of a tour of the western United States, Alaska, and Canada. The events that took place at the start of the journey may have been an omen of things to come.

On June 24, 1923, a car carrying four Secret Service officers went off the road at Lookout Mountain, Colorado, killing all of the passengers.

When Harding died suddenly on August 2, 1923, during a stay in San Francisco, his doctor listed the official cause of death as food poisoning.

Through the years, some believe that Mrs. Harding may have poisoned the president because of his constant straying with other women. The suspicion arose as there was never an autopsy performed, and the body has never been exhumed.

If First Lady Florence Harding did kill her husband, she took her secret to the grave as she died sixteen months later on November 21, 1924, of kidney disease.

Calvin Coolidge was sworn in as the nation's new president following the death of Warren Harding. But for more than four hours, the United States didn't have a commander in chief.

Harding died at 10:30 pm (Eastern Time) on August 2, 1923, in San Francisco, and Coolidge was not sworn into office until 2:47 am (Eastern Time) on August 3 at his father's Vermont farm. As there was no television and most of the population was asleep, hardly anyone noticed.

Coolidge was given the oath by his father, John, a notary public, while he was visiting the family home in Plymouth Notch, Vermont. Using a phone at the general store, the only one in town, they had called the attorney general to get the precise wording of the oath.

Coolidge was sworn in by the light of a kerosene lamp in the parlor and used his mother's Bible even though it was not the custom to use one in Vermont when public officials were sworn into office. At 3:00 am, employees of the phone company arrived to install a phone for the new president. Coolidge used it at 3:30 am to call Secretary of State Charles Evans Hughes and then went back to bed.

Later that morning, John Coolidge used the phone and then ordered it removed. Uceremoniously, at 7:00 am the new president left his father's house by car to catch a train to Washington, D.C.

Before he was president, Calvin Coolidge was the lieutenant governor of Massachusetts, which meant that one of his duties was to preside over the state senate. During his tenure, he ended up in the middle of a dispute between two legislators, which ended in one telling the other that he could "go to Hell!"

The insulted politician went to see Coolidge to ask him to do something about it. Coolidge said calmly with his usual deadpan expression, "I have looked up the law, Senator, and you don't have to go."

President Coolidge didn't say much, earning him the nickname "Silent Cal." A White House dinner guest once made a bet that she could get Coolidge to say more than two words. When she told the president of her wager, he replied, "You lose." To uphold his reputation as a man of few words, Coolidge refused to use the telephone while in office.

Being the president of the United States is a twenty-four-hours-a-day job. However, Calvin Coolidge eased the burdens of his office by confining himself to four hours of work each day and taking a nap every afternoon.

Following in that tradition, in 1935 all plane flights over the White House were barred. Not for security concerns but because they were disturbing Franklin Roosevelt's sleep.

A great amount of power comes with being the president of the United States. Calvin Coolidge owned a cat named Tiger. One day when the small feline could not be found, the leader of the free world asked local radio stations to broadcast a "missing cat" bulletin.

Tiger was recovered but later ran away again and was never found.

William Jennings Bryan ran for president three times (1896, 1900, and 1908) and lost. But that's nothing compared to Norman Thomas.

A member of the Socialist Party, he ran for governor of New York (1924); mayor of New York City (1925 and 1929); and for U.S. president (1928, 1932, 1936, 1940, 1944, and 1948). His record was perfect—he lost every time.

Calvin Coolidge won the presidential election of 1924 and was sworn into office on March 4, 1925. But it was a dark victory as the First Family was still in mourning when the electoral landslide was announced.

On July 7, 1924, the president's son Calvin Coolidge Jr. died from blood poisoning after he developed a blister on his foot while playing tennis. "Cal" had been away at school at Mercersburg Academy in Pennsylvania and had returned to the White House to spend summer vacation with his parents and his older brother John. The popular teenager was scheduled to graduate the following summer.

Just a few days after the tennis match, Cal's blister became infected, and it poisoned his blood. On July 6, the doctors said his condition was terminal, although a final attempt to surgically remove the poison was made at Walter Reed Army Hospital, where the young man died.

Although Coolidge was elected president four months later, he said in his autobiography that when his son died, "the power and the glory of the presidency went with him." First Lady Grace Coolidge said that her husband "lost his zest for living."

Because the Coolidges were still grieving over the death of their sixteen-year-old son, the inaugural festivities were limited to a brief parade, and only charity balls were held that evening.

In July 1925, one of the most famous legal cases in the nation's history took place. It is known as the Scopes Monkey Trial.

John T. Scopes, the defendant, was a high school science teacher in Dayton, Tennessee, who was accused of teaching Darwin's Theory of Evolution, which violated the state law. The trial turned into a legal showdown featuring two of the country's most famous attorneys, Clarence Darrow and William Jennings Bryan.

When he was in high school in Salem, Illinois, Scopes had once called Bryan, the individual who was now prosecuting him, "the greatest man produced in the United States since Thomas Jefferson."

In reality, Scopes never taught evolution. After the trial, he admitted to reporter William K. Hutchinson of the International News Service, "I didn't violate the law," further explaining that he had omitted the evolution lesson, but the lawyers had coached his students on what to say on the stand. Hutchinson did not file his story until after the Scopes appeal was decided in 1927.

Scopes also admitted the truth to the wife of Dr. Charles Francis Potter whose husband had served as an adviser on the Bible for Scopes's defense team. In addition to teaching science, the defendant was also the school's football coach.

"Tornado Alley" is a region of the Central Plains that spawns a large number of twisters each year and includes portions of Texas, Oklahoma, and Kansas. But the deadliest tornado in U.S. history didn't take place in this area.

It touched down near Annapolis, Missouri, on March 18, 1925. The Tri-State Tornado, as it was called, killed a record 689 people and injured thousands as it cut a destructive path across Missouri, Illinois, and Indiana.

Missouri can also claim the world's heaviest recorded rainfall: twelve inches in one hour, which occurred in the town of Holt on June 22, 1947.

Perhaps that's why Missouri can call itself the "Show Me State."

In May 1927, Charles Lindbergh became the first pilot to successfully fly an airplane solo across the Atlantic from New York to Paris. But he wasn't the first to make a flight across the ocean.

On June 16, 1919, British aviators John Alcock and Arthur Brown made the first nonstop transatlantic flight. They flew a modified World War I bomber from St. John's, Newfoundland, to Clifden, Ireland. Winston Churchill presented them with the *Daily Mail* prize of £10,000 for the first crossing of the Atlantic Ocean in "less than 72 consecutive hours." They were knighted by King George V.

Lindbergh's trip was actually the sixty-seventh across the Atlantic, but he was the first to perform the feat as a solo pilot.

Lindbergh's flight made newspaper headlines throughout the world. But there was another major story that shared front-page status with the historic plane trip. Unfortunately, unlike Lindbergh's journey, the other story would not have a happy ending.

The Bath School Disaster was a series of three bombings in Bath Township, Michigan, on May 18, 1927, that killed forty-five people and injured fifty-eight. Most of the victims were children in the second to sixth grades (7–12 years of age) attending the Bath Consolidated School. Their deaths constituted the deadliest act of mass murder at a school in U.S. history.

The perpetrator was school board member Andrew Kehoe, who was upset by a property tax that had been levied to fund the construction of a new school building. He blamed the additional tax for financial hardships which led to foreclosure proceedings against his farm. These events apparently provoked Kehoe to plan his attack.

The plot took hold that morning as the angry local resident killed his wife and burned down his farm. He then set off a series of explosions, destroying the school. The final blast killed Kehoe himself and the school superintendent.

Two days later, Lindbergh's plane lifted off for Paris.

In 1928, Herbert Hoover was elected as the nation's thirty-first president. As secretary of commerce in 1927, he was the first person to appear on an intercity television broadcast. When television became more widespread, Hoover didn't watch it much except to catch an occasional baseball game.

In 1928, Commander Richard Byrd launched an expedition to the Antarctic. It was highlighted on November 28, 1929, when he and his crew made the celebrated first flight to the South Pole and back.

On March 4, 1929, the commander and his mates were listening to a special live shortwave radio broadcast inside their recently built base camp at Little America in the Antarctic. It was President Herbert Hoover taking the oath and delivering his inaugural address, the broadcast being carried by shortwave to Tokyo, Leningrad, and to the Little America camp, ten thousand miles away.

During Herbert Hoover's presidency, the president's son, Allan, had two pet alligators that were sometimes permitted to wander loose around the mansion.

This wasn't the first time that the species had been a resident at the White House. John Quincy Adams was given a gator by the Marquis de Lafayette and kept it in a bathroom of the East Room.

One of the members of the presidential cabinet is the secretary of war. In 1929, Herbert Hoover waited until he'd been in office forty days before calling in the man holding that office, James W. Good.

Hoover asked Good, "Do you know of anything particular going on in your sphere about which I should be informed?"

"Not a thing in the world, Mr. President," Good replied. That was the last time the president and his secretary of war had occasion to get together. Good died suddenly on November 18, 1929, from peritonitis caused by a ruptured appendix.

When the Stock Market crashed in 1929, many people were forced to sell everything that they owned. Among that unfortunate group was Frank Epperson.

On a cold night in 1905, as an eleven-year-old living in San Francisco, he had put a mixing stick in a glass filled with flavored powder and water. It was left on his back porch overnight, where it was found frozen the next morning.

Frank had invented the Epsicle, which eventually became known as the Popsicle. By 1924, Frank had patented "a handled, frozen confection or ice lollipop." But like so many, the creator was hurt by the crash and sold his patent to Popsicle after 1929.

"I was flat broke and had to liquidate all my assets," he recalled years later. "I haven't been the same since."

Epperson died in 1983.

The Teapot Dome Scandal revealed that former secretary of the interior Albert Fall accepted a $100,000 bribe to lease oil-rich public land to private corporations.

On October 25, 1929, Fall, who had been out of office for six years, was found guilty of bribery related to the scandal, making him the first presidential cabinet member to go to prison for his actions in office. But most of the country wasn't paying attention because Fall's verdict came during the same week that the Stock Market crashed.

Many of America's most notorious criminals of the 1920s were sentenced to prison. Among those was the well-known mobster Al Capone. Beginning in 1929, Capone spent eight months at Eastern State Penitentiary in Philadelphia after being picked up on charges of carrying a concealed weapon following the St. Valentine's Day Massacre.

But Capone's detainment didn't resemble the usual sentence served by most convicts as he used his ample amounts of cash to buy favors and live in comfort.

Eastern State was the nation's first true penitentiary with its policy of separate confinement. It was also a place that housed the most unusual inmate in U.S. history.

In 1924, five years before Capone's arrival, Pennsylvania governor Gifford Pinchot sentenced Pep the "Cat-Murdering Dog" to a life sentence at Eastern State. The canine was banished from the family home when he allegedly murdered the governor's wife's beloved cat.

Prison records reflect that Pep was assigned an inmate number (no. C2559), which is seen in his official mug shot (see figure 12.2).

Many Americans suffered through the period known as the Great Depression. However, Michael J. Cullen was not one of them.

He worked for eleven years at the Kroger Grocery & Bakery Company in Herrin, Illinois.

During that time, he came up with the idea of a "supermarket." It would be a large store with more selections and low prices.

Cullen proposed his idea in a letter to his bosses at Kroger but received no reply. In 1930, in the midst of the nation's economic nightmare, the son of Irish immigrants took a major risk by quitting his job and moving his family to Long Island, New York, to open his own store.

On August 4, the world's first supermarket, King Kullen Grocery, opened for business and was soon a huge success. Within two years, Cullen's stores were doing more than $6 million in revenue (more than $75 million in today's market). By 1936, there were seventeen King Kullen supermarkets.

Figure 12.2 Pep the Dog's official mug shot taken in 1924. *Eastern State Penitentiary*

Cullen died that same year from complications from an appendix operation, but fifty-two of his stores still survive today.

While officials at Kroger ignored Cullen's idea at the time, they didn't totally dismiss the concept. Today, Kroger is the country's largest supermarket chain.

The president has the power to issue executive orders to help officers and agencies of the executive branch manage the operations within the federal government.

On June 24, 1931, President Herbert Hoover signed Executive Order 5658. This executive order was about—wait for it—executive orders! It explained all the helpful details one needs to know about grammar, spelling, margins, selecting a title, and even what size paper to use (8½ × 11).

File this item under the history of government waste.

New York City's Empire State Building was the world's tallest structure from 1931 to 1973. There is a mast that sits atop the towering edifice, but contrary to popular belief, it was not built especially for King Kong to climb during the final scene of the movie.

The tower's top column was originally planned as a docking area for dirigibles. But there were a number of problems with that idea, the first being that it was more than a thousand feet above the ground. Passengers would have had to carefully maneuver down a gangway, while battling high winds, onto a narrow, open walkway near the top of the mast.

A couple of airships attempted to make drops of items, like newspapers, using ropes, but this proved to be too dangerous. Those efforts ended any hopes of using the mast as an airship terminal.

John Tauranac, author of *The Empire State Building: The Making of a Landmark*, called the airship plan "the looniest building scheme since the Tower of Babel."

Through the decades, the mast has remained and proven to be quite useful as a radio and television transmitter. It also has two popular and lucrative observation decks, and it is, of course, the well-recognized location where King Kong made his last stand.

The Stock Market crashed in October 1929. That fact is well known and is included in every history textbook.

There is also another little known chapter to the economic fallout of that year. The market recovered rather quickly after tumbling from 380 points in mid-October to below 200 in November. But by April 1930, the Dow Jones was back above 290, and many believed that the worst had passed.

However, the financial death blow arrived when another crash struck which had long-lasting consequences. Starting in June 1930, the Dow plunged from over 270 to 41.22 on July 8, 1932. Since the drop was spread out over a two-year period, the 85 percent decline didn't represent sudden economic death but more of a slow torture.

Things didn't improve, and the market didn't hit bottom until August 12, 1932, when the Dow sank to a low of 63 which is where it had begun in 1896. This also marked the end of Herbert Hoover's chances of re-election.

In 1932, Charles Lindbergh's baby son was kidnapped and murdered. What the public didn't know was that the famed aviator actually had three families. In addition to his wife and six children in the United States, he also had two other families in Germany that produced five more children.

Lindbergh was able to maintain his secret personal life until his death in 1974.

On March 7, 1932, unemployed autoworkers and union organizers rioted outside the Ford River Rouge plant in Dearborn, Michigan. The turmoil had begun as a protest march with a plan of presenting a list of demands to chairman Henry Ford. But the situation turned violent when displaced workers clashed with the police and plant security.

When it was over, four protesters were dead, with dozens more wounded from gunfire. About twenty-five Dearborn police officers were injured by thrown rocks and other debris.

But everyone wasn't upset with Henry Ford; in fact, some well-known customers were singing his praises. On April 13, 1934, the chairman received a letter from the notorious gangster Clyde Barrow. Barrow praised the automaker's product, saying, "I have driven Fords exclusively when I could get away with one."

A month later, Ford picked up another endorsement. This testimonial was from Public Enemy Number One John Dillinger, who wrote, "Dear Mr. Ford—I want to thank you for building the Ford V-8 as fast and as sturdy a car as you did, otherwise I would not have gotten away from the coppers in that Wisconsin, Minnesota, case. Yours till I have the pleasure of seeing you—John Dillinger."

But the two gangsters met their fate just weeks afterward. Barrow along with his criminal partner Bonnie Parker was killed on May 23, 1934. They were ambushed by lawmen while riding in a Ford V-8.

Dillinger could have used a getaway car on July 22, 1934, when FBI agents gunned him down in an alley next to the Biograph Theater in Chicago.

New York City is a maze of streets, roads, and bridges that help keep its massive population moving. The man who designed most of those pathways was city planner Robert Moses.

In a forty-four-year span, from 1924 to 1968, Moses was never elected to public office but served as chairman of the Triborough Bridge and Tunnel Authority, city park commissioner, and city construction coordinator. Some have referred to him as the most powerful politician in NYC during those years.

Over his tenure, he transformed the Big Apple into a haven of mass transit as it transitioned into the automobile age. Under Moses, the metropolitan area came to have more highway miles than its California counterpart Los Angeles.

Many of Moses's ideas for the area, including additional major bridges, revolved around the continuous movement of automobiles. His concepts are especially innovative considering that Moses never learned how to drive.

If an individual killed fifty-three people, he or she would be considered a serial killer. But there was a person who took down that number and was considered a hero.

Frank Hamer was a Texas Ranger who killed fifty-three lawbreakers in the line of duty from 1906 to 1948, the most famous of these being the gangsters Clyde Barrow and Bonnie Parker. The deaths of Barrow and Parker took place during an ambush in 1934.

Always looking for justice to be served, at the outbreak of war in Europe in 1939 Hamer and forty-nine other retired Texas Rangers offered their services to the King of Great Britain to help protect that country in case of a Nazi invasion. The offer was appreciated by the royals who turned it down.

Although Hamer was wounded seventeen times during his career, it was complications from previous heat stroke that sent the Ranger to his last roundup in 1955 at age seventy-one.

In 1932, President Herbert Hoover ran for re-election. Faced with an impending defeat in November due to the poor economy, some Republicans spoke of rejecting their incumbent and drafting former president Calvin Coolidge to run against the Democrats' nominee Franklin Roosevelt.

But the former commander in chief made it clear that he was not interested in running again and that he would publicly reject any effort to draft him. Looking back, that appears to have been the ex-president's last good idea as Coolidge died in 1933.

Franklin Roosevelt defeated Herbert Hoover in the election of 1932. But the star of the campaigns that season was actor and humorist Will

Rogers, who was actually nominated for the nation's highest office and personally addressed both the Republican and Democratic conventions.

One of his best-remembered lines from those events was the observation that "most ordinary voters would like to be able to cast two ballots, one against Hoover and one against Roosevelt."

The weeks between the time that a person is elected president until they take the oath of office is referred to as the transition period. Franklin Roosevelt had a most eventful time on February 15, 1933, as he was the target of an assassination attempt during his transition.

Luck was definitely on FDR's side that day in Miami as it should have been an easy shot for the gunman. There were five rounds fired at just twenty-five feet. But the assassin, anarchist Giuseppe Zangara, lost his balance while standing atop a wobbly chair and instead of hitting president-elect Roosevelt, he fatally wounded Anton Cermak, the mayor of Chicago, who was shaking hands with FDR.

The mayor's last words to the president-elect were, "I am glad it was me instead of you."

It is a tradition for the outgoing president and his successor to ride together to the inauguration ceremony. In 1933, Herbert Hoover and Franklin Roosevelt rode in the same car to the steps of the Capitol Building but never said a word to each other. Following the ceremony, they never saw each other again.

Originally, the United States Mint made $10, $5, and $2.50 coins of solid gold. But on April 5, 1933, President Roosevelt issued an executive order that required all citizens to relinquish any gold in their possession to the U.S. government. That included coins, bullion, and certificates. He ordered all gold coins removed from circulation and returned to the U.S. Treasury, where millions were melted into gold bars.

The penalty for those who failed to comply was ten years in prison, a $10,000 fine, or both. On December 31, 1974, with Executive Order 11825, President Gerald Ford repealed FDR's order of 1933.

Since then, the value of the precious metal has continued to increase. Among American gold coins is the 1933 U.S. Gold Double Eagle, which is considered the most valuable coinage in history. Most were melted down during the confiscation of gold by the government that year. But a few did survive.

In 1996, British numismatist Stephen Fenton had one in his possession when he arrived in New York. But he was immediately arrested by the Secret Service as part of a sting operation because it was thought that the famous coin had been stolen.

The action set off a prolonged court battle over ownership of the Double Eagle, which resulted in a settlement. It was decided that the piece would be sold at auction, with the proceeds split between Fenton and the U.S. Mint.

That decision was quite profitable as the rare coin was purchased at auction on July 30, 2002, for $7,590,000. But like so many other gold coinage, there was a time shortly before the sale that it might also have been destroyed, but unlike the others, that wouldn't be from a president's executive order.

During the period that the two sides were in negotiations, the valuable coin was stored in the treasury vaults at the World Trade Center. It was relocated to Fort Knox just two months before the 9/11 terrorist attacks.

Many people were looking for ways to make money during the Great Depression. One of the more successful enterprises was a concession that earned $862,000 in just five months at the 1933 Chicago World's Fair. It was a restroom that charged 5¢ per visit.

Many historians and others view Eleanor Roosevelt as politically liberal. While her beliefs may have swayed to the left, she was a firm supporter of the Constitution's Second Amendment.

Shortly after moving into the White House in 1933, the First Lady informed the Secret Service that they wouldn't be allowed to accompany her at all times. At that point, they issued her a revolver.

After her husband's passing in 1945, Eleanor moved to New York City where, following multiple death threats, she applied for and received a concealed weapons permit.

Franklin Roosevelt was paralyzed from polio and served his entire presidency without the use of his legs.

Unknown to the public was an unwritten agreement among the press not to photograph FDR in positions that highlighted his handicap. During his twelve years in the White House, there were only three pictures taken of him in a wheelchair among the 125,000 photographs in the Roosevelt library. Two of those photos were taken by one of FDR's longtime female companions (and sixth cousin) Daisy Suckley.

On June 2, 1933, the first White House swimming pool was completed. It was built with private funds to help FDR with his therapy for polio.

The Dust Bowl centered on the panhandles of Texas and Oklahoma and adjacent parts of the central United States.

Figure 12.3 This is one of the three existing photos showing FDR in his wheelchair. With him are his dog Fala and Ruthie Bie, a friend's granddaughter. *National Archives*

On May 9, 1934, a strong two-day dust storm removed massive amounts of Great Plains topsoil in one of the worst such episodes during the Dust Bowl. The clouds of dirt blew all the way to Chicago, where it fell like snow. Two days later, the same storm reached cities in the east such as Buffalo, Boston, New York City, and Washington, DC.

So much of the plains topsoil made its way into the atmosphere that it caused red snow to fall on New England.

The flamboyant U.S. senator Huey Long of Louisiana was shot on September 8, 1935, in the state capitol building at Baton Rouge. He died two days later.

There were many who were not surprised by the act as the colorful political figure had his share of enemies, but most were taken aback when it was revealed that the man who shot Long was a doctor.

Dr. Carl Weiss was described as a brilliant physician and a calm, sensitive family man. He was also a native of the capital city of Baton Rouge.

On the day of the shooting Dr. Weiss seemed entirely normal, and in fact he confirmed plans to carry out an operation the following morning. He was killed at the scene after being shot sixty-one times by Long's bodyguards.

The reason for the murder is still unknown, but it is believed to have centered around a political dispute between Long's and Weiss's in-laws.

Hoover Dam was a Depression Era project that was completed in 1936. But there was more to this massive undertaking than just another construction job. There were 112 deaths associated with the building of the structure.

On December 20, 1922, J. G. Tierney became the first person to die on the project. He was a surveyor who drowned while looking for an ideal spot for the dam. Ironically, his son, Patrick W. Tierney, was the last man to die working on the project, thirteen years to the day later when he fell from an intake tower.

The dam was originally named Boulder Dam, but the name was changed in honor of President Herbert Hoover. The name change took place after Franklin Roosevelt died.

Gambling was illegal in Boulder City, Nevada, where most of the workers resided. The reason was that the government did not want the laborers on the project to gamble away their wages. But that didn't keep the workers from making a wager as Las Vegas was only twenty miles away.

The Boulder City charter, approved by the residents, prohibited gambling within Boulder City's limits. This provision still exists, making Boulder City one of only two locations in Nevada where gambling is illegal (the other is the town of Panaca).

Franklin Roosevelt's first of a record three re-elections took place in 1936, and his second inauguration was historic.

It was on January 20, 1937, making it the first one not held on March 4 due to a change made by the Twentieth Amendment to the U.S. Constitution. But Mother Nature wasn't cooperative. Sleet and freezing rain pelted the nation's capital. Between 11:00 am and 1:00 pm, 0.69 inches of rain fell. When the ceremony began at 12:23 pm, the temperature was an almost freezing 33 degrees Fahrenheit.

But FDR demanded that the proceedings should continue as scheduled. He rode in an open car with half an inch of water on the floor. At the inaugural parade, the president stood for an hour and a half in an uncovered viewing stand while getting soaked.

The total rainfall for the day was 1.77 inches, which remains a record for the area on the day of January 20. Unlike William Henry Harrison, who became ill and died a month after his inauguration, FDR came through the event and lived to tell about it.

San Francisco's Golden Gate Bridge opened on May 27, 1937. One of its most interesting statistics is that only eleven workers died during construction, a new safety record for the time. In the 1930s, bridge builders could normally expect one fatality per every $1 million in costs. The projected budget of the Golden Gate was estimated at $35 million.

One of its safety innovations was a net suspended under the flooring of the bridge. Over a four-year span, the man-made web saved the lives of nineteen workers during construction. Their death-defying adventures earned the group the nickname the "Half Way to Hell Club."

The Golden Gate Bridge connects the northern tip of the San Francisco Peninsula to Marin County on the California coast. As one of the tallest bridges in the world, the structure has attracted its share of "jumpers."

While a handful of an estimated 1,300 jumpers have walked the Golden Gate's plank and survived, the others needed to find a location outside the city to be buried in.

That was because, as the massive bridge was being finished, San Francisco residents voted to no longer build cemeteries within the city proper. As a result, a site south of the city limits was selected for a new national cemetery.

Franklin Roosevelt served longer than any other president. He also appointed the longest-serving Supreme Court justice.

William O. Douglas took his seat on the nation's highest court in April 1939 and retired in November 1975. That's thirty-six years and seven months, which means he began before the United States entered World War II and finished after the end of the Vietnam War.

Douglas was on the court during the presidential terms of Franklin D. Roosevelt, Truman, Eisenhower, Kennedy, Johnson, Nixon, and Ford. In addition to serving several presidents, he was also busy away from the court as he was married four times.

The Magna Carta is one of history's most important documents. The creation of the U.S. Constitution was influenced by the well-known British charter of 1215.

At the 1939 New York World's Fair, the copy of the Magna Carta belonging to Lincoln Cathedral left Britain for the first time to be displayed in the British Pavilion at the fair. Within months, the Brits entered World War II, and it was deemed safer for the more than seven-hundred-year-old document to remain in America until peace could be resumed. The Magna Carta was taken to Fort Knox and placed next to the original copy of the Constitution until it was returned home in 1947.

Also in the vault with the two historic documents were the English Royal jewels, the gold reserves of several occupied European nations, the Declaration of Independence, the original draft of Lincoln's Gettysburg

Address, the Articles of Confederation, and the three volumes of a Guten-
berg Bible.

Franklin D. Roosevelt's plan to help the United States out of the Great
Depression was called the New Deal.

In 1939, a group of political and business leaders in Sheridan, Wyoming,
who were unhappy with FDR's strategy proposed the creation of the new
state of Absaroka that included parts of Wyoming, Montana, and South
Dakota.

A. R. Swickard, the street commissioner of Sheridan, appointed himself
governor. License plates were issued, and Miss Absaroka 1939 was crowned.
But the movement was unsuccessful and fairly short-lived.

Smoking is not allowed in most public places. In the late 1930s and early
1940s, while the Nazi regime was slaughtering people in concentration camps
and on the battlefield, they also had one of the first effective anti-smoking
campaigns.

Hitler was so opposed to lighting up that he began one of the most expensive and successful anti-tobacco movements in history. The Third Reich
banned smoking in restaurants and public transportation systems, citing
public health concerns, while limiting advertising of smoking and cigarettes.

Germany instituted a high tobacco tax, and the supplies of cigarettes to
the Wehrmacht were rationed. Several of the country's health organizations
even began claiming that smoking heightened the risks of miscarriages by
pregnant women, which is now a commonly accepted fact.

In 1940, the statistics of annual cigarette consumption per capita had
Germany at only 749, while Americans smoked over 3,000. Among those
who were known as heavy smokers were President Roosevelt and General
Eisenhower.

It was said that when it was learned that Hitler had committed suicide,
several of those inside his Berlin bunker lit up a smoke to celebrate.

Franklin Roosevelt was so popular with his fellow citizens that he is the
only president to be elected to four terms in office.

Like most leaders, FDR received many letters, especially from children,
but didn't have the time to reply to many of them. In 1940, however, he
did respond through an official at the American Embassy to a letter from a
thirteen-year-old who was attending a private boarding school in Cuba. The
child's teacher was so impressed that she posted FDR's letter on the classroom bulletin board for a week.

That young boy who wrote to FDR and got a response was Fidel Castro.

Sam Houston had the distinction of serving as the governor of Tennessee and as the governor of Texas. His son was Andrew Jackson Houston.

On April 21, 1941, eighty-six-year-old Andrew was appointed by Texas governor W. Lee O'Daniel to fill the unexpired term of Senator Morris Sheppard, who had died. When Andrew was born, his father held the same U.S. Senate seat that Andrew would soon occupy.

On June 2, 1941, the son of the Texas legend became the oldest man ever to become a freshman U.S. senator. But Houston's political career was short-lived. He passed away just twenty-four days after taking the oath—the shortest term of any Texan in Congress.

Following Houston's death, O'Daniel decided to hold a special election for the seat and included himself as a candidate. He defeated Lyndon Johnson by 1,306 votes in one of the more controversial elections in state history. His victory made him the only person to ever defeat LBJ for elected office.

Franklin Roosevelt appointed many justices to the Supreme Court. His nine selections rank only behind George Washington's fourteen.

Many citizens don't realize that nowhere in the Constitution does it say that Supreme Court justices have to be lawyers or have any legal training. In fact, several justices in the court's history never attended law school.

Included in that lot is one of FDR's choices, James Byrnes, who was nominated on June 12, 1941, and confirmed by the Senate that same day. After only sixteen months of service, Byrnes resigned from the court on October 3, 1942, to serve as director of the Office of Economic Stabilization, making it the shortest tenure for the nation's highest court.

Byrnes not only never attended law school, he also didn't go to high school or college. He did apprentice under a lawyer, and was admitted to the bar in 1903.

The man without a diploma was from South Carolina and was elected to the House of Representatives in 1910, the U.S. Senate in 1931, and concluded his political career with a term as governor of his home state, beginning in 1951.

· *13* ·

World War II: That German Guy Sure Has a Strange-Looking Mustache

We are not retreating—We are advancing in another direction.

—General Douglas MacArthur

*T*he United States didn't enter World War II until December 1941. A prewar Gallup poll showed 88 percent of Americans opposed U.S. involvement in the latest European conflict.

In a 1940 (election-year) speech, Franklin Roosevelt stated, "I have said this before, but I shall say it again and again and again: Your boys are not going to be sent into any foreign wars."

But FDR didn't tell the public about Tyler Kent. He was a code clerk at the U.S. Embassy in London who discovered secret dispatches between the president and British prime minister Winston Churchill. These revealed that FDR, despite his campaign promises, was determined to engage America in the conflict.

Kent was arrested for smuggling some of the documents out of the embassy as he planned to alert the public. The American was tried in a secret British court and confined to a prison until the war's end.

Kent was then deported to the United States, where he died in 1988.

Hitler was not a German. He was actually born in Austria. The home country of the man who was responsible for the deaths of millions of people was the first to abolish capital punishment, in 1787.

For many years, there was a story that Hitler's mother, Klara, considered having an abortion when she was pregnant with him. There is actually no evidence to prove or disprove that story, although it is known that she was a devout Catholic, which may have been a factor in her decision.

However, the odds were against young Adolf surviving to adulthood. Alois Hitler married Klara Polzl on the morning of January 7, 1885, before he went to work for the day.

Four months later their first son, Gustav, was born, and a daughter, Ida, followed in September 1886, but both infants died of diphtheria during the winter of 1886–1887. A third child, Otto, was born and died in 1887.

Adolf arrived on April 20, 1889, followed by Edmund in March 1894 and Paula in January 1896. Edmund died of the measles at age five. Only two of Klara's children, Adolf and Paula, survived childhood.

Germany's Adolf Hitler and Italy's Benito Mussolini were allies during World War II. But long before they were comrades, Hitler idolized the Italian dictator. In 1927 he wrote to Mussolini requesting an autographed photo. Hitler received a handwritten reply from Il Duce: "Request refused."

Winston Churchill was the prime minister of Britain during World War II. But in March of 1938, Churchill was in personal financial trouble as his brokerage account was £18,000 in the red. At that point, he decided to place an ad in the *London Times* to advertise his home, Chartwell, for sale, inviting offers of £20,000.

A few days before the notice was to appear, Sir Henry Strakosch, a wealthy banker and businessman, agreed to pay off Churchill's debts, and Chartwell was withdrawn from the market.

Strakosch realized the importance of the war effort and Churchill's role in it. He was a Jew who had been born in Czechoslovakia, which was taken over by the Nazis a few months later.

General Douglas MacArthur was a U.S. military hero during World War II. In the 1920s, the general was assigned to the Philippines until he returned to Washington, D.C., in 1930 to serve as U.S. Army chief of staff. Accompanying the general was his much younger girlfriend Isabel Rosario Cooper.

It was an affair that MacArthur wanted kept quiet, but Drew Pearson, a reporter for the *Washington Post*, was threatening to expose the entire episode. The general filed a libel action against the journalist, trying to keep the matter under wraps. But when Pearson added Cooper to his list of witnesses to be deposed, MacArthur dropped the suit and subsequently paid the newsman $15,000 to keep his secret.

Allegedly, the money was delivered by the general's aide, Major Dwight D. Eisenhower as Isabel was hustled back to the Philippines.

Was MacArthur afraid that the president or one of his military superiors might find out about his young girlfriend? Not hardly; he was hiding the affair from his overbearing mother.

Mary MacArthur (also known as "Pinky") had lived at the West Point Hotel during her son's four years at the academy. From the window of her suite, she had an unobstructed view of room 1123 in the cadet barracks, so she could monitor her son's study habits.

It may have been a bit intrusive, but it worked, as Douglas graduated at the top of the Class of 1903.

France fell to the Nazis on June 25, 1940. It was known as "Hitler's revenge" because the Führer required the French to sign the surrender documents at Compiègne in the same rail car in which Germany had been compelled to sign the armistice ending World War I. He had the train car taken from a museum and returned to the surrender location, which he personally attended.

Before the Allies liberated France in 1944, Hitler ordered the monument dynamited, and the following year he had the carriage itself destroyed to prevent a possible second German armistice or surrender from being signed in that same car.

Figure 13.1 Hitler and his inner circle prepare to enter the train car where it all began. *Bild Bundes*

As the leader of Germany, Adolf Hitler had his own personal transportation. The Führer's Special Train (*Führersonderzug* in German) was one which he frequently used to travel between various strategic locations throughout Europe. It also served as his headquarters, and in 1940 the train was named *Führersonderzug . . . "Amerika."*

The USS *Arizona* was one of the ships destroyed during the attack on Pearl Harbor. Today it stands as a permanent memorial to those who lost their lives on that morning. When the *Arizona* was bombarded by the Japanese, twenty-three of the thirty-seven sets of brothers on board the ship were killed.

The attack on Pearl Harbor was a surprise assault by the Japanese military. In reality, it should not have been.

Writers had been cautioning about a possible bombardment at that location for quite some time. Among the works warning of this were Hector Bywater's *Sea Power in the Pacific* (1921) and *The Great Pacific War: A History of the American-Japanese Campaign of 1931–33* (1925), as well as a January 21, 1930, *Saturday Evening Post* article by Lieutenant Stephen Jurika Jr. in which a simulated attack on Pearl Harbor by aircraft from the USS *Saratoga* was reviewed.

Prior to the attack on Pearl Harbor, the United States was not fighting in World War II. On November 29, 1941, most of the members of the military were focused on the annual Army-Navy football game that was being played in Philadelphia.

The contest's souvenir program carried a picture of the USS *Arizona* with the caption "It is significant that despite the claims of air enthusiasts no battleship has yet been sunk by bombs."

Nine days later, the *Arizona* was among the ships that were sunk at Pearl Harbor.

General Douglas MacArthur was fired by President Truman during the Korean War for disobeying a direct order. Truth be told, Mac could have been in trouble years earlier after the bombing of Pearl Harbor.

Despite hours of warning after the attack, MacArthur, who was based in the Philippines, failed to place his aircraft in the sky, such that the bulk of his planes, including a large B-17 bomber force, were destroyed on the ground.

Perhaps a bigger error was his failure to stockpile food, ammunition, and medical supplies on the Bataan Peninsula. The plan was known as "Rainbow 5," but MacArthur did not start taking action until after the Japanese had arrived in the Philippines, and by then it was too late.

The Japanese attacked the American fleet at Pearl Harbor, Hawaii, on December 7, 1941.

On the day after the assault, President Roosevelt rode to Congress to deliver his declaration of war in a limousine that was once owned by the notorious gangster Al Capone. The Secret Service wanted to take extra measures to protect the president but didn't have a suitable vehicle so they used an armor-plated 1928 Cadillac Town Sedan that had been confiscated by the Department of the Treasury following the mobster's tax evasion conviction.

At the time, Al didn't need the luxury ride. He had been released from prison due to his failing health and was quietly residing at his estate at Palm Island, Florida.

The U.S. military suffered heavy losses at Pearl Harbor. Many of those were lower ranked personnel, but the first American general killed in World War II was Herbert Arthur Dargue.

He died on December 12, 1941, when his plane crashed in California. Dargue was on his way to Hawaii where he was slated to become the new U.S. Army commander at a location that had been attacked just five days earlier—Pearl Harbor.

The construction of the Panama Canal was highly publicized and is considered to be one of engineering's wonders of the world.

Perhaps even more amazing, although lesser known, was the building of the Alaska-Canada (Alcan) Highway, covering 1,523 miles from Dawson Creek, British Columbia, to Delta Junction, Alaska. The needs of World War II dictated its quick completion, thus it was begun on March 8, 1942, and finished on October 28, 1942.

This amazing project had taken just over eight months and was built by the U.S. Army Corps of Engineers.

The United States gained a major naval victory at the Battle of Midway. But among the ships that were lost in the fighting was the aircraft carrier *Yorktown*.

It was actually a miracle that the watercraft was at Midway. During the Battle of the Coral Sea just a month earlier, the ship had been severely damaged.

Despite estimates that the carrier would require several months of repairs, the Pearl Harbor Naval Shipyard worked around the clock, and in just seventy-two hours, the *Yorktown* was restored to a battle-ready state. Her flight deck was patched, and whole sections of internal frames were cut out and replaced. Just three days after putting into dry dock at Pearl Harbor, the *Yorktown* was again under way.

The ship played a key role at the Battle of Midway but was sunk by a Japanese submarine on June 7, 1942. In 1998, the wreck of the *Yorktown* was found and photographed by the renowned oceanographer Dr. Robert D. Ballard, who also discovered the wreck of the *Titanic*.

General George Patton was a strict disciplinarian with the troops that he commanded.

But he had a reputation for bending the rules to suit himself.

His self-promotion went as far as items of his uniform. Even his side-arm wasn't the regular military issue. While others carried a standard pistol, Patton holstered an ivory-stocked, silver-plated Colt .45, better known as the "Peacemaker," which was made famous by the legendary lawmen of the Old West, the Texas Rangers.

The general was reputed to have killed two of Pancho Villa's men with the weapon in 1916 while hunting the outlaw in Mexico with General Pershing.

In 1970, George C. Scott won an Academy Award for Best Actor in a biographical film portrayal of the famous tank commander. But Scott didn't accept the Oscar because he believed that actors shouldn't be in competition with each other. Today the Oscar is on display at the Virginia Military Institute which Patton attended (1903–1904) before receiving his appointment to the United States Military Academy at West Point.

On November 23, 1942, the SS *Benlomond* was torpedoed by a German U-boat in the Atlantic, 750 miles off the Azores. Second Steward Poon Lim (born in Hong Kong), along with some shipmates of the U.K. Merchant Navy, abandoned ship, and Lim was able to secure one of the ship's large rafts.

Climbing aboard, he found himself alone but with some basic provisions. With careful managing of these supplies, a little fishing, and collecting rainwater, Lim survived 133 days alone and adrift on the South Atlantic before being rescued by a fisherman. He had unintentionally set the record for the longest recorded survival alone on a raft.

By the time he was rescued, Lim had drifted far beyond his original departure point. He was picked up by a fishing boat off Salinas, Brazil, on April 5, 1943, and was able to walk ashore.

Lim was awarded the U.S. Merchant Marine Combat Bar with one star along with the British Empire Medal. Poon Lim returned to the sea, working with the United States Line as chief steward until he retired in 1983.

Many companies in the United States produced goods for the troops during World War II. Among those was the military production division of the Ford Motor Company which exceeded the output of the entire country of Italy. During 1942, Ford halted its civilian line and shifted to total military production.

Due to the high number of casualties in World War II, medics and doctors were kept busy on the battlefield. When blood supplies were running low in the Pacific, physicians discovered that the liquid inside young coconuts (not to be confused with regular coconut milk) could be used as a substitute for blood plasma.

One of the main reasons that it was used was because of its purity.

M&M's Chocolate Candy has been a popular snack food for many years. But its creation has some history behind it.

Forrest Mars Sr. got the idea for M&M's during a visit to Spain while the country was engaged in a civil war in the late 1930s. He noticed soldiers eating pellets of chocolate encased in a hard, sugary coating which prevented the candy from melting. When Mars returned home, he used that candy as the model to create the recipe for M&M's.

With the outset of World War II, those little chocolate pellets became popular with American troops. They were included in the soldiers' C-rations because they withstood extreme temperatures, especially in the South Pacific's tropical environment.

That's why M&M's have always melted "in your mouth, and not in your hand."

The Soviet Union's dictator Josef Stalin was cruel and ruthless. He was accused of having thousands of his own people sent away to death camps.

Stalin's son Yakov Dzhugashvili was a 2nd lieutenant in the artillery corps. He was captured on May 16, 1942, and interned in the Sachsenhausen Concentration Camp.

In 1943, an attempt was made by the Germans to exchange Yakov for Field Marshal Friedrich von Paulus, who was captured after the fall of Stalingrad. The request was refused by Stalin. Although he grieved for his thirty-six-year-old son, the Soviet premier was quoted as saying, "I will not exchange a private for a field marshal."

On April 14, 1943, Yakov was shot while trying to escape. Some sources say he committed suicide by throwing himself at the perimeter fence to force the guards to fire upon him. Von Paulus was designated a war criminal and was not released until 1953. He died four years later.

Japanese admiral Isoroku Yamamoto was one of the primary planners of the attack on Pearl Harbor. He studied at Harvard University (1919–1921) during his tour as an admiral's aide, and served two postings as a naval atta-ché in Washington, D.C. He learned a great deal about the country and was fundamentally opposed to going to war with the United States.

While his countrymen cheered the attack on Pearl Harbor, which Yamamoto designed, the admiral was skeptical, saying, "I fear all we have done is to awaken a sleeping giant and fill him with a terrible resolve."

Some might say that the talented Japanese military officer was also clairvoyant because on April 18, 1943, his plane was ambushed much like the attack that he had planned on the U.S. fleet two years earlier. The aircraft was shot down by an American squadron over New Guinea. There were no survivors.

Hitler's SS squadron was his elite force. Heinrich Himmler was the chief of the feared brigade, and was so treacherous that he had his nephew, 1st Lieutenant Hans Himmler, demoted and sentenced to death for revealing SS secrets while he was drunk.

The sentence was commuted, and Hans was sent to the front as a para-chutist. He was again charged with making remarks about the regime and banished to the dreaded Dachau concentration camp near Munich, where he was "liquidated" on suspicion of being a homosexual.

During World War II, Native American soldiers were used to pass se-cret information by utilizing their tribal languages. Among the most famous were the Navajo Code Talkers.

But the chatter of Native Americans wasn't the only method of steg-anography. Chess games, crossword puzzles, student grades, and newspaper clippings were also used to pass secret messages.

The United States fought the Japanese on the Empire's soil during World War II. But Japan also attacked some of America's home turf.

On February 23, 1942, an Imperial Japanese Navy submarine launched shells at an oil refinery near Santa Barbara, California. About sixteen rounds were fired from the enemy's guns. There were no casualties, although a couple of explosions did damage to some local ranches.

On June 21, 1942, another Japanese submarine fired on Fort Stevens, Oregon, in the first attack on a mainland U.S. military base in 130 years. The vessel was retaliating for the Doolittle Raid, a surprise attack by U.S. B-25 bombers, a few months earlier. Most of the damage was limited to the fort's baseball diamond. No one was injured.

And on September 9, 1942, Japanese pilot Nobuo Fujita flew a float-plane from a long-range submarine aircraft carrier, the I-25, near the coast of southern Oregon and headed east toward Mt. Emily. His mission was to drop an incendiary (fire) bomb on the thick forest and cause a massive fire.

However, luck wasn't with Fujita. He released the bomb over the target area, but it only left a small crater about three feet in diameter and nearly a foot deep.

In 1943 Japan invaded the Aleutian Islands, which started the One Thousand Mile War. It was the first battle fought on American soil since the Civil War because Alaska was a U.S. territory at that time. The islands of Agattu, Attu, and Kiska were the only parts of North America occupied by Japanese troops during World War II.

From late 1944 until early 1945, the Japanese launched over nine thousand "Balloon Bombs," of which three hundred were found or observed in the United States. They were discovered in Alaska, Washington, Oregon, California, Arizona, Idaho, Montana, Utah, Wyoming, Colorado, Texas, Kansas, Nebraska, South Dakota, North Dakota, Michigan, and Iowa, as well as in Mexico and Canada.

But the weapons weren't very efficient, with a kill rate of just 0.067.

On July 5, 1943, the town of Boise City, Oklahoma, became the only community in the continental United States to be bombed during World War II, but the bombers were American pilots. The attack by a B-17 Flying Fortress occurred at approximately 12:30 am. The pilots were performing target practice but became disoriented and mistook the lights around the town square as their target. No one was killed in the surprise bombing (only practice bombs were used, and the square was deserted at the time), which proved embarrassing for the flight crew.

For the fiftieth anniversary of the error, the pilots were brought back as guests of honor to Boise City.

The presidential plane is code-named Air Force One. The first dedicated aircraft proposed for presidential use was a C-87A VIP transport aircraft.

This plane was modified in 1943 for use as a presidential conveyor. It was nicknamed the *Guess Where II* and was intended to carry President Franklin D. Roosevelt on international trips.

However, after a review of the C-87's highly controversial safety record in service, the Secret Service flatly refused to approve it as a presidential transport. In an effort to avoid government waste, the suspect aircraft was then used to take senior members of the Roosevelt administration on various trips.

Another plane, a Boeing C-54, nicknamed the *Sacred Cow* by the White House press corps, replaced the *Guess Where II* as the first presidential aircraft.

There were many new weapons that were used during World War II. But one of the more improbable projects was a plan to release myriads of bats bearing incendiary devices over Japanese cities.

The idea made sense to a small group of Marine Corps strategists who developed it and then convinced top military brass, along with President Roosevelt, to back the bizarre scheme.

The unorthodox experiments were carried out in the secrecy of Bandera, Texas; Carlsbad, New Mexico; and El Centro, California, in 1942–1943. Although the experiments were riddled with failures and uncertainty, the team pressed forward with the offbeat undertaking.

During one particular test in early July of 1943 at the Carlsbad Air Force Base, six bats were armed with bombs and released for a publicity photo-op with the media. However, the winged creatures proved to be livelier than expected and quickly flew toward the buildings of a brand-new auxiliary air field.

The aerial bat squad roosted on a barracks building, a control tower, an office, an airplane hangar, and, according to some accounts, a general's car and a fuel tank. Then they blew up.

The fires caused by the swooping mammals sparked other blazes. Black smoke rose into the sky as the entire complex burned to the ground. That brought a fiery conclusion to the bat-bombers experiment.

When troops are accidentally shot at by their fellow soldiers, that is known as "friendly fire." There was a close call on November 14, 1943, during World War II when a torpedo fired from an American submarine barely missed the battleship USS *Iowa*.

The ship was going through a training exercise off Bermuda when the mishap occurred. Along with the crew aboard the *Iowa* at the time was President Franklin Roosevelt and the Joint Chiefs of Staff.

The United States used spies during World War II, although one became more famous for her work in the kitchen than for her covert operations.

Julia Child is best remembered for her cookbooks and television programs, most notably *The French Chef*, which premiered in 1963.

After the United States entered World War II, Julia felt the need to serve her country. She was too tall to join the military (she stood 6 feet 2 inches), so she volunteered her services to the Office of Strategic Services (OSS), which was the forerunner of today's Central Intelligence Agency (CIA). The Smith College graduate was one of 4,500 women who served in the OSS.

Julia started out at OSS Headquarters in Washington, D.C. She then worked with the OSS Emergency Sea Rescue Equipment Section, where she helped develop shark repellent. The compound was a critical tool during World War II and used as a coating on explosives that targeted German U-boats. Before the introduction of the repellent, curious sharks would sometimes set off the explosives when they bumped into them.

During her last two years in the OSS, Julia served as chief of the registry. Having top security clearance, she knew every incoming and outgoing message that passed through her office. It was during her time of service that she met her husband Paul, who was also an OSS officer.

After the war the ex-spy attended the famous Le Cordon Bleu cooking school in Paris, which started her career as a master chef. Years later, she parlayed those experiences into her successful endeavors as a television personality and best-selling author.

Julia passed away in 2004, but her various cooking shows continue to run on television. Few viewers realize that before she revealed her secret recipes for the kitchen, she was a top intelligence officer during World War II.

Millions of U.S. soldiers fought against Germany in World War II. One of those who received little attention over the years was William Patrick "Willy" Stuart-Houston, a hospital corpsman in the U.S. Navy.

His real name was William Patrick Hitler, and he was der Führer's nephew. Willy was the son of Adolf's half-brother Alois Hitler Jr., and grew up in Liverpool, England, where he was born. He was working in a German bank when his uncle became chancellor.

In 1939, Willy left Germany after a dispute with the dictator and came to the United States, along with his mother, for a lecture tour. They remained in the country after World War II broke out, and in 1944 Willy was given special permission to join the U.S. Navy by Franklin Roosevelt. He was wounded and received the Purple Heart for his service.

In 1947 he changed his name, eventually married, and had a family. Willy died in 1987 in New York, where he is buried.

A great deal of planning went into the preparation for the D-Day invasion. U.S. forces conducted a series of exercises on a stretch of beach called Slapton Sands, near Plymouth, England. In an area comprising around 30,000 acres, a total of 3,000 people (750 families) and 180 farms with livestock were evacuated. This enormous task had to be completed in six weeks.

On April 27, 1944, an exercise at Lyme Bay known as Operation Tiger turned into an actual attack as Allied landing craft were attacked by nine German torpedo boats. Two of the landing craft were sunk and others damaged.

The casualties included 638 killed (197 sailors and 441 soldiers) and hundreds injured. This was more than ten times greater than the casualties sustained in the real assault on Utah Beach on June 6 (43 Americans killed, 63 wounded).

Including casualties from other ships and those killed by friendly fire on shore, a total of 946 Americans gave their lives during an exercise that was scheduled to be just a dress rehearsal for D-Day.

General Dwight D. Eisenhower was the mastermind behind the D-Day invasion. But he didn't inherit his talent as a commander from his parents as they were members of the Mennonite River Brethren, a religion that preaches pacifism and is opposed to war and violence of any kind.

The plans for the D-Day invasion were created by General Dwight D. Eisenhower at his headquarters in Europe. He laid out the specifics of his strategy to President Roosevelt while the two were aboard the presidential yacht, the USS *Sequoia*. But it wouldn't be the last time that this vessel would be a part of history.

It was also the place where Harry Truman was when he decided to drop the atomic bomb on Hiroshima and where Richard Nixon finalized his decision to resign.

There was a large air assault using a massive number of paratroopers on D-Day. On June 5, 1944, Private Charles Hillman, serving with the U.S. 101st Airborne Division, was one of those on his way to Normandy for a date with destiny.

Like any trained jumper, as the time drew near, Private Hillman carried out a final inspection of his equipment. He was surprised to see that his gear had been packed by the Pioneer Parachute Company in his hometown of Manchester, Connecticut, where his mother worked part time as an inspector. He was further surprised when he saw her initials on the inspection tag.

The D-Day invasion was so top secret that the public received no details until it was well underway. On June 6, 1944, when the Allied forces landed in France, the ringing sound of the Liberty Bell was broadcast over the radio to all parts of the United States.

The only U.S. battleship to be present at both the Japanese attack on Pearl Harbor on December 7, 1941, and at the D-Day invasion on June 6, 1944, was the USS *Nevada*. After suffering severe damage in Hawaii, the vessel returned thirty-one months later to take part in the invasion of Europe.

At the 1944 Democratic National Convention in Chicago, Franklin D. Roosevelt was nominated for an unprecedented fourth term as the nation's leader. But FDR was not present on any of the days (July 19–21) of the convention. That's because he was dying.

In late March, FDR had what is believed to have been either a mild heart attack or stroke. After two weeks of medical tests, his doctors ordered him to take four weeks of rest, which he did at multimillionaire Bernard Baruch's plantation in South Carolina.

Following that, from July 13, 1944, to August 17, 1944, the frail president spent time relaxing in San Diego, Honolulu, Alaska, and Seattle. One didn't have to possess a medical degree to see that FDR's health had failed dramatically during his third term in office.

Aware of the risk that Roosevelt would die during his fourth term, the party regulars insisted that Vice President Henry A. Wallace, who was seen as too pro-Soviet, be dropped from the ticket. After considering former senator and Supreme Court justice James Byrnes of South Carolina, and being turned down by Indiana governor Henry F. Schricker, Roosevelt replaced Wallace with a little-known senator from Missouri, Harry Truman.

The foresight of this political maneuvering proved to be advantageous as on January 20, 1945, Truman was sworn in as vice president and then became the nation's commander in chief when Roosevelt died just eighty days later.

Franklin Roosevelt's health continued to fail in his last year in office (1944–1945). During that time, his thirty-eight-year-old daughter Anna served as a "super aide" to her dad. She was described as a combination of a personal secretary and chief of staff.

But the casual observer didn't need more evidence than the events of the day as to further proof of FDR's deteriorating health. Rather than traveling to the Capitol for his inauguration, the president took the oath of office on the South Portico of the White House. His inaugural address was the second shortest in history—just 559 words.

The traditional post-address luncheon with members of Congress, the inaugural parade up Pennsylvania Avenue, and subsequent evening festivities were all scrapped. The official word from the White House was that all of the events were scaled back due to the war effort, but most observers also felt that the frail leader was not physically up to a major celebration.

Germany's Autobahn is one of the most famous highway systems in the world. Most of it was built during Hitler's regime.

Toward the end of World War II, stretches of the well-known roadway were used as makeshift runways for Luftwaffe fighters and bombers. It was also used by U.S. Army troops to pursue Hitler's troops into Berlin.

Many future presidents served in the military during World War II. Among those was Gerald Ford, who like most, faced constant danger.

On December 17, 1944, while serving aboard the light aircraft carrier USS *Monterey*, Ford was almost blown overboard during a typhoon in the South Pacific. The storm was known as Typhoon Cobra and it sank three destroyers with a total loss of 790 lives. Nine other warships were damaged, and over one hundred aircraft were wrecked or washed overboard.

On the *Monterey*, while wearing a gas mask, Ford led a fire team into the carrier's hangar area, where airplanes, broken from their moorings and in flames, slid across the deck as the ship lurched. They spent most of the night putting out fires. Admiral Chester Nimitz said that the typhoon's impact "represented a more crippling blow to the 3rd Fleet than it might be expected to suffer in anything less than a major action."

Due to the damage suffered from Cobra, the *Monterey* returned to Bremerton, Washington, for overhaul but rejoined the fleet for the final few victorious weeks of the war in 1945.

Joseph Goebbels was Hitler's minister of propaganda. It was his duty to make the Nazi regime look powerful through the use of books and film.

Goebbels used actual German soldiers in many of those movies. One of those was the costliest motion picture ever made by the Nazis. It was called *Kolberg*.

The film was intended to boost the morale of the Germans in the last phase of World War II. It was based on the autobiography of Joachim Nettelbeck, the mayor of Kolberg, and it told the 1807 story of the successful defense of the fortress town against Napoleon's powerful French troops.

Kolberg, begun in 1943, was made at a cost of more than eight million marks (around $20 million). In comparison, the biggest movie of that era, *Gone with the Wind*, cost about $4 million. Thousands of soldiers were used in the production, even though every man was badly needed at the front lines.

The film was finally completed at the Babelsberg Studios in Potsdam while the town and nearby Berlin were being steadily bombed.

The movie opened in a provisional cinema in Berlin on January 30, 1945. It was also screened in the Reich chancellery after the broadcast of Hitler's last radio address that same day. *Kolberg* ran under the constant threat of air raids until the fall of Berlin in May 1945, but the film came far too late for Goebbels's desired propaganda effect because many theaters throughout Germany had already been destroyed.

President Franklin Roosevelt died shortly before Germany surrendered to end the war in Europe. He passed away on April 12, 1945, after serving the longest tenure of any American president—twelve years and one month. At the end, he was eighty-two days into his fourth term.

Also at that time, FDR's two archenemies took their final bows. Two weeks after Roosevelt's death, Italian dictator Benito Mussolini was executed by a mob near Lake Como. Three days later, Hitler committed suicide in his Berlin bunker.

Franklin Roosevelt was at his retreat in Warm Springs, Georgia, when he died in April 1945. But the president was not alone.

The person who was with him at the time of his death was his long-time mistress, Lucy Mercer. First Lady Eleanor Roosevelt was in Washington, D.C., when she was notified of her husband's passing.

During his first inauguration speech in 1933, Franklin Roosevelt had said, "The only thing we have to fear is fear itself."

But Roosevelt feared more than just fear. FDR had an acute case of triskaidekaphobia, or fear of the number 13. He would invite his secretary to come to dinner with him if there were otherwise going to be thirteen guests present at the function.

If his party was going to travel on the 13th of the month, he would reschedule the departure for 11:50 pm on the 12th or 12:10 am on the 14th. He avoided the date even in death, passing away on April 12, 1945.

Had FDR made it just one more day, his death would have been on Friday the 13th.

Franklin Roosevelt had been an avid stamp collector since his youth. A year after his death, his family sold his collection at auction for almost $200,000.

Franklin Roosevelt died before he could write his memoirs. But years earlier, while recovering from polio, FDR worked at various projects. He spent some time writing a movie script based on the history of the ship *Old Ironsides*, but he never succeeded in selling the product to Hollywood.

President Harry Truman ordered the dropping of the first atomic bomb on August 6, 1945. What many didn't realize at the time was that the

Manhattan Project was so secret that FDR had not even informed his fourth-term vice president that it existed. In fact, when Truman's 1943 senatorial investigations into war-production expenditures led him to ask questions about a suspicious plant in Minneapolis, which was secretly connected with the research, he received a stern phone call from FDR's secretary of war Harry Stimson warning him not to inquire further.

America's secret development of the atomic bomb began in 1939 with Roosevelt's support. When the president died on April 12, 1945, Truman was immediately sworn in and, soon after, informed by Stimson of a new and terrible weapon being developed by physicists in New Mexico. In his diary that night, Truman noted that he had been told that the United States was "perfecting an explosive great enough to destroy the whole world."

On April 24, Stimson and Leslie Groves, the Army general in charge of the project, brought Truman a file full of reports and details on the Manhattan Project. Three and a half months later, the first of two atomic bombs was unleashed by the man who had had no prior knowledge of the weapon before becoming president.

Harry Truman became president upon FDR's death in 1945. But that's not the job he had aspired to attain.

Figure 13.2 In 1961, former President Harry Truman returned to the White House to play for the crowd in the East Room. That's concert pianist Eugene List (R) admiring his technique. You might notice President Kennedy sitting in the front row. *National Archives*

As a boy, Truman dreamed of being a concert pianist. He had even had an opportunity as a youngster to meet the great Polish keyboard artist Jan Paderewski. But his dreams of playing in concert halls were dashed at the age of fifteen when he was forced to go to work to help support his family.

However, he never lost his love for the piano and would constantly play, along with his daughter Margaret, in the White House.

It was Harry Truman who made the historic decision to use atomic weapons to end World War II. However, the president made a mistake years earlier that almost cost him his life.

On Sunday March 27, 1938, while serving as a U.S. senator, Truman was returning to the nation's capital from Hagerstown, Maryland, with his wife and daughter. The future commander in chief was driving his new Plymouth when he ran a stop sign at an intersection. Another car broadsided Truman's vehicle, causing it to roll over several times.

Amazingly, no one in either automobile was hurt, and the senator later said that his view of the stop sign had been blocked by a parked car.

Although Truman's brand-new vehicle was a total loss, no citations were issued by the police. His daughter Margaret recalled, "It was a miracle that we escaped alive. Dad had a cut over his forehead and Mother had a wrenched back."

She also said that her father always drove too fast.

An atomic bomb destroyed the city of Hiroshima, Japan, on August 6, 1945. It was the first time that the weapon had been used against an enemy in combat but it wasn't the first to be detonated.

On July 16, 1945, the world's first atomic bomb was set off at the Alamogordo Bombing and Gunnery Range located 230 miles south of Los Alamos, New Mexico. Around 260 personnel were present for the top-secret operation, but none were closer than 5.6 miles.

In 1952, the site of the explosion was bulldozed, and was listed on the National Register of Historic Places on October 15, 1966.

Harry Truman may have made the biggest military decision of all time when he elected to drop the two atomic bombs on Japan. However, as a young man, the commander in chief applied to but was rejected for admission to West Point. The reason was his poor eyesight.

One of the longtime activities of schoolyard children is the dog pile. The object is for the youngsters to create a human tower atop the unlucky individual on the bottom. However, the behavior isn't restricted to kids.

The United States dropped the first atomic bomb on the Japanese city of Hiroshima on August 6, 1945. Two days later, the Soviet Union declared war on Japan because the Japanese were in no position to defend themselves.

Following the second nuclear attack, the Japanese surrendered on August 14, and like the other Allies, the Soviets claimed their share of the victory, proving that the dog pile is an adult activity too.

Hiroshima wasn't the only target for an atomic bomb as there were other cities that were being considered, including Kyoto, Yokohama, and Kokura. Some thought Kyoto would be selected, but Henry L. Stimson, the secretary of war at the time, vetoed that choice. He had admired the area since he and his wife had honeymooned there in 1893.

The United States dropped two nuclear bombs on Japan to end World War II. But years later, America dropped two nukes on itself.

In 1961, two hydrogen bombs were accidentally expelled on the tiny farming town of Faro, twelve miles north of Seymour Johnson Air Force Base in Goldsboro, North Carolina, after a B-52 aircraft broke up in midair. The two weapons were released after the crew abandoned the aircraft, which had suffered a mid-flight structural failure.

Three of the bomber's eight crew members died in the crash. Both bombs had gone through several steps in the arming sequence, but fortunately neither of them detonated.

In 1942, General Douglas MacArthur was awarded the nation's highest military decoration—the Medal of Honor. But he wasn't the first in the family to claim the award.

His father, Captain Arthur MacArthur Jr., was decorated for his actions during the Civil War. The MacArthurs are the first father-son combination to win the Medal of Honor.

The Japanese surrendered following the dropping of the second atomic bomb on the city of Nagasaki. When Emperor Hirohito announced the decision on the radio, it was the first time that the citizens of the country had ever heard his voice.

Physicist J. Robert Oppenheimer was the scientific director of the Manhattan Project. After the bombing of Hiroshima and Nagasaki, Oppenheimer told President Truman that America's atomic scientists had "blood on our hands." The undaunted Truman responded, "Never mind. It'll all come out in the wash."

"The Manhattan Project" was the top-secret code name for the development of the atomic bomb. During the days of the classified undertaking, all applicants for menial jobs at the plant where the bomb was being built did not get hired if they could read. This was because government authorities didn't want the staff reading secret documents.

There was a book titled *The World Set Free*. It was written by the famed British author H. G. Wells about nuclear weapons that would be able to destroy cities.

That may not seem worth mentioning except that Wells wrote the book in 1913, a year before the outbreak of World War I, and decades before the first nuclear chain reaction in 1942.

The dropping of the atomic bomb on Nagasaki, which took place on August 9, 1945, was the last action of World War II. Later that day, Hirohito notified the Allies that Japan would surrender.

But there were some who didn't hear the news and were still fighting. On August 15, the USS *Heerman* shot down a Japanese plane attempting a Kamikaze attack. Also, unknown to the Japanese government, the U.S. forces already had plans in place for their next nuclear strike to take place on August 17 or 18 following the Nagasaki blast.

Then there was Lieutenant Hiroo Onoda, who held out from December 1944 until March 1974 on Lubang Island in the Philippines. He surrendered to his former commanding officer, who was brought to the scene, in March 1974.

A few months later, in November 1974, the last-known Japanese holdout, Private Teruo Nakamura, was discovered on Morotai Island in Indonesia where he had been doing his duty since 1944.

Audie Murphy was arguably the greatest American combat soldier of World War II and perhaps of all of American history. The Farmersville, Texas, native won over twenty combat

Figure 13.3 Audie Murphy . . . from battlefield warrior to a man of letters.

awards including the Medal of Honor, five Bronze Stars, two Silver Stars, and the French Croix de Guerre.

After the war, he wrote his best-selling autobiography *To Hell and Back* and became a movie star.

Murphy, a battlefield warrior who went to school only until the eighth grade, was also a successful country-western songwriter, and he penned a few poems.

The famous war crimes trials were held at Nuremberg, Germany. But because it was a series of international tribunals, there were language barriers that needed to be rectified.

IBM had created the first simultaneous translation device, and the company offered to donate as much equipment as the court needed. Each headset had a switch to choose one of four languages (English, German, French, or Russian), and if someone spoke too quickly, a yellow light would turn on to slow them down, or even a red light to stop them altogether.

The other first at this trial was the introduction of a new word into the English language: "genocide."

Many of the surviving Nazi officials were put on trial as war criminals at Nuremberg, Germany, in 1945 and 1946. Among those who received a life sentence was Rudolf Hess, a deputy of the Nazi Party.

Hess, along with six other convicted war criminals, was sent to Germany's Spandau Prison. Of the seven, only four served out their full sentences, with the remaining three being released partway into their time due to ill health.

Between 1966 and 1987, Hess was the only prisoner residing inside the walls of Spandau. His lone companion was the warden, Eugene K. Bird, who became a close friend. Bird wrote a book titled *The Loneliest Man in the World* about Hess's imprisonment.

In 1987, the lone inmate committed suicide at the age of ninety-three. A short time later, the prison was demolished.

Nearly sixteen million Americans served in the Armed Forces during World War II. One was Elbert Lewis of Odessa, Texas, who was in the U.S. Navy.

On March 4, 1995, the eighty-year-old veteran received a letter notifying him to register for the draft. It was from the Selective Service Board, stating that he had not registered for the draft as required by law when he turned eighteen.

The letter mistakenly indicated that Lewis was born November 11, 1976, instead of November 11, 1914. Having read this, the former serviceman disposed of the notification.

• *14* •

1945–1949: The Forties Are Finished and Dewey Lost Again

Lady Astor once told Winston Churchill, "If you were my husband, I would poison your coffee." Churchill replied, "If you were my wife, I would drink it."

Combat pilots go through a great deal of training and preparation. On December 5, 1945, five TBM Avenger torpedo bombers, known as Navy Flight 19, disappeared during an overwater navigation training flight from a naval air station at Fort Lauderdale, Florida.

The assignment was a combination of bombing and navigation, which other flights had or were scheduled to undertake that day. All nine airmen on the detail were lost, as were all twelve crew members of a PBM Mariner flying boat which was assumed to have exploded in midair while searching for survivors.

The Navy conducted an inquiry into the incident, eventually publishing a five-hundred-page report that suggested the pilots may have become disoriented and mistakenly headed out to sea, where they ran out of fuel and crashed into the ocean. But a general lack of evidence led to the disappearance eventually being listed as "cause unknown."

There are also those who believe that they were victims of the storied Bermuda Triangle.

The term "Iron Curtain" was included in Winston Churchill's famous Sinews of Peace address of March 5, 1946, at Westminster College in Fulton, Missouri. For the next several decades, it was used to describe the Soviet domination of Eastern Europe.

It was probably fitting that Churchill gave that speech in the United States. His mother, Jennie Jerome Churchill, was an American citizen who gave birth to Sir Winston in a ladies' cloakroom after she went into labor during a dance at Blenheim Palace in Woodstock, England.

A cataclysmic disaster of April 16, 1947, started with a mid-morning fire and the detonation of approximately 2,300 tons of ammonium nitrate onboard a ship in the port of Texas City, Texas, killing at least 581 people.

The explosion created such force that a two-ton anchor of the French freighter *Grand Camp* was hurled 1.62 miles across Texas City and found in a ten-foot crater. It now rests in the town's memorial park. The ship's other anchor, weighing five tons, was propelled one-half mile to the entrance of the Texas City dike, and it now rests on a Texas-shaped memorial at the entrance.

The president of the United States travels in chauffeur-driven limousines. But on July 6, 1947, when on a return trip to Washington, D.C., from Charlottesville, Virginia, President Harry Truman did something that would be unheard of today as he took over the wheel of the limo and drove back to the White House.

A lover of cruising, he was also known to have climbed into the driver's seat on other occasions while serving as chief executive. The president had a strong dislike for General Motors products because he was denied use of them during his 1948 presidential campaign. So when it came time to replace the presidential limo, it was Ford's Lincoln Division that got the job.

On October 14, 1947, U.S. Air Force captain Chuck Yeager became the first pilot to fly faster than the speed of sound. What the flight coordinators at California's Edwards Air Force Base did not know is that two nights before his historic journey, Yeager broke two ribs after falling from a horse. He didn't reveal the injury to flight doctors for fear that he would be grounded.

The nation of Israel was created in 1948 as an independent Jewish state. In 1952 the country's first president, Chaim Weizman, died, which meant there would be an election.

As talk of potential candidates emerged, one name came to the forefront—Albert Einstein. Many were enthusiastic about the possibility, even though the Princeton University professor believed in coexistence with the Arabs and didn't know Hebrew, the official language of the new state.

However, some believed that as a mathematics genius, Einstein could solve any problems that might arise with the economy. When he was contacted by an Israeli envoy, the seventy-three-year-old naturalized U.S. citizen replied, "I have neither the natural ability nor the experience to deal with human beings."

The nation's first "Tornado Warning" was issued on March 25, 1948, in Oklahoma City just minutes before a devastating twister struck Tinker Air Force Base. It caused $6 million in damage, but due to precautions taken after the alert, no injuries were reported.

The event marked the second time that a tornado had touched down on the base in six days. The damage from the first twister to military aircraft was substantial. The cost came to around $10.25 million.

That wasn't the last time that the base would face off against the elements. On May 3, 1999, a tornado with a mile-wide funnel caused approximately $16 million in damage and ultimately claimed the lives of five Tinker personnel.

In 1948, after serving out the remainder of Franklin Roosevelt's term, Harry Truman was elected to four years of his own as president of the United States. During much of Truman's presidency, the interior of the White House, with the exception of the third floor, was being completely gutted and renovated.

This meant that the First Family lived at Blair House, directly across Pennsylvania Avenue, and best known as the official residence for visiting dignitaries.

Harry Truman is the only president who grew up in Missouri. But he almost didn't grow up at all.

Little Harry developed diphtheria in 1894 at age ten. He was paralyzed for several months and had to be wheeled around in a baby carriage. Diphtheria antitoxin was unavailable at that time, so he was treated with ipecac and whiskey. Because of that, he developed a severe distaste for both.

On January 30, 1948, political and spiritual leader Mohandas Gandhi was assassinated in New Delhi, India. Also on that same day in Dayton, Ohio, aviation pioneer Orville Wright died of heart failure. Wright was seventy-seven years old, Gandhi was seventy-eight.

Every four years, the political parties in the United States hold their conventions to nominate their presidential candidates. Major cities always make bids to host these events. In 1948, three political parties—Republican, Democratic, and National Progressive—all selected Philadelphia as their national convention site. They nominated Thomas E. Dewey, Harry S. Truman, and Henry A. Wallace, respectively. Truman won.

Governor Thomas Dewey of New York was favored to defeat Harry Truman in the election of 1948. It was a classic example of what has played out so many times when the pre-election polls are wrong.

On election night, Dewey asked his wife Frances, "How will it be to sleep with the president of the United States?"

She replied, "A high honor, and quite frankly, darling, I'm looking forward to it."

The next morning, at breakfast, after Dewey's defeat, Frances inquired, "Tell me Tom, am I going to Washington or is Harry coming here?"

Most of the nation's presidents since 1900 either were or became wealthy. But that wasn't the case for Harry Truman, who was having a hard time breaking even. During his tenure, the government paid the White House staff and servants but did not feed them. First Lady Bess Truman tried cutting the staff (which ran between twenty-five and thirty) but had to discard that plan because the housework didn't get done.

Feeding the help, plus family and friends, meant that Truman had to pay for about two thousand meals a month. In the Roosevelt era, the monthly food bill sometimes soared to $7,000; Bess Truman cut it to about $2,000. On quiet nights with the family, the president often dined on leftovers.

Truman confided to friends that after paying his $30,000 income tax bill, he averaged about $80 a week in take-home pay.

The president is the person who hires and fires members of the cabinet. On March 28, 1949, Harry Truman dismissed Secretary of Defense James Forrestal because the two disagreed over policy matters.

The pressure of his job in addition to his firing caused Forrestal to act erratically. He was checked into Bethesda Naval Hospital and placed on the sixteenth floor, which had been built for FDR. After prior suicide attempts, on May 22, 1949, Forrestal fell to his death from his high-rise window. He is buried at Arlington National Cemetery.

To this day, there are those who don't believe that Forrestal's demise was suicide but think that he might have been murdered, even though the case is officially closed.

• 15 •

The Fifties: In the Event of a Nuclear Attack, Get Under a Table!

I have no use for bodyguards, but I have very specific use for two highly trained certified public accountants.

—Elvis Presley

General Douglas MacArthur was the supreme commander of the U.N. Forces in the Korean War even though he never actually spent a single night in the country during the conflict.

MacArthur did make an appearance in Pyongyang on October 20, 1950, when American troops entered the North Korean capital.

"Any celebrities here to greet me?" he asked as he stepped off the plane—adding, in a mocking reference to North Korean leader Kim Il Sung, "Where is Kim Buck Tooth?"

That evening, the general got back on his plane and returned to Tokyo where he was directing the war while simultaneously serving as supreme commander of U.S. Occupation Forces in Japan.

MacArthur's running of the Korean War was one of history's most unusual commands. Over the years, he took thirteen photo-op trips to Korea but never stayed at one location for more than a few hours. He also never spent a full day or night in the country, always opting to return to Japan.

The Medal of Honor recipient ran the war from his luxurious office on the sixth floor of the Dai-ichi Mutual Life Insurance building in Tokyo which overlooked the Imperial Palace. It was said that the general enjoyed making Emperor Hirohito look up to him.

The Korean War kept the dividing line of North and South Korea at the 38th parallel. The peace talks between the factions lasted two years and seventeen days. A total of 575 meetings took place before an agreement was reached. That was equal to almost the entire length of the war, which began on June 25, 1950, and ended on July 27, 1953.

On November 1, 1950, two Puerto Rican nationalists attempted to assassinate President Harry Truman. The First Family was residing at Blair House across Pennsylvania Avenue while renovations were going on at the executive mansion. That's where the pair attempted to ambush the nation's leader.

The main front door was open because of the warm weather, but its screen door was locked. It was a setting which would never be allowed to take place in today's world.

During the shootout that followed in front of the residence, one gunmen was killed and the other captured. As for the president, he was taking a nap upstairs in Blair House when the shooting began and was unharmed.

Douglas MacArthur was relieved of his command in Korea when he was fired by President Truman. The general returned home to the United States where he received a hero's welcome, including a ticker tape parade through New York City. At that juncture, MacArthur hadn't been in the United States for almost fifteen years due to his continuous overseas duties.

In the summer of 1953, two years after he had dismissed the general, Truman made a trip to New York City. For eight nights, he stayed at the Waldorf-Astoria Hotel in a suite five floors below MacArthur's apartment where he resided. The hotel staff made sure that the two men never crossed paths.

Many citizens know that the Constitution and the Declaration of Independence are housed in the National Archives Building. What most don't realize is how they got there.

During the 1920s and 1930s, the famous documents were on display at the Library of Congress. On December 13, 1952, they were transferred to the newly erected National Archives Building.

The transfer itself had become considerably more complex than the day in 1920 when Herbert Putnam, the librarian of Congress, transported the founding documents in his Model-T Ford truck. For the big move thirty-two years later, the Constitution and the Declaration of Independence were placed in helium-filled cases, enclosed in wooden crates, laid on mattresses in an armored Marine Corps personnel carrier, and escorted by ceremonial troops, two tanks, and four servicemen carrying submachine guns down Pennsylvania and Constitution Avenues to the National Archives.

The transfer was successful, and today they reside in the facility along with other items from the nation's history.

Dwight D. Eisenhower was sworn in as president on January 20, 1953. The tradition of the president-elect going first to the White House to meet the outgoing president before proceeding to the Capitol began in 1877 with Rutherford B. Hayes and incumbent Ulysses S. Grant.

That ritual continued until January 20, 1953, when Ike and his wife Mamie refused to go inside the White House to join the Trumans for coffee. Even though he won the election, the incoming president was still upset over remarks that his predecessor had made about him and Senator Joe McCarthy during the campaign.

Having been spurned, Truman emerged on the White House steps after a few moments wearing a bogus smile, but several veteran reporters on the scene understood what had just taken place. The contentiousness continued in the car on the way to the Capitol.

Eisenhower, one of the heroes of World War II, asked Truman who had released his son John from active duty in Korea so he could attend the inauguration. John, a West Point graduate like his father, was embarrassed that he had been called home. Truman stated that he had given the order, which infuriated Ike.

After the ceremony, the outgoing commander in chief went directly home to Independence, Missouri.

Over the years, the long-distance sparring continued as each man did his best to avoid the other. On November 25, 1963, the two old rivals found themselves together once again sharing a limousine—this time they were among the mourners at President Kennedy's funeral. When it was over, the pair of ex–world leaders returned to Blair House for food and fellowship. They sat and talked about the past for over an hour, and at the conclusion of the afternoon, the former presidents buried the hatchet. It was their final face-to-face meeting.

Most American citizens have to pay their federal income tax by April 15 of each year. That included Joseph Nunan.

After retirement, Nunan had several run-ins with the Internal Revenue Service (IRS). In 1952, he was convicted of tax evasion after concealing an income of more than $90,000. Included was $1,800 that he had won on a bet that Harry Truman would be victorious in the election of 1948, which he had neglected to declare on his taxes. He was sentenced to five years in federal prison.

In case you're wondering what Nunan did for a living before retiring, from 1944 until 1947 he was the head of the IRS.

Senator Joseph McCarthy of Wisconsin made headlines in the 1950s with hearings that were held to expose Communists in the government. While the probe made him a national celebrity, his overreaching eventually led to his political downfall.

McCarthy, a Republican, established a bond with the powerful Democratic Kennedy family, and he became a close friend of Joe Kennedy Sr., himself a fervent anti-Communist. He dated two of Kennedy's daughters, Patricia and Eunice, and was godfather to Robert F. Kennedy's first child, Kathleen. She was lieutenant governor of Maryland from 1993 to 2003.

In most states, if you don't prefer the candidates who are on the ballot, then you may write in the name of the individual of your choice.

Upon the death of U.S. senator Burnet Rhett Maybank in 1954, former governor Strom Thurmond ran as a write-in candidate for senator against the nominee of the South Carolina Democratic Party, Edgar Brown. He defeated Brown in the primary, eventually becoming the first person in U.S. history to be elected to a major office on a write-in ballot.

In 2010, incumbent U.S. senator Lisa Murkowski of Alaska made history as she staged a successful write-in campaign in the general election after having been defeated in the Republican primary a few weeks earlier.

In 1955, President Eisenhower suffered a massive heart attack while visiting his in-laws in Denver. But that wasn't Ike's only bout with health problems.

In 1956, Eisenhower had to decide whether to run for a second term. Health concerns were a major part of this decision. At one point, he had considered passing up a return to office.

After declaring to run again, he was struck on June 9 with a bowel obstruction that required immediate surgery. The blockage could have killed him but the operation was successful, and a few weeks later, he won re-election.

But that wasn't the last of Ike's health issues. Just a few months into his second term, the sixty-seven-year-old president suffered a stroke. There was speculation that Eisenhower's health issues stemmed from the fact that during his military days, he was a four-pack-a-day cigarette smoker. In 1949, he quit cold turkey.

The popular leader successfully completed his second term and then retired to his Gettysburg farm, where he lived quietly until his passing in 1969.

Ulysses S. Grant and Dwight D. Eisenhower were different individually but their career paths were nearly identical. Each man graduated from West Point; each was the commander and winning general of a major war; and each won two terms as president.

In the case of both, their two electoral victories were the only time that either had run for public office.

President Franklin Roosevelt was crippled by polio and died on April 12, 1945. Exactly ten years to the day later, the vaccine for the disease was announced.

The polio serum was discovered by Dr. Jonas Salk of the University of Pittsburgh Medical Center. His discovery is among the biggest medical breakthroughs ever.

Salk graduated from high school when he was just fifteen and intended to become a lawyer. A few years later, his fiancée's father, a wealthy Manhattan dentist, viewed Salk as a "social inferior" and would not agree to the marriage until the young medical student could be listed as an MD on the wedding invitations.

In June 1939, Salk received his medical degree from New York University Medical School and was married the next day to his fiancée Donna Lindsay.

Jonas Salk's anti-polio vaccine was introduced in 1955 while he was doing research at the University of Pittsburgh Medical School. He needed healthy human test subjects to test the vaccine so he volunteered himself and his entire family for a trial. The gamble paid off as everyone tested positive for anti-polio antibodies. He also refused to patent the vaccine, and he never received financial compensation for his discovery.

An individual named Basil O'Connor supplied most of the funding for Salk's research. O'Connor was Franklin Roosevelt's best friend and former law partner.

The public has become accustomed to seeing the libraries of U.S. presidents constructed after they have left office. The Truman Library was the first to be created under the provisions of the 1955 Presidential Libraries Act.

What many don't realize is that Truman actively participated in the day-to-day operation of his library, which opened in 1957. He personally conducted impromptu "press conferences" for visiting school students, for example. Truman frequently arrived before the staff and would often answer the phone to give directions and answer questions, telling surprised callers that he was the "man himself."

U.S. presidents receive a government pension after they have left office. They are also given allowances for office space, staff compensation, communications services, medical expenses, printing, and postage, along with Secret Service protection for ten years.

Prior to 1958, the U.S. federal government provided no pension or other retirement benefits to former presidents. Several former chief executives, like Thomas Jefferson and James Monroe, were broke when they died. In 1912, steel magnate Andrew Carnegie offered to endow a $25,000 annual pension for ex-presidents but Congress rejected the idea.

It was in 1955 that former president Harry Truman's limited financial resources prompted legislation to provide benefits to past chief executives. When he retired from office in 1953, Truman's primary income was a monthly military pension of $112.56. When offered corporate positions at large salaries, he declined, stating, "You don't want me. You want the office of the president, and that doesn't belong to me. It belongs to the American people and it's not for sale."

When the Former Presidents Act took effect in 1958 there were two living former presidents: the wealthy Herbert Hoover and Truman, who each received an annual salary of $25,000. Harry once observed about the workings of the federal government, "You want a friend in Washington? Get a dog."

Alaska became the nation's 49th and largest state on January 3, 1959. In 1926, thirteen-year-old Benny Benson from Cognac, Alaska, won a contest when he designed a flag for the territory. Thirty-three years later, when Alaska became a state, Benny's creation from his boyhood days became the official state flag.

In April 1959, NASA selected its first group of astronauts, who were known as the "Mercury 7." But two men who were considered the country's top pilots at that time, Chuck Yeager and Scott Crossfield, were not invited to try out for the program.

Yeager was the first man to break the sound barrier (in 1947) and Crossfield, the designer of the famous X-15 rocket plane, was the first to fly at Mach II (in 1953). Both pilots were fiercely independent, and the government wasn't convinced that they would follow NASA's orders.

If America's first group of astronauts were known as the "Mercury 7," who were the "Mercury 13"? They were a group of thirteen of America's top female pilots who, as part of a privately-funded program, underwent some of the same physiological screening tests as the original astronauts selected by

NASA. The Mercury 13 were not part of NASA's astronaut program, they never flew in space, and they never actually met as a group.

Among the group was record-setting pilot Jerrie Cobb, who became the first American woman, and the only one of the Mercury 13, to undergo and pass all three phases of testing. Unfortunately, she and the others never got an opportunity to fly into space.

The government canceled the women's program based on a new ruling that all astronauts must be jet pilots. Since all jet pilots were military, and the military didn't allow women to fly jets, none of the Mercury 13 were eligible to be astronauts at that time.

In 1959, U.S. Air Force test pilot Donald "Deke" Slayton was selected as one of America's Mercury astronauts. However, he was the only member of the original seven who didn't fly in a Mercury spacecraft due to an irregular heartbeat.

Slayton continued working at NASA, and in 1972 he was medically cleared to fly in space. Sixteen years after being selected as an astronaut, he was part of the first international mission, Apollo-Soyuz, July 15–24, 1975.

Hawaii became the nation's 50th state on August 21, 1959. With its many beautiful beaches, it has long been a popular tourist destination. NASA sent astronauts there during the 1960s but not to vacation or surf.

They were there to train for their future trips to the moon. Some of that time was spent on the hardened lava beds of the big island which were used to simulate the lunar surface.

The Cuban Revolution of 1959 resulted in Fidel Castro taking over power on the island. But not all of the members of the Castro family were on board with the ideas of the new dictator.

Alina Fernández Revuelta lived under her father's rule from when he took power until she fled the country in 1993 with her daughter (Castro's granddaughter) because of her dissenting political views. She lived for several years in Columbus, Georgia, and now resides in South Florida, where she has a nightly radio show.

Another daughter, Francisca Pupo (born 1953) and her husband now reside in Miami, Florida. The dictator's sister Juanita Castro has been living in the United States since the early 1960s.

Congressman Mario Rafael Diaz-Balart is the nephew of Castro's first wife, Mirta Diaz-Balart. His brother, Lincoln Diaz-Balart, is also a congressman, representing the 21st District of Florida.

The last two states to join the Union were Alaska and Hawaii. That meant that the flag would need to be changed.

Robert Heft was living with his grandparents in Lancaster, Ohio. The seventeen-year-old high school student was in search of a class project when he thought of redesigning the American flag in light of the recent addition of Alaska as a state. His teacher, Stanley Pratt, told Heft that his design lacked originality and gave him a B- on the project.

The teacher offered his student a challenge, saying he would raise the grade to an A if Heft could get the U.S. Congress to accept his flag design. He even went as far as to put the promise in writing.

Heft sent his flag design to Walter Moeller, his Ohio congressman. Moeller succeeded in having the young man's depiction adopted as the new U.S. flag on July 4, 1960.

Heft's original flag has flown over the White House, every state capital building in the Union, and eighty-eight U.S. embassies. It was eventually presented to the originator, who was offered as much as $350,000 for it.

Robert died in 2009, but he did have the foresight to obtain copyrights for designs of U.S. flags with 51 to 60 stars just in case any new states are ever added. His history teacher Stanley Pratt also kept his word and raised his grade from a B- to an A.

· *16* ·

It's the Sixties: Far Out, Man

The pay is good and I can walk to work.

—John F. Kennedy answering a question from the press
on what he liked about being president

In 1960, American pilot Francis Gary Powers was shot down over the
Soviet Union in a U-2 spy plane. He was held prisoner by the Soviets for two
years until he was returned to the United States.

Powers had been given a silver dollar that split open to reveal a pin charged
with a powerful toxin, allowing him to commit suicide if captured. The military pilot chose not to use the pin after his plane was gunned down and he
parachuted to the ground. His Soviet captors tried it on a dog, which died in
ninety seconds.

After his release, Powers became an airborne traffic reporter for television station KNBC in Los Angeles. In 1977, having survived being shot
down by Soviet planes and held in a Soviet prison, the Air Force veteran died
in a helicopter crash while covering Southern California's brush fires for the
local network.

The tiny village of Dixville Notch, New Hampshire, is best known in
connection with its longstanding practice of middle-of-the-night voting in
the U.S. presidential election and the New Hampshire primary (the first
primary election in the U.S. presidential nomination process).

The tradition started with the 1960 election as all the eligible voters in
Dixville Notch gathered at midnight in the ballroom of the Balsams Hotel.
The electors cast their ballots, and the polls officially closed one minute later.
The result of the Dixville Notch vote in both the New Hampshire primary

and the general election is traditionally broadcast around the country immediately afterward.

A similar tradition in the community of Hart's Location, New Hampshire, began in 1948. It was discontinued in the 1960s in light of the abundance of media attention but was revived in 1996.

John F. Kennedy defeated Richard Nixon, the sitting vice president, in the election of 1960. What many voters were not aware of was that the pair had something in common: they were both intense anti-Communists.

This was so much so that in Nixon's Senate campaign of 1950, JFK personally delivered a $1,000 campaign contribution to the candidate while his dad, Joe Kennedy Sr., kicked in a donation of $150,000.

From 1947 to 1950, Kennedy and Nixon were working colleagues as both were members of the U.S. House of Representatives.

Terrorists used two large passenger jets to attack New York City on September 11, 2001. But that wasn't the first time that there had been a disaster in the sky over the Big Apple involving passenger aircraft.

On December 16, 1960, United Airlines Flight 826 collided with TWA Flight 266 over New York City, a disaster in which one plane crashed into Staten Island and the other into Park Slope, a Brooklyn neighborhood. The accident killed all 84 people aboard Flight 826, 44 on Flight 266, and 6 people on the ground.

The planes were traveling in heavy clouds when they collided. It marked the first time that a "black box" flight recorder was used to provide extensive details in an air disaster investigation.

When John F. Kennedy was elected president in 1960, he had to relinquish his seat in the U.S. Senate.

In terms of a successor, that seemed simple as JFK's father, Joseph Kennedy Sr., wanted his son Ted to assume the seat. But there was an age problem since Ted Kennedy was only twenty-eight and the required minimum age for a U.S. senator is thirty.

Joe Sr. had used many of his high-placed connections to get JFK elected to the Senate in 1952 and he wanted to keep the seat in the family. The old man once said, "I bought and paid for that Senate seat and as long as there is a Kennedy alive, it will be a Kennedy in it."

The Kennedys called on an old family friend, Ben Smith, for help. Smith had been JFK's roommate at Harvard University and actually had some political experience, having served as mayor of Gloucester, Massachusetts, from 1954 to 1955.

Joe Sr. and JFK, who had been reelected to a second Senate term of six years in 1958, advised Governor Foster Furcolo of Massachusetts to appoint Smith to fill the vacated seat "in the interest of promoting party unity." But the intention was that Smith was to be a "seat-warmer" until the president elect's brother turned thirty.

Ben served in the Senate until 1962 when he promptly resigned so that a special election could be held in November. As planned by Joe Sr., the voters elected Ted Kennedy, who served the remainder of Smith's term and was reelected in every election until his death in 2009.

His passing produced another special election for the seat in 2010. But despite Joe Sr.'s promise that "as long as there is a Kennedy alive, it will be a Kennedy in it," no member of the famous political family ran for the office. The seat, which had been controlled by the Kennedys for fifty-six years, was won by Scott Brown, a Republican.

Senator Ted Kennedy graduated from Harvard, following in the footsteps of his father and three older brothers, Joe Jr., JFK, and Robert. But the future senator was expelled from the Ivy League institution in 1951 when he convinced another individual to take a Spanish exam for him. He reapplied two years later and after being readmitted, graduated in 1956.

The 1961 Bay of Pigs invasion by Cuban refugees and the CIA ended in disaster as all of the 1,500 Cubans who were involved were either captured or killed. So what went wrong?

The CIA's information that showed that the Bay of Pigs was an unpopulated area was years out of date. As it turned out, the bay was Fidel Castro's favorite fishing ground, and he was building a resort there that included a seaside cabin for himself. Thus it was constantly patrolled by the Cuban military.

On May 5, 1961, astronaut Alan Shepard became the first American to go into space. Ten years later, he became the fifth American to walk on the moon. But who knew that Shepard broke the record for the longest golf shot ever?

While on the lunar surface, the astronaut struck two golf balls with a six iron, driving the second, as he jokingly put it, "miles and miles and miles."

Hey Jack Nicklaus, how about that?

President Kennedy gave a speech on May 25, 1961, in which he predicted that the United States would put men on the moon before the end of the decade. That did happen.

But it was Richard Nixon, the man whom JFK defeated in the election of 1960, who became the first president to talk to humans who were on another celestial body. He did so when he spoke from the White House by radio-telephone on July 21, 1969, to astronauts who were on the moon.

In July 1961, Gus Grissom became the second American to travel into space. But when he returned to Earth, his spacecraft, nicknamed *Liberty Bell 7*, sank in the Atlantic Ocean following the splashdown.

Almost thirty-eight years to the day after it went to the bottom, the spacecraft was recovered from the ocean floor. It was found at a depth of more than 15,000 feet—3,000 feet deeper than the wreck of the *Titanic.*

Liberty Bell 7 is now on exhibit at the Cosmosphere in Hutchinson, Kansas.

On February 3, 1962, President Kennedy expanded a trade embargo against Cuba that had begun in 1960. It was done in response to the Castro regime imposing further restrictions over the Cuban people. This meant that the United States would no longer purchase goods from Cuba, including its world-famous cigars.

That was bad news for JFK, who was an avid cigar smoker. He had originally planned that the embargo would not include Cuban tobacco products. Richard Goodwin, who had been an assistant to presidents Kennedy and Johnson, revealed that JFK told him in early 1962, "We tried to exempt cigars, but the cigar manufacturers in Tampa objected. I guess we're out of luck."

The night before the embargo began, the stogie-loving president sent his press secretary Pierre Salinger to buy a stockpile of Cuban cigars. The following morning, Salinger returned with 1,200 H. Upmann Petit Corona cigars. JFK left no evidence of his stash as he ordered all of the special boxes burned in the White House furnace after they were empty and the product was stored safely away.

In May 1962, Salinger met with Soviet Premier Khrushchev in Moscow. At the end of the meeting, Khrushchev, who did not smoke, gave Salinger a box of 150 Cuban cigars that he had received from Fidel Castro. Upon his return Salinger passed them on to Kennedy.

The president jokingly said he was going to destroy them, to which Salinger quipped, "I know, one by one."

It is also reputed that in the 1990s, a number of boxes of Cuban cigars that were confiscated at airports would eventually make their way to President Bill Clinton who, like Kennedy, was a patron of the banned tobacco.

The United States and the Soviet Union were on the brink of nuclear war in October 1962 during the Cuban Missile Crisis. Everyone knows that cooler heads eventually prevailed, but at the time, few realized that it was a journalist who helped prevent the ultimate conflict.

John Scali was an ABC News reporter who became an intermediary between the factions during the crisis. In October 1962, a year after he joined the network, Scali carried a critical message from the KGB's Colonel Aleksandr Fomin to U.S. officials. That was the beginning of several proposals that led to a cool down between the superpowers.

Scali's role in the negotiations did not become known until 1964. He left ABC in 1971 to serve as a foreign affairs adviser in the Nixon administration before becoming U.S. ambassador to the United Nations in 1973.

Lessons are taught in schools about the Cuban Missile Crisis, but hardly anyone, outside of Minnesota, has ever heard of the Duluth Missile Crisis.

On October 25, 1962, while the Americans and Soviets were staring each other down, a guard at an airbase in Duluth spotted an intruder attempting to scale the perimeter fence. He fired on the trespasser and raised the alarm, which also activated sirens at all bases in the area.

However, at Volk Field Air Base in Wisconsin, the alarm had been wired incorrectly. Instead of sounding a sabotage warning, it ordered a fleet of F-106A Delta Dart Interceptors armed with nuclear missiles to take off. As there are no practice alert drills when DEFCON 3 (U.S. Defense Readiness Condition 3) is activated, the pilots believed a nuclear war with the Soviet Union had begun. As the aircraft were about to take off, a car from the air traffic control tower rushed toward them and they were signaled to stop.

The pilots were notified that the intruder who had started the rapid chain of events back in Duluth, Minnesota, had been identified. It was a bear that had been wandering in the area.

John F. Kennedy was the first U.S. president of the Catholic faith, and he attended confession regularly. But JFK was constantly concerned that a priest might recognize his distinctive voice and reveal his sins to the world.

On Good Friday afternoon in 1963, the nation's chief executive went to a Catholic Church in Palm Beach, Florida, with a group of fellow Catholic Secret Service agents, hoping not to be recognized. As he entered the confessional, the priest greeted him with a pleasant, "Good evening, Mr. President." JFK replied, "Good evening, Father," and immediately left the church.

Under the terms of the U.S. Constitution, a defendant has the right to remain silent and must be notified of that fact when they are arrested. It was the main argument in the famous Supreme Court case *Miranda v. Arizona*. It is also the reason that today, when someone is arrested, they are immediately read their rights.

But what about Ernesto Miranda, whose name is always associated with a person being read their rights? In 1963, he was arrested in Phoenix, Arizona, for stealing $8 from a bank worker and charged with armed robbery. He already had a previous record for an armed holdup, along with juvenile offenses that included attempted rape, assault, and burglary. While in police custody, he signed a written confession to the robbery and to kidnapping and raping an eighteen-year-old woman eleven days before that robbery.

Following his conviction, Miranda's lawyers appealed on the grounds that their client did not know that he was protected from self-incrimination. After the Supreme Court decision set aside his initial conviction for rape, the State of Arizona retried him. At the second trial, even though his confession was excluded from evidence, he was again convicted and spent eleven years in prison. He was paroled in 1972.

In 1976, Miranda was stabbed to death during a bar fight in Phoenix. In a bizarre twist of fate, a suspect was arrested, but he chose to exercise his right to remain silent after being read his Miranda rights. The suspect was released and supposedly fled to Mexico. The Miranda murder case was closed, and the victim's murderer was never apprehended.

President Kennedy was assassinated on November 22, 1963. Five months earlier on June 6, 1963, JFK had hosted the annual reception at the White House for Boys State representatives from all fifty states.

Among them was a seventeen-year-old from Hot Springs, Arkansas, who got the opportunity to shake hands with the president and decided at that point that he might someday like to become the nation's chief executive. And thirty years later, Bill Clinton did just that.

John F. Kennedy was assassinated while riding in the back of a convertible. That was the last time that a U.S. president has ridden in an open-top vehicle.

Many people have been told that John F. Kennedy was one of the most popular presidents of all time. But JFK's approval rating in the southern states was 33 percent in the fall of 1963, which gave his campaign team cause for concern.

Thus the decision was made by the Kennedy brain trust that they needed to begin their 1964 re-election campaign a year early and that it would get underway in Texas. During the tour, there were stops in San Antonio, Houston, and Fort Worth before that final historic day in Dallas. As with those of many presidents, JFK's approval ratings, like his legacy, have grown since he left office.

Figure 16.1 President Kennedy smiles during his final moments. *Walt Cisco*

On the day that John F. Kennedy was assassinated, November 22, 1963, both he and Richard Nixon were in Dallas. The former vice president was speaking at a convention of Pepsi-Cola executives, and then flew to New York City.

He stated that he first heard the news about the president's murder while taking a cab ride from the airport into the Big Apple. Nixon's plane had landed at Idlewild Airport, which one month later was renamed John F. Kennedy International.

JFK and his vice president Lyndon Johnson often disagreed on various issues. On the night of November 21, 1963, in Room 850 of the Hotel Texas in Fort Worth, President Kennedy and LBJ were engaged in a heated exchange over the seating arrangements for the motorcade the next day.

The argument was so loud that the First Lady heard it from outside the presidential suite. Johnson insisted that his good friend Texas governor John Connally should ride with him in the rear vehicle rather than in the president's lead car. When Kennedy refused, Johnson stormed out of the room, prompting JFK to give his last dictated words to his secretary Evelyn Lincoln: "Johnson will not be on the ticket." It was an indication that JFK planned to replace LBJ during his run for a second term.

The following afternoon, Vice President Johnson was riding with U.S. senator Ralph Yarborough two cars behind Kennedy's open-top limousine when the shooting began in Dallas. Unfortunately, Governor Connally was sitting directly in front of the president and was seriously wounded.

The Kennedy assassination took place on the streets of Dallas, Texas. Later that afternoon, Police Officer J. D. Tippett was shot and killed by Lee Harvey Oswald. Since then, local cops have continued to have a tough time whenever a president or a presidential candidate has come to Big D.

On February 22, 2008, Dallas police officer Senior Corporal Victor Lozada was killed in an accident escorting candidate Hillary Clinton on a campaign stop through downtown. Lozada's family filed a lawsuit against Clinton and the City of Dallas, which was dismissed in 2011.

On August 9, 2010, Dallas police officer Senior Corporal Michael Manis was injured in a motorcade that was escorting President Barack Obama from Love Field Airport to a private Democratic fund-raiser. Manis was released from the hospital the following day.

Both officers were aboard police motorcycles at the time of their crashes.

President Kennedy died of gunshot wounds, and there are many who still have questions about the identity of his assassin.

There was another real-life mystery that took place on October 12, 1964, as JFK's close friend and former neighbor Mary Pinchot Meyer was gunned down while strolling along a walking path in Washington, D.C. A suspect was arrested and put on trial for the murder, but he was acquitted. To this day, the case officially remains unsolved.

The murder of accused Kennedy assassin Lee Harvey Oswald by Dallas nightclub owner Jack Ruby took place live on national television as the suspect was being transferred from the city jail.

As a boy, Ruby (whose real name was Jacob Rubinstein) grew up in Chicago and ran errands for mobster Al Capone.

Before Oswald was shot, President Kennedy had died at Parkland Hospital. Two days later on November 24, 1963, after being gunned down by Jack Ruby, Oswald was taken to the same emergency ward, and he died among some of the doctors who had treated Kennedy.

On January 3, 1967, Ruby succumbed to lung cancer. Like Kennedy and Oswald, he died at Parkland Hospital.

Jack Ruby was convicted of murdering Lee Harvey Oswald and sentenced to death. But before the punishment could be carried out, he died of cancer in 1967. However, on April 26, 1964 (about five weeks after the conviction), Ruby made an unsuccessful suicide attempt by ramming his head into the wall of his cell.

Before becoming president, Lyndon Johnson had served in the U.S. Senate. He won his first election to the chamber in 1948. When it was over, it was discovered that 202 deceased individuals had cast ballots, giving him a winning margin of just 87 votes.

Nonetheless, the election was certified and Johnson was off to the nation's capital. The victory led to his famous nickname, "Landslide Lyndon."

It's a known fact that presidents often ride in helicopters, and Lyndon Johnson was one who enjoyed them. He loved them so much, in fact, that his desk chair in the Oval Office was actually a vinyl helicopter seat—green, with a built-in ashtray.

On one occasion, Johnson was at an airfield and heading for the wrong helicopter when a young Air Force corporal pointed to the presidential aircraft and said, "This is your helicopter sir," to which Johnson replied, "They're all my helicopters, son."

U.S. presidents frequently meet with leaders of foreign countries. German chancellor Ludwig Erhard once said to LBJ during a visit to Texas, "I understand you where born in a log cabin," to which Johnson replied, "No, no, no. You have me confused with Abe Lincoln. I was born in a manger."

President Lyndon Johnson was busy with the Vietnam War and unrest in the inner cities during the 1960s. He also had to keep an eye on his brother, Sam Houston Johnson. Sam enjoyed drinking too much and passing bad checks, which led LBJ to place him under Secret Service surveillance.

In 1967, fighting in the Vietnam War was raging on with no end in sight. But back home, sixty-seven American cities were struck by riots in the summer of that same year.

Richard Nixon was elected the nation's thirty-seventh president in 1968. However, in 1937, Nixon, who had just graduated from Duke University Law School, applied for a job with the FBI . . . and was rejected.

Most crimes carry a statute of limitations. It sets forth the maximum amount of time following a misdeed during which a defendant can be tried for the offense that has been committed. However, there is no statute of limitations for murder. It also only applies when no one has been indicted for the crime.

In November 1968, Luis Armando Pena Soltren hijacked a packed Pan American Airways flight from New York to Puerto Rico, ordering the crew to fly to Cuba. He was finally captured by the FBI in October 2009. The sixty-six-year-old Puerto Rican national, who had since been living as a fugitive in Cuba, was arrested upon his arrival from Havana at New York's JFK Airport after making arrangements with U.S. officials to surrender himself.

Soltren, who was the FBI's longest-wanted fugitive, was accompanied by security personnel on his flight back to the United States. He told authorities that he wanted to come home because he missed his family. In January 2011 he was sentenced to fifteen years in prison after pleading guilty in federal court.

No one was injured in the hijacking but Soltren had been indicted for the crime in 1968 by the district attorney in New York City. That meant that there was no statute of limitations in the case and that Soltren remained a wanted fugitive.

Richard Nixon was Dwight Eisenhower's vice president. On December 22, 1968, Julie Nixon, daughter of Richard Nixon, married David Eisenhower, grandson of Dwight Eisenhower. Her dad had been elected president just forty-seven days earlier.

The ceremony at New York City's Marble Collegiate Church took just fifteen minutes, the shortest wedding in First Family history.

The Christmas of 1968 was Lyndon Johnson's last as president. Although the peace talks continued in Paris, the war was still continuing in Vietnam.

On December 23, 1968, LBJ sent Christmas greetings to the American troops in Southeast Asia, which included his two sons-in-law, Maj. Charles Robb of the Marine Corps and Airman 1st Class Patrick Nugent of the Air National Guard.

Small children are taught that water is used to put out fires. But on June 22, 1969, an oil slick and debris in the Cuyahoga River caught fire in Cleveland, Ohio.

The fire lasted just thirty minutes, but it did approximately $50,000 in damage—principally to railroad bridges spanning the river. It is unclear what caused the blaze, but most people believe sparks from a passing train probably ignited the river.

This was not the first time that the Cuyahoga had caught on fire. Flames erupted from the river in 1868, 1883, 1887, 1912, 1922, 1936, 1941, 1948, and 1952. The 1952 fire caused over $1.5 million in damage. The event helped lead to the passage of the Clean Water Act in 1972.

In July 1969, Neil Armstrong and Buzz Aldrin landed safely on the moon. But on May 6, 1968, Armstrong had been forced to eject from a lunar landing research vehicle. He lost control of the craft about two hundred feet above the ground while training for the moon mission at Ellington Air Force Base in Texas.

Armstrong parachuted to safety and suffered minor injuries. The training craft was a total loss.

Figure 16.2 After the crash, Neil Armstrong parachutes safely back to Earth. *NASA*

U.S. astronaut Neil Armstrong was the first human being to walk on the moon, although a mistake with his paperwork almost kept him on Earth.

Years earlier, Armstrong's astronaut application had arrived at NASA about a week past the June 1, 1962, deadline. Dick Day, with whom the pilot had worked closely at Edwards Air Force Base, was later employed at the Manned Spacecraft Center, and saw the past-due arrival of the application. He slipped it into the pile of on-time candidates' paperwork before anyone noticed, and seven years later, Armstrong made history.

The U.S. space program had six moon landings between 1969 and 1972. NASA scientists estimate that the footprints of the astronauts who were on those missions should last ten million years since the moon has no atmosphere.

The Vietnam Moratorium took place on October 15, 1969. It was the largest demonstration in U.S. history, with over one million participants at home and another million throughout the world. At the time, Bill Clinton was a twenty-three-year-old Rhodes Scholar at Oxford. He helped organize and participate in a demonstration during the Vietnam Moratorium outside the U.S. embassy in London.

But thirty years later, the perspective of the former war protester changed. During the last two years of Clinton's presidency, U.S. military aircraft routinely attacked anti-aircraft installations in Iraq.

• *17* •

The Seventies: There Were Crooks in the White House and Everyone Had Disco Fever!

If Lincoln were alive today, he'd be turning over in his grave.

—President Gerald Ford

$\mathcal{O}$n May 4, 1970, four students were shot dead by soldiers from the Ohio National Guard during an anti-war protest at Kent State University. The Guard had been sent in on the orders of Governor James Rhodes.

But Rhodes had an interesting life during his own college days. He dropped out of school (Ohio State) after one quarter during the Great Depression. He then opened a gambling operation across the street from the university called Jimmy's Place. It was known for running a numbers racket (an illegal lottery) from 1936 to 1938.

Apollo 15 was one of the NASA missions that put astronauts on the moon. It took place in 1971, and it wasn't without controversy.

The crew had the idea of creating a financial windfall from their lunar journey. They took 398 commemorative postage-stamp covers with them on their trip to the moon, the covers having been provided by a German stamp dealer. The agreement was that upon their return, 100 of the covers would be purchased by the dealer and the other 298 retained by the crew.

Although the flight team had broken no laws or regulations, the covers were confiscated by NASA. The episode caused Congress, a group with a reputation of using the rules to their own advantage, to begin asking questions about the episode. Meanwhile, legal action against the space administration was started by the Apollo astronauts to recover their property.

The crew's 298 covers were not returned until 1983. In their lawsuit, the crew cited the fact that NASA had entered into a partnership with the U.S. Postal Service to sell covers that had been flown on the Space Shuttle. Needless to say, the entire affair was an embarrassment for the space agency.

For the record, the market value of the postal covers has climbed steadily over the years. One of them was sold at a 2008 auction for $18,000.

Pilot Amelia Earhart and her navigator Fred Noonan disappeared in 1937. Neither the plane nor the bodies were ever recovered, and the episode has become one of the biggest mysteries in the nation's annals.

History repeated itself on October 16, 1972, when a plane carrying Congressmen Hale Boggs and Nick Begich disappeared while on a campaign flight from Anchorage to Juneau, Alaska. As in the more famous 1937 incident, neither the plane nor the bodies were ever found.

Most of the time in Congress, issues are decided with a roll-call vote. On January 23, 1973, during the 93rd Congress, the first electronic tally was held in the House Chamber. It took just fifteen minutes to roll call the votes of the members, a process which had previously taken thirty to forty-five minutes.

Some of the most damaging testimony against President Nixon during the Watergate hearings was provided in 1973 by White House counsel John Dean. He is best remembered for this response to a question during the hearings: "I began by telling the president that there was a cancer growing on the presidency and that if the cancer was not removed the president himself would be killed by it."

What the committee didn't know was that a year earlier, the government's star witness "borrowed" $4,850 from a White House safe that contained leftover cash from Nixon's 1968 campaign. He used the money for his honeymoon.

On October 10, 1973, Vice President Spiro Agnew resigned from office because he was facing charges of tax evasion and money laundering. He later plead no contest.

Agnew was the second vice president to resign from office. In 1832, John C. Calhoun quit the nation's second-highest government position because of his differences with his boss Andrew Jackson. Following his departure, he ran for the U.S. Senate seat in South Carolina and won.

All records indicate that Calhoun, as opposed to Agnew, paid his taxes.

Spiro Agnew was Richard Nixon's vice president. But back in 1968, the Republican candidate ignored recommendations from some advisers to choose Michigan governor George W. Romney as his running mate, opting for a complete unknown in Agnew, who had been the politically unsung governor of Maryland for less than two years.

Congressman and future president Gerald Ford was said to have laughed aloud when told the news because he was sure Nixon was joking. Ironically, Ford was Agnew's replacement as vice president after Agnew resigned in disgrace. The Michigan Republican was in line to become Speaker of the House, the job he actually wanted, and would have gotten it if he hadn't accepted Nixon's offer to become second in command after Agnew resigned. When the episode was over, Nixon and Agnew never spoke again.

One of the most high-profile Supreme Court cases ever was *Roe v. Wade*, which held that a mother may abort her pregnancy for any reason up until the "point at which the fetus becomes viable." The viability issue is determined by each state's law.

While most know of the case, many don't realize that the defendant, Jane Roe, whose real name was Norma McCorvey, never had an abortion and successfully gave birth to a daughter in 1970. She later became an advocate of the pro-life movement.

Many Americans believe that, in the history of the country, there has never been an occurrence like the Watergate break-in. That's not really true, although at the time there hadn't been anything like it in forty-two years.

In June 1930, President Hoover ordered Glen Howell, a naval intelligence officer, and his civilian assistant Robert J. Peterkin to break into the Democratic National Headquarters in New York City.

Their job was to recover a file that was critical of the Hoover administration. They carried out the order but never found the alleged file, and unlike the Watergate burglars, they didn't get caught.

By February 1974, the Watergate investigation was in full swing. Federal judge John Sirica became famous for his role as the chief magistrate presiding over the scandal. He rose to national prominence when he demanded that President Richard Nixon turn over his private recordings of White House conversations. The action led to Nixon's eventual resignation.

However Judge Sirica had a skeleton in his own closet as his father, an Italian immigrant, was arrested for bootlegging during Prohibition.

Two of the presidential candidates in 2008 were Democrat Hillary Clinton and Republican Fred Thompson. But it wasn't the first time that the duo was part of a major event as they first participated in a historic proceeding more than thirty-five years earlier.

In 1973, Thompson was appointed as counsel to assist Republicans on the Senate Watergate Committee, a special body convened by the U.S. Senate to investigate the Watergate scandal.

Thompson is sometimes credited with supplying Republican Senator Howard Baker's famous question, "What did the president know, and when did he know it?"

During 1974, Hillary Clinton (Rodham at that time) was a member of the impeachment inquiry staff advising the House Committee on the Judiciary during Watergate. She helped research procedures of impeachment and the historical grounds and standards for the indictment.

The pair, who were assisting senators in the investigation, would both be elected to the Senate decades later.

The beginning of Richard Nixon's downfall came with the break-in at the Democratic Party headquarters at the Watergate Hotel. But that wasn't the only time that Nixon was associated with a burglary.

During his days as a law student at Duke University, the future president and several classmates broke into the dean's office to get a look at their grades because they hadn't been posted on time.

Richard Nixon tried to rely on the precedent of executive privilege to withhold White House tape recordings during the Watergate investigation but was unsuccessful. Even though he was a lawyer, perhaps Nixon didn't know that maneuver had already been unsuccessfully attempted by another president.

When Aaron Burr was tried for treason in 1807, he subpoenaed certain documents from Thomas Jefferson which he felt were needed for his defense. Jefferson raised the executive privilege issue, but Chief Justice John Marshall ruled that the president was subject to a subpoena like anyone else, but also subject to certain national security protections.

Jefferson eventually complied with Marshall's order, and Burr was acquitted.

Richard Nixon was in the process of being impeached prior to his resignation. While the public was focused on the Watergate burglary, many didn't realize that one of the charges against him was bribery.

Item 21 in the Articles of Impeachment stated that in June, July, and August 1972, the re-election campaign of President Nixon solicited and obtained contributions totaling $200,000 from Ray Kroc, chairman of the board of McDonald's. The donation was in exchange for permission from the Price Commission to raise the price of McDonald's Quarter Pounder with Cheese.

The request was first denied on May 21, 1972, but then granted on September 8, 1972, in violation of Article II, Section 4 of the Constitution and Sections 201, 372, 872 and 1505 of the Criminal Code.

Perhaps best-selling author Tom Clancy said it best: "The difference between fiction and reality? Fiction has to make sense."

The actions of Richard Nixon led to his eventual resignation as president. But he wasn't the only one in his family who was known for his questionable dealings.

The president's brother Donald was a restaurateur and not a very good one. In 1954 he was running a chain of Nixon's drive-ins in Whittier, California, and fell upon some tough financial times. In an effort to keep the business afloat, he accepted a $205,000 loan from billionaire Howard Hughes.

But "Big Don," as he called himself, never paid back the money. Voters questioned why a businessman of Hughes's stature with a financial interest in airlines, movie studios, and Las Vegas hotels would suddenly become involved in a few small-time burger joints even though they happened to be run by the then vice president's brother. At any rate, the Hughes loan wasn't enough and the chain went under the following year.

During World War II, future president Gerald Ford served in the Navy and fought against the Japanese forces. In November 1974, he became the first American president to visit Japan.

In a strange twist, Hirohito, who was the Japanese emperor during World War II, greeted the U.S. president and ex-combat veteran when he arrived.

When Gerald Ford became president, he and his family moved into the White House. One night Ford was locked out of the executive mansion while walking his golden retriever, Liberty, on the grounds. Upon realizing what had happened, the Secret Service let him in.

Bill Clinton is probably the most famous politician from Arkansas. But before Clinton entered the political arena, the folks in the Razorback state were following the adventures of Congressman Wilbur Mills.

He was first elected to the House of Representatives in 1938 and eventually became chairman of the powerful Ways and Means Committee in 1957. But like the 42nd president, Mills had an appreciation for attractive younger women.

At 2:00 am on October 9, 1974, the congressman's car was stopped by police in Washington, D.C., because it was being operated without headlights.

When police approached the vehicle, they immediately noticed that the sixty-five-year-old Mills was intoxicated and that his face had been cut in a scuffle with his girlfriend Annabelle Battistella, better known as Fanne Foxe, a stripper from Argentina. At one point the thirty-eight-year-old showgirl leaped from the vehicle and jumped into the nearby Tidal Basin near the Jefferson Memorial in a half-baked attempt to escape. The tawdry episode became front-page news the following day.

Despite the scandal, in November 1974 Mills's constituency back home in Arkansas re-elected the aged playboy to Congress. However, on November 30, 1974, a drunken Mills was accompanied by Foxe's husband onstage at the Pilgrim Theatre in Boston, a burlesque house where she was performing.

Following the show, the inebriated elected official held an impromptu press conference in Foxe's dressing room. Soon after this second public incident, Mills stepped down from his chairmanship of the Ways and Means Committee, acknowledged his excessive drinking, and joined Alcoholics Anonymous.

The congressman later confessed that during the time of his affair with Foxe, he was consuming a half-gallon of vodka every night!

He did not seek re-election in 1976 and devoted his time to counseling individual alcoholics. Mills died in 1992, six months before Bill Clinton was elected president.

At the end of the Vietnam War, many Vietnamese citizens fled the country during the fall of Saigon.

General Nguyễn Ngoc Loan was the Republic of Vietnam's chief of the National Police, and as the evacuation took place, he was among the masses who escaped and moved to the United States. Upon his relocation, the former law enforcement official opened a pizza restaurant at Rolling Valley Mall, in the suburb of Burke, Virginia.

Prior to fleeing his home country, Nguyễn had gained international attention on February 1, 1968, when he was photographed executing a Viet Cong prisoner in Saigon during the Tet Offensive.

The disturbing picture was taken by Eddie Adams of the Associated Press and was awarded a Pulitzer Prize.

In 1976, the United States observed its bicentennial. While citizens celebrated the nation's anniversary, Richard Honeck died on December 28. In 1899, he and an accomplice had murdered Walter F. Koeller as revenge for testifying against them in an arson case.

Honeck was arrested in Chicago and sentenced to life in prison, but in many similar cases, punishment for that type of crime tended to be twenty-five years or less. In this instance, Honeck spent almost his entire natural life in prison.

The convicted felon, the son of a wealthy farm-equipment dealer, had been working as a telegraph operator. When sentenced, the twenty-two-year-old was remanded to the dreary Joliet Correctional Center in Illinois, but trouble followed him when in 1912 he stabbed an assistant warden.

Honeck was then transferred to the Menard Penitentiary in Chester, Illinois, where he spent the final thirty-five years of his sentence peacefully, working in the prison bakery. During his entire stay, he received only two visitors—one from a friend in 1904 and the other from Associated Press reporter Bob Poos in the same year as his parole.

On December 20, 1963, eighty-four-year-old Honeck was finally released. His niece took him in, and the two lived in Oregon until his death at the age of ninety-seven.

Honeck is believed to have served the longest sentence, 23,418 days, of any inmate in U.S. history.

The Iranian hostage crisis was a diplomatic standoff between Iran and the United States. It began when a group of Islamist students and militants took over the U.S. Embassy in Tehran. Fifty-two American citizens were held for 444 days, from November 4, 1979, to January 20, 1981.

A few months earlier, there was another hostage incident. But rather than wait for the U.S. government to help, a private citizen masterminded a plan to rescue his people.

In February 1979, two employees of Electronic Data Systems (EDS) of Dallas, Texas, were taken hostage by the Iranian government. At the time, EDS was owned by billionaire businessman and future presidential candidate H. Ross Perot, who took the initiative and directed a rescue mission composed of EDS employees and led by retired Green Beret colonel Arthur "Bull" Simons, a hero of the Vietnam War. Perot, a Naval Academy graduate and former officer, went to Iran and entered the prison where his men were held.

The two Americans, along with eleven thousand Iranian prisoners, escaped to freedom. Simons and the rescue party fled across the mountains into Turkey, and subsequently returned to the United States. Three months later, Colonel Simons died of a heart attack while on vacation in Vail, Colorado.

United States' missile defenses were often on high alert during the Cold War. At 8:50 am, on November 9, 1979, a warning appeared on the computers at four American command centers (including the Pentagon and the Strategic Air Command's bunker located deep beneath Cheyenne Mountain) that a massive Soviet ICBM strike was en route to the United States.

Minuteman nuclear missiles were prepared to launch a retaliatory attack, and the National Emergency Airborne Command Post (a Boeing 747 modified to resist the effects of electromagnetic impulses and radiation) took off, although the president was not on board.

Senior officers quickly convened a threat assessment conference. However, after six tense minutes, early-warning satellites and radar showed that no Russian missiles had been launched. It was later discovered that a training video depicting a massive Soviet attack had accidentally been loaded into the early-warning computers and had generated the false alarm. After an investigation of the incident, a new off-site facility was created to run training tapes.

• *18* •

The Eighties: The President Looks Just Like This Guy That I Saw the Other Night in an Old Movie!

But there are advantages to being elected president. The day after I was elected, I had my high school grades classified Top Secret.

—Ronald Reagan

*W*ashington's Mount St. Helens, a live volcano, erupted on May 18, 1980. The blast resulted in the largest landslide in recorded history as lava and ash swept down the area killing fifty-seven people. In all, approximately twenty-three square miles of material was removed from the mountain.

One of the area's residents was eighty-three-year-old Harry Truman (not the former president). He lived there with his sixteen cats and refused to leave when the warnings were issued. It was the place that he had called home for fifty-four years.

During an interview, Truman stated, "I have lived up here a long time and wouldn't last two weeks if I had to move to some apartment down in Longview."

True to his word, Harry and all of his cats never left their dwelling and perished in the eruption.

You might be old enough to remember the massive eruption of the Mount St. Helens volcano in 1980. But you probably weren't around for Wyoming's Yellowstone Caldera, sometimes referred to as the "Yellowstone Supervolcano." The last full-scale eruption of the Caldera took place nearly 640,000 years ago, ejecting approximately 240 cubic miles of rock and dust into the sky. The most recent lava flow occurred about 70,000 years ago, while the largest violent eruption excavated the West Thumb of Lake Yellowstone around 150,000 years ago.

If you do remember it, write a book.

Eighteen years old is the legal age for adulthood. But that minor obstacle didn't detour Brian Zimmerman.

In 1983, at the age of eleven, he was elected mayor of the community of Crabb, Texas. Brian won by a landslide over two adult candidates, garnering twenty-three of the thirty votes cast. The election was no publicity stunt as his stated goal as mayor was to incorporate his unincorporated hometown of approximately two hundred people to avoid annexation by neighboring Houston.

Mayor Zimmerman held that an impending annexation would result in even higher taxes than incorporation, which instead would give the south Texas town some control over tax rates. The other major issue was that incorporation would force him out of his position as mayor, since Texas law stated that mayors of incorporated communities must be at least eighteen years of age.

The middle school student's incorporation bid was ultimately unsuccessful, but he was reelected as mayor following the referendum. His unique mayorship garnered considerable attention that included articles in *People* magazine and the *New York Times*. In 1988, his story was chronicled in a made-for-TV movie called *Lone Star Kid*.

In 1996 Zimmerman died of a heart attack in Houston at the age of twenty-four, but today the town of Crabb remains unincorporated.

The right to a speedy trial is guaranteed by the Constitution's Sixth Amendment and is intended to ensure that defendants are not subjected to unreasonably lengthy incarceration prior to a fair trial.

But the Sixth Amendment primarily applies to criminal trials and not to civil litigation. On February 6, 1984, at the St. Clair County Court House in Belleville, Illinois, what would be the longest trial in U.S. history was just getting underway.

It was the case of *Kemner v. Monsanto Co.*, which centered on an alleged toxic spill in Sturgeon, Missouri. The process included 67 plaintiffs, 182 witnesses, 6,000 separate exhibits, and a transcript of more than 100,000 pages.

The trial concluded on August 26, 1987, mercifully ending after 657 long days of testimony. The jury deliberation took another two months. Finally on October 22, 1987, the plaintiffs were awarded punitive damages of $16,250,000.

The proceedings took so long that one of the plaintiffs died before the verdict was reached. But as Benjamin Franklin once said, "Time is money."

In November 1984, Ronald Reagan was reelected as the nation's president. He is considered one of history's most conservative political leaders.

However, Reagan had started out as a registered Democrat, an admirer of Franklin D. Roosevelt, and a supporter of the New Deal. But by the early 1950s, his political philosophy had moved to the right where he became an icon for the conservative wing of the GOP.

Space Shuttle *Challenger* exploded seventy-three seconds after takeoff on January 28, 1986. All seven crew members were killed, and the shuttle program was shut down for the next three years while changes were made to the fleet.

Time passed, and two large chunks of *Challenger*'s left wing washed ashore ten years later. Both pieces were found in the surf on Cocoa Beach, Florida, some twenty miles south of the Kennedy Space Center.

Some believe that the crew of Space Shuttle *Challenger* were the first American astronauts killed in the line of duty. That's only partially true.

They were the first U.S. astronauts to die in space, but by then many Americans had forgotten an event nineteen years earlier. On January 27, 1967, the crew of Apollo 1—Gus Grissom (the second American in space), Ed White, and Roger Chaffee—became trapped inside their command module when it caught fire and burned during a launch pad test at Cape Kennedy. There were no survivors.

The mission had been intended to be used to test the new Apollo command and service modules in Earth's orbit. It was to be the first phase of the program that would eventually land a man on the moon.

In 1987, the United States and the Soviet Union signed the Intermediate-Range Nuclear Forces Treaty, eliminating intermediate range (300–3,400 miles) nuclear and conventional ground-launched ballistic and cruise missiles.

In a separate move in 1983, the Chico (California) City Council banned all atomic weapons, enacting a mandatory $500 fine for anyone detonating a nuclear device within city limits.

As of 2014, there is no record of anyone having been charged with this offense.

In 1988, among the field for the Democratic nomination for president was Gary Hart, U.S. senator from Colorado.

When Hart declared his candidacy on April 13, 1987, he was already the party's front-runner. But rumors quickly began circulating that the senator was having an extramarital affair.

In an interview that appeared in the *New York Times* on May 3, 1987, Hart responded to the innuendos by daring the press corps, "Follow me around. I don't care. I'm serious. If anybody wants to put a tail on me, go ahead. They'll be very bored."

Unfortunately for Hart, he probably never read *The Monkey's Paw* (1902) by W. W. Jacobs with the famous warning "Be careful what you wish for, you may receive it" (Anonymous).

The media leaped at the challenge, and shortly thereafter, discovered that the candidate was keeping time with Donna Rice, a marketing representative for a pharmaceutical company in South Florida. On June 2, 1987, a photograph appeared in the press showing Hart relaxing on a dock with Rice sitting on his lap.

The picture created a nationwide scandal as the public devoured every detail. Among the items was a yacht where the pair would rendezvous, which was appropriately named *Monkey Business*.

At that point, Hart dropped out of the race. But, like a boxer trying to make a comeback, he reentered the contest in December before finally withdrawing for good in March 1988. The negative publicity also cost Rice her pharmaceutical job.

Today she is the president of Enough Is Enough, an anti-pornography movement which seeks to make the Internet safer for families and children. Gary Hart remained with his wife but never held political office again.

In 1988 the Democrats nominated Massachusetts governor Michael Dukakis for president. He was a New England liberal who selected a Southern moderate to give his nomination speech at the convention that year. Most who heard the address from the little-known governor thought it was boring and, at thirty-two minutes, much too long.

Some pundits predicted that the speaker had no future in politics. But four years later, Dukakis's nominating orator surprised them all, and Bill Clinton was elected president.

George H. W. Bush was elected the forty-first president in 1988. But many years earlier, he was the youngest pilot in the Navy when he received his wings. He flew fifty-eight combat missions and was shot down twice during World War II.

However, Bush's life was in peril just months before entering the service. As a high school senior, he almost died from a staph infection in his right arm. He spent weeks recovering at Massachusetts General Hospital. Antibiotics, in the form of sulfa drugs, were available in that era, but, curiously, they were not used.

Following his recovery, Bush graduated from Phillips Academy in Massachusetts and enlisted in the Navy.

One of the popular definitions for karma is "What goes around, comes around." There are many examples of it in politics. One took place in 1988 when George H. W. Bush defeated Michael Dukakis in the presidential election. Prior to that, Lloyd Bentsen had defeated Bush in 1970 for a U.S. Senate seat from Texas.

In 1988, Bentsen was Dukakis's vice presidential nominee when they lost to Bush and his running mate Dan Quayle.

Four U.S. presidents were born in Massachusetts. They were John Adams, John Quincy Adams, John Fitzgerald Kennedy, and George Herbert Walker Bush.

The four former chief executives were not only born in the same state, all of them were from Norfolk County.

Barbara Bush is both the wife and mother of U.S. presidents. The only other person who held that distinction was Abigail Adams.

But Mrs. Bush has another connection to the White House. Her maiden name was Barbara Pierce, and she is a distant cousin of former president Franklin Pierce. That makes her the only person who is a mother, wife, and cousin of a U.S. president.

The Nineties: Denials, Trials, and the .com Market!

I love California, I practically grew up in Phoenix.

—Vice President Dan Quayle

$\mathcal{J}$ohn Adams and George H. W. Bush each had sons who also served as president. Most everyone already knows that, but there are a few other similarities about the presidential pair.

Both were born in Massachusetts and attended Ivy League colleges: Harvard for Adams, Yale for Bush. They both served as ambassadors and were elected as vice president for two terms, serving under popular, older presidents—George Washington and Ronald Reagan, respectively.

Adams and Bush are the sole presidents elected immediately after two terms as vice president, and both were single-term presidents. Both were defeated in their re-election bids by younger Southerners (Jefferson and Clinton, respectively). Their sons shared their first names, were also Ivy League graduates, lost the popular vote but won the electoral contest, and succeeded two-term Southern presidents (Monroe and Clinton).

Both the Adams and Bush families are descendants of the Mayflower Pilgrims.

One of the heroes of the Gulf War of 1991 was General Norman Schwartzkopf Jr. But Schwartzkopf's father was also well known for his service. Norman Sr. was a lead investigator in the kidnapping of the Lindbergh baby in 1932.

The trial for the offense that was referred to as the "Crime of the Century" began just a few months after General Schwartzkopf was born.

The success of Operation Desert Storm in 1991 resulted in a military victory over Iraq in just six weeks. During that brief war, Allied Forces lost just 4 tanks out of the 3,360 that were deployed. However, the Iraqi military lost 4,000 tanks out of 4,230 they used.

Even so, ten years later Iraqi president Saddam Hussein was still trying to claim victory when he said, "Iraq has triumphed over the enemies of the (Arab) nation and over its enemies."

George H. W. Bush was among a group of six presidents who served in the armed forces during World War II.

While he was president, First Lady Barbara Bush once accompanied her husband on a state visit to Japan in January 1992. During a formal luncheon at the Imperial Palace in Tokyo, she found herself seated beside Japan's Emperor Hirohito. "Was the former palace so old that it crumbled?" she asked, noting the building's modern features.

"No," Hirohito abruptly replied. "I'm afraid that you bombed it."

The Twenty-Seventh Amendment to the U.S. Constitution was ratified in 1992. It states that congressional salaries for representatives may only take effect after the beginning of the next term of office.

It took a while to pass the measure as the amendment was originally submitted by James Madison in 1789. From 1789 to 1791, the compensation proposal was ratified by the legislatures of only six states out of the ten that were required. As more states entered the Union, the ratification threshold increased.

It was finalized on May 5, 1992, by the elected officials of Alabama. After all was said and done, it only took 202 years for the Twenty-Seventh Amendment to become law, which might explain why things tend to move slowly in the nation's capital.

There's that old question "What have you done for me lately?" In the election of 1992, Arkansas governor Bill Clinton defeated the incumbent president George H. W. Bush. One year before his loss, Bush had an approval rating of 89 percent.

Timothy McVeigh orchestrated the Oklahoma City Bombing of April 19, 1995, that killed 168 persons. At first he was not arrested for his part in the attack and, at one point, nearly got away.

About ninety minutes after the explosion, McVeigh was taken into custody by an Oklahoma Highway Patrol officer a short distance from Oklahoma City after being pulled over for not having a license plate on his car. It was also discovered that he had no insurance in addition to carrying an unregistered pistol and a knife.

At that point, he was taken north to the Noble County Jail in Perry. Two days later, shortly before he was to be released on bail, McVeigh was identified as the prime suspect in the bombing and charged in the crime. He was then transferred into federal custody.

When Timothy McVeigh, a former Gulf War veteran, was taken into custody for the Oklahoma City Bombing, he was wearing a rather interesting T-shirt that had a picture of Abraham Lincoln and the motto "Sic Semper Tyrannis." Those were the famous words shouted by John Wilkes Booth after he shot Lincoln.

On the back of the shirt was a tree with a picture of three blood droplets and the Thomas Jefferson quote "The tree of liberty must be refreshed from time to time with the blood of patriots and tyrants."

Bill Clinton was reelected as president in 1996. In each of his White House victories, he never received 50 percent of the popular vote even though since that time, he has been the most successful fund-raiser for the Democratic Party.

Bill Clinton, the commander in chief of the military, admitted having an affair with a twenty-two-year-old White House intern but completed his second term as president. In 1998, U.S. Army major general David Hale was forced to retire because he had affairs with the wives of several of his subordinate officers.

The Space Shuttle program flew from 1981 to 2011. It is considered to be one of the most successful ventures ever. There were also some prehistoric items that were involved on selected missions.

A skull from the dinosaur Coelophysis, borrowed from Pittsburgh's Carnegie Museum of Natural History, was taken into space on the shuttle *Endeavor* in January 1998. It also traveled to the space station MIR.

A Maiasaura bone fragment and piece of its eggshell flew with astronaut Loren Acton on an eight-day mission (Spacelab 2) in 1985.

Everyone in the White House who is under Secret Service protection has a code name. For example, Ronald Reagan was "Rawhide" and Bill Clinton was "Eagle."

But Clinton's troublesome younger brother Roger also had his own code name. It was "Headache."

The moniker seemed a perfect fit as the president's sibling had served prison time for dealing cocaine. Before leaving office, the chief executive issued a presidential pardon for "Headache."

In 1998, President Bill Clinton was receiving a great deal of criticism over his affair with intern Monica Lewinsky. One of the voices leading the attack was Speaker of the House Newt Gingrich. But what Gingrich wasn't telling people was that Clinton wasn't the only one straying from his marriage.

Gingrich himself was cheating on his wife of seventeen years, Marianne Ginther, during the impeachment proceedings. It turns out that the Speaker was conducting private business with Callista Bisek, a woman twenty-three years his junior, behind his spouse's back.

In May 1999, the Georgia congressman called Marianne at her mother's home. After wishing his eighty-four-year-old mother-in-law a happy birthday, he followed that up by telling his wife that he wanted a divorce. Gingrich left her eight months later upon finding out she had been diagnosed with multiple sclerosis.

But Marianne was his second wife. His first spouse, Jackie Battley, got pressed by the politician to sign divorce papers while she was in the hospital recovering from cancer surgery.

Gingrich didn't find any of the accusations hypocritical because he said that Clinton committed perjury by lying under oath about the Lewinsky affair: "The President of the United States got in trouble for committing a felony in front of a sitting federal judge."

In December 1998, Bill Clinton became the second president to be impeached by the House of Representatives. The charges included perjury, abuse of powers, and obstruction of justice.

One of the congressmen who voted to impeach Clinton was Mark Sanford of South Carolina. In 2003, he became governor of the state, but it was discovered in 2009 that he was having an affair. Prior to the scandal, it was believed that Sanford might be a Republican candidate for president in 2012. His wife later divorced him.

But just like the phoenix (and other politicians), Sanford rose from the ashes to resurrect his career in 2013 when he was elected to the U.S. House of Representatives.

Two other former congressman who voted for Clinton's impeachment, John Ensign of Nevada and Chip Pickering of Mississippi, also later admitted that they had been involved in extramarital affairs.

As for Clinton, it is believed that he is the first sitting president to officially go through marriage counseling while serving in office.

Two presidents (Andrew Johnson and Bill Clinton) have been impeached but neither was removed from office. But that isn't the case with governors.

William Holden, North Carolina (1871); David Butler, Nebraska (1871); William Sulzer, New York (1913); James Ferguson, Texas (1917); John C. Walton, Oklahoma (1923); Henry S. Johnston, Oklahoma (1929); Evan Mecham, Arizona (1988); and Rod Blagojevich, Illinois (2009) were each given the heave-ho by their respective states.

Oklahoma came close to having three on the list. Just three days after leaving office in January 1975, Governor David Hall was indicted on federal racketeering and extortion charges. Following his trial and conviction, Hall served nineteen months of a three-year sentence at a federal prison in Tucson, Arizona.

Vice President Al Gore once said, "During my service in the United States Congress, I took the initiative in creating the Internet." Gore made that statement during an interview on March 9, 1999, as he was seeking to become the Democratic presidential nominee.

Apparently, the former vice president never heard of ARPANET (Advanced Research Projects Agency Network), which was created by the Advanced Research Projects Agency of the United States Department of Defense during the Cold War. It was the world's first operational packet switching network and the predecessor of the global Internet.

The first message ever to be sent over the ARPANET (via the first host-to-host connection) was sent at 10:30 pm on October 29, 1969. At the time, Gore was a U.S. Army private finishing basic training at Fort Dix, New Jersey.

Sorry Al . . . better luck next time.

· 20 ·

The Twenty-First Century:
Terrorism and Twitter

Throughout our history, the words of the Declaration have inspired immigrants from around the world to set sail to our shores.
These immigrants have helped transform 13 small colonies into a
great and growing nation of more than 300 [*sic*] people.

—President George W. Bush,
Charlottesville, Virginia, July 4, 2008

$\mathcal{T}$ed Kennedy (2009) and Robert Byrd (2010) each served over forty years
in the U.S. Senate and were still in office when they died.

However in 2000, Mel Carnahan of Missouri was elected to the U.S.
Senate. There was just one small matter of importance—he was already dead.

Carnahan was the Show-Me State's former governor who was killed in
an airplane crash on October 17, 2000, while on his way to a campaign event.
Missouri election law did not allow the candidate's name to be removed from
the ballot so his widow Jean became the unofficial surrogate nominee.

After being dead for three weeks, on November 7, 2000, the late Mel
Carnahan won the election by a 2 percent margin. His wife served the first
twenty-two months of the term before Jim Talent won a special election to
serve out the remaining years.

Al Gore is one of the few presidential candidates who didn't win his
home state. Had he been able to get a victory in Tennessee, he would have
been elected president in 2000.

There was a great deal of confusion that took place with the results in Florida during the 2000 presidential election. Many citizens wondered how something like this could happen. Meanwhile, historians were saying to themselves, "Not again."

In November 1876, although there were no voting machines during that time, Democrat Samuel Tilden won 250,000 more votes than Republican Rutherford B. Hayes but neither man gained an undisputed electoral-vote majority. To reach the 185 electoral votes necessary for election, Tilden needed one more ballot; Hayes needed twenty.

The states that controlled those twenty disputed electoral votes were Oregon, South Carolina, Louisiana, and . . . wait for it . . . yes, of course . . . Florida. There was no recount but there was an election committee which made the final decision.

Even though Tilden got a quarter of a million more votes, Hayes won the election.

The famous attorney Clarence Darrow once said, "History repeats itself, and that's one thing that's wrong with history." No doubt Samuel Tilden and Al Gore would agree with Darrow.

Before he became president, George W. Bush was twice elected governor of Texas. But he lost his debut election when he ran for Congress in 1978, although it wasn't the first time that a member of the Bush family was defeated in an initial attempt to gain public office.

In 1964, George W.'s father lost his first election. It was for a U.S. Senate seat.

In 2000, former First Lady Hillary Rodham Clinton was elected U.S. Senator from New York. A few months before the election, she and former president Bill Clinton purchased a home in Massapequa to establish her as an official New York resident since they had never lived in the state.

However, this was not an original tactic by Mrs. Clinton. In the past, New York voters elected Robert F. Kennedy (1965) and Daniel Patrick Moynihan (1977) to the Senate, both of whom had moved to the Empire State only a short time before running for office.

Also, Mrs. Clinton wasn't always a Democrat. In 1964 she worked as a volunteer for the campaign of Republican presidential nominee Barry Goldwater.

The following year as a college freshman, she served as president of the Wellesley College Young Republicans.

As a college student, Bill Clinton used his political connections to stay out of the military during the Vietnam War. These actions have lead some to refer to him as a "draft dodger."

On November 16, 2000, Clinton became the first U.S. president to visit Vietnam since the end of the war.

On his final day as president, Bill Clinton signed a number of pardons, including one for his brother Roger who had been arrested on drug charges several years earlier. But Roger wasn't the only Clinton family member who stepped on the wrong side of the law.

When Clinton's brother-in-law Hugh Rodham, an attorney, successfully lobbied the president to pardon two of his clients, Carlos Vignali Jr. (cocaine trafficking) and Almon Glenn Braswell (mail fraud and perjury), it was discovered that Rodham had pocketed a hefty $400,000 in legal fees for the effort. Both the outgoing president and First Lady, Rodham's sister, demanded that he return the cash, which he did.

Almost anyone who was around can remember what took place on September 11, 2001. But few recall what happened the day before.

Secretary of Defense Donald Rumsfeld held a press conference on September 10 to announce that the Pentagon could not account for a major portion of its budget.

"According to some estimates we cannot track $2.3 trillion in transactions," Rumsfeld admitted. That was followed by Jim Minnery of the Defense Finance and Accounting Service who said, "We know it's gone. But we don't know what they spent it on."

The subject abruptly disappeared when the attacks took place the next day.

Terrorists attacked New York City's World Trade Center on September 11, 2001, killing nearly three thousand citizens. The event is often referred to as 9/11.

The next major terrorist aggression took place at the train station in Madrid, Spain, on March 11, 2004, killing 191 and injuring over 2,000. That attack in Madrid took place 911 days after New York.

On September 11, 2012, eleven years to the day after the original attacks, the United States was again under siege. The American consulate in Benghazi, Libya, was burned and Ambassador J. Christopher Stevens along with three others, including two former Navy Seals, were murdered. That was in addition to the storming of the U.S. Embassy in Egypt on the same day.

The numerals 9 and 11 have become an unpleasant symbol of the costliest terror attack in history.

Planes were used during the attacks on 9/11. Two of them slammed into the twin towers in New York City. But this was not the first time that an aircraft crashed into a Gotham skyscraper.

On July 28, 1945, a U.S. Army Air Corps B-25 hit the side of the Empire State Building. It was a rainy, overcast day, and the pilot had ranged out of the landing pattern. Fourteen people were killed and dozens were injured. This event took place during the final weeks of World War II.

The pilot was attempting to land in Newark, New Jersey, the same place where one of the hijacked jets had taken off from on 9/11.

Terrorist Osama bin Laden was the individual who was behind the 9/11 attacks. But the mastermind had a number of relatives living in the United States at the time of the deadly act. Among them was his brother, Abdullah M. bin Laden, a 1994 graduate of Harvard Law School, who was living in Cambridge, Massachusetts.

At least thirteen relatives of the terrorist leader, accompanied by bodyguards and associates, left the United States on a chartered flight eight days after the September 11, 2001, attacks. They departed from Boston's Logan Airport—the place where two of the four hijacked planes had taken off.

Space Shuttle *Columbia* exploded on February 1, 2003, while returning to earth from a mission. The entire crew was killed, but that wasn't the shuttle's first brush with death.

On March 19, 1981, two workers died and five were injured while setting up a ground test of the spacecraft at NASA.

President George Washington commissioned fourteen copies of the Bill of Rights. One was taken from the North Carolina Statehouse by a Union soldier during the Civil War in 1865.

In 2003, the document was recovered by the FBI in Philadelphia during an undercover operation when an individual attempted to sell it. The copy was believed to have been in North Carolina during its final period of captivity, but officials were uncertain where it had been for most of the past 138 years. It is worth an estimated $30 million.

In 2003, Iraqis in Baghdad toppled a huge statue of their deposed president Saddam Hussein. But that wasn't the first time that a crowd got worked up about an unpopular ruler.

The Declaration of Independence was read aloud to George Washington and his troops in New York City on July 9, 1776. The crowd that had gathered there became so excited upon hearing the words of the powerful document that a statue of King George was torn from its pedestal and melted into 42,000 patriot bullets.

In December 2003, former Iraqi dictator Saddam Hussein was captured by U.S. troops near his hometown of Tikrit. He was tried and eventually executed on December 30, 2006.

But back in 1980, the Middle Eastern tyrant received the key to the city of Detroit. Saddam's bond with the Motor City started in 1979 when the Rev. Jacob Yasso of the Chaldean Sacred Heart Church congratulated him on his presidency. In return, Yasso's church received a $250,000 contribution.

A year later, Yasso traveled with about two dozen people to Baghdad as guests of the Iraqi government and were invited to one of Saddam's palaces. It was there that the dictator was presented with the key to the city, courtesy of Detroit's mayor Coleman Young. At that point, Saddam donated another $200,000.

Unfortunately the money didn't last long in the Motor City as in 2013, Detroit filed for bankruptcy.

Hurricane Katrina struck the Gulf Coast in 2005 doing massive amounts of damage. One of the hardest hit areas was New Orleans.

This wasn't the first time that the "Big Easy" had to overcome hardship. In 1832, a cholera outbreak killed over 4,000 people; in 1853, yellow fever killed 7,790; and a second round of yellow fever struck in 1867 and took another 3,000 lives.

During a presidential election year, the first primary contest is always held in New Hampshire. What may have gotten overlooked in 2008 was that Hillary Rodham Clinton, not Barack Obama, won the New Hampshire Democratic presidential primary. That made her the first woman in U.S. history to win a presidential primary contest.

In 2008, senators Barack Obama, Hillary Rodham Clinton, and John McCain were presidential candidates. Because of that fact, they each missed a number of sessions in the U.S. Senate.

Most voters were probably unaware that while they were watching the trio campaign across the country, the three were in violation of a federal law.

In 1906, Congressman John Wesley Gaines of Tennessee discovered a little known edict from 1856 that stated that members of Congress are docked a day's pay anytime that they are absent. The only exception is for illness. To this day, no member of Congress has had their pay slashed by campaigning for higher office.

There were many bank failures that contributed to the Great Depression. Of the more than 25,000 depositories that were in business in 1929, fewer than 15,000 survived to 1933. The public saw $140 billion disappear through bank failures.

Yet the mother of all bank boo-boos didn't happen during the Great Depression. In 2007, Washington Mutual held assets valued at $327.9 billion, making it the sixth-largest bank in the United States.

But by September 25, 2008, those numbers had shrunk to $33 billion in assets and $8 billion in debt, forcing the institution to be placed in receivership of the federal government. The action was taken due to the withdrawal of $16.4 billion (9 percent of the bank's total assets) in deposits, during a ten-day bank run. The next day, September 26, Washington Mutual filed for Chapter 11 bankruptcy, making it the largest bank failure in American financial history.

Following the court proceedings, Washington Mutual was taken over by J.P. Morgan Chase.

In 2009, George W. Bush left office with the lowest approval rating (22 percent) of any president. In contrast, the forty-third president had also enjoyed the highest rating of any president (92 percent) following the 9/11 attacks in 2001.

His administration had fifty-two months of uninterrupted job growth (longest ever) from September 2003 to December 2007, creating 8.3 million new jobs. But Bush's numbers tumbled in his final year, which marked the beginning of a recession and the bursting of the housing bubble.

It's not unlike what happened to his dad, who had an approval rating of 89 percent in February 1991 during the Gulf War, but by July 1992 had sunk to 29 percent.

Will Rogers once said, "Being a hero is about the shortest-lived profession on earth."

It's not unusual for U.S. presidents to visit several foreign countries each year. During his first one hundred days in office, Barack Obama made separate journeys to Europe, Canada, and Mexico.

Presidential international trips began in 1906 when Theodore Roosevelt went to Central America to review the construction of the Panama Canal, making him the first president to travel outside the country while in office.

In states that have an income tax, citizens must file a tax form. But the Rhode Island Individual Income Tax Return form (RI-1040) is the only state tax return with frowny and smiley faces. They appear on the "This is the amount you owe" and "This is the amount you over paid" lines, respectively.

In 2010, a British Petroleum oil rig blew up in the Gulf of Mexico, causing one of the largest oil spills in history. It was big news on all of the media outlets for weeks.

What those reporters didn't recall was that the 1910 Lakeview Gusher in Kern County, California, lost over four million barrels of "black gold." During the gusher's life of 544 days, it was estimated that some 9.4 million barrels of oil poured out. However, about five million were saved for sale. The large flow created a creek of crude oil running downhill from the well site.

In 2010, the nation watched Illinois governor Rod Blagojevich go on trial for corruption. He was accused of attempting to sell the U.S. Senate seat that was once occupied by Barack Obama.

But "Blago" was just following in the footsteps of others before him because there were three other former Illinois governors—Otto Kerner Jr., Dan Walker, and George Ryan—who also had their share of self-inflicted problems.

Kerner was governor from 1961 to 1968 and later served as a judge on the U.S. Court of Appeals. He was found guilty in 1973 of bribery, conspiracy, perjury, and related charges for taking payoffs from a racetrack operator in exchange for choice racing dates and two expressway exits to funnel fans to the horse races. After resigning his judgeship, Kerner was sentenced to three years in federal prison and fined $50,000.

Walker's crimes were committed after he served as governor from 1973 to 1977. He was convicted of fraud related to his stewardship of the First American Savings & Loan Association of Oak Brook, Illinois. News reports at the time indicated that he received more than one million in fraudulent loans for his business and repairs on his yacht, *Governor's Lady*. Walker served eighteen months of a seven-year sentence in federal prison.

Ryan was Blagojevich's predecessor. He began serving a six-year prison sentence after being convicted in April 2006 on racketeering and fraud charges. A decade-long investigation began with the sale of driver's licenses for bribes and led to the conviction of dozens of people who worked for Ryan when he was secretary of state and governor.

In August 2010, Alaska's former longtime U.S. senator Ted Stevens was killed in a plane crash. No doubt passengers departing from the airport in Anchorage feel safer knowing that it was named in honor of Senator Stevens in 2000.

On May 1, 2011, United States troops killed terrorist Osama bin Laden during a covert military attack. It was announced to the world later that evening by President Obama.

It was exactly sixty-six years to the day after German radio announced that Adolf Hitler was dead. Hitler had actually died one day earlier.

There is another old saying that bad news comes in threes. In a three-week period in 2011, there was some pretty bad news for three prominent politicians.

On May 17, 2011, former California governor Arnold Schwarzenegger announced that in 1997 he fathered an illegitimate child during his marriage to Maria Shriver. The couple had announced their separation a few days earlier.

On June 3, 2011, a federal grand jury indicted former U.S. senator and 2008 presidential candidate John Edwards on charges of conspiracy, making false statements, and violating campaign law.

A two-year investigation charged that Edwards and campaign aide Andrew Young orchestrated payments between donors and the candidate's former mistress and videographer Rielle Hunter. In 2008, Hunter gave birth to a baby fathered by Edwards while his wife was battling cancer.

In 2012 the one-time legislator from North Carolina was acquitted on one charge of campaign finance fraud, and a mistrial was declared on the five other counts on which the jury was deadlocked.

And on June 6, 2011, at a news conference, a tearful Congressman Anthony Weiner acknowledged that he sent inappropriate and explicit photos and messages to women through his Twitter account. A few days later, it was announced that Weiner and his wife of one year were expecting their first child.

You may be familiar with the phrase "when Hell freezes over."

It is a historical fact that this has previously taken place and has happened many times over the years. The town of Hell, Michigan (population 266) usually freezes over every winter.

Figure 20.1 In Michigan, Hell freezes over every year. *Sswonk*

• 21 •

Never Follow a Legend

I may be a living legend, but that sure don't help when I've got to change a flat tire.

—Roy Orbison, Hall of Fame Recording Artist

*T*here is an old saying that applies in any profession "Never follow a legend." In many cases this is true as there are a number of successors throughout history who have failed to live up to the deeds of their predecessors. Here are a few examples.

Christopher Columbus made the first successful voyage to the New World. But little is known about Alonso de Ojeda who was with Columbus on his second voyage (1493–1496). Three years later, in May 1499, Alonso again journeyed to the New World, this time on his own account, but it was his navigator Amerigo Vespucci who would be remembered in the history books by discovering that, contrary to Columbus's beliefs, the land they had reached was not Asia but rather an entirely unknown land mass. So much for Alonso.

The Pilgrims came to the New World in 1620 aboard the *Mayflower.* There was a second ship, also called the *Mayflower,* that made the voyage from London to Plymouth Colony in 1629 carrying thirty-five passengers, many from the Pilgrim congregation in Leiden that organized the first voyage.

It was not the same ship that made the original crossing with the first settlers. This journey began in May and reached Plymouth in August. The ship also made the trip from England to America in 1630, 1633, 1634, and

231

1639. It attempted the journey again in 1641, departing from London in October of that year under master John Cole, with 140 passengers bound for Virginia, but it never arrived. On October 18, 1642, a deposition was made in England regarding the loss.

But only the first *Mayflower* and its voyage is featured in most history books.

The first person to sign the Declaration of Independence was John Hancock. He wrote his name in very large script because he wanted to be sure that his enemy King George III of Britain would be able to see it. Today, spectators can easily catch a glimpse of his famous signature at the National Archives.

However, it seems that Hancock may have been the second signer. On July 4, 1776, the original Declaration of Independence was signed by only two people, Charles Thomson as secretary and Hancock as president of the Continental Congress. The original signed document was then taken to John Dunlap, a Philadelphia printer. He printed five hundred Hancock/Thomson "typed-signed" broadsides, which were distributed to the members of Congress and King George III.

The original Declaration of Independence that was actually signed by Thomson and Hancock, however, was lost in transition. On August 2, 1776, the delegates returned to Philadelphia to sign a newly prepared document, but for some unknown reason Thomson was not invited to sign even though he may have been the first to place his name on the original.

During the Revolutionary War, George Washington was commander of the Continental Army. His second in command was the gifted major general Nathaniel Greene who won a series of important battles in South Carolina and Georgia. Unlike many of Washington's top officers, Greene did not pursue a political career as he twice turned down offers to become secretary of war.

George Washington selected Alexander Hamilton as the first secretary of treasury. Hamilton is credited with establishing the nation's banking system which is still used today, and his face adorns the ten-dollar bill. But after almost six years on the job, he resigned to return to practicing law.

In 1795, Washington appointed the auditor of the federal treasury, Oliver Wolcott Jr. as Hamilton's successor. Wolcott resigned in 1800 due to unpopularity after a campaign against him was pursued in the press that, among other things, falsely accused him of setting fire to the State Department building.

John Jay was the first chief justice of the Supreme Court. On June 28, 1795, Jay resigned his post after being elected governor of New York. Associate Justice John Rutledge, a respected statesman and signer of the Constitution, was immediately chosen by George Washington to head the court. But over the next six months, Rutledge's support faded due to incidents which may have been related to mental illness. On December 15, 1795, Rutledge's nomination was rejected by the Senate.

John Adams was the second president of the United States. Unfortunately, he was sandwiched between two of the greatest leaders in the nation's history—Washington and Jefferson. They each got two terms in office, Adams just one.

Almost everyone has learned about Lewis and Clark's amazing journey west establishing the Oregon Trail. About twenty years later, explorer Jedediah Smith and his company not only made it to Oregon as had their predecessors but traveled down the west coast as far as San Diego. But today, Lewis and Clark continue to garner most of the attention when it comes to westward expansion.

Francis Scott Key wrote the poem "The Star Spangled Banner" as Fort McHenry was being attacked during the War of 1812. However, the music was composed by John Stafford Smith for the Anacreontic Society, a London social club. The tune, known as "Anacreon," was also employed for the national anthem of Luxembourg until 1895.
But while Key made it to your history book, Smith was forgotten.

In August 1814 during the War of 1812, British troops invaded Washington, D.C., setting fire to the White House and the Capitol Building.
But what was the next stop was for the Brits? On August 27, Captain James Gordon advanced to Fort Washington, Maryland, two days after burning the nation's capital. He prepared to shell the fort as its commandant, Captain Samuel T. Dyson, evacuated his troops. After the Americans left, the British flotilla blew up the encampment. After the fort's destruction, the British headed to the town of Alexandria.

When Davy Crockett lost the election for his congressional seat in 1835, he set out for Texas to restart his political career. But who was the man who defeated the legend?
Adam Huntsman was a lawyer and a friend of Andrew Jackson, and he had little use for the famous frontiersman turned congressman. But even with

support from the president, the shine quickly came off Huntsman's apple as he was defeated for re-election in 1837.

In the meantime, Crockett had risen to iconic status, especially in his home state of Tennessee, following the Battle of the Alamo. Today he is recognized as the state's most famous hero while Huntsman is just an afterthought.

While much time is spent reflecting on Fort Sumter as the opening battle of the Civil War, the same cannot be said of the second battle—the Battle of Sewell's Point in Norfolk, Virginia. It took place on May 18–19, 1861, and consisted of an exchange of cannon fire between the Union gunboat USS *Monticello* and Confederate batteries. There were a total of ten casualties but no deaths, and no winner was declared.

The biggest battle of the Civil War was Gettysburg, but where did the combatants next meet?

During July 4–5, 1863, General Lee's battered and beaten army began its retreat from Gettysburg, moving southwest on the Fairfield Road toward Hagerstown and Williamsport, screened by J. E. B. Stuart's cavalry.

On July 11, Lee entrenched a line, protecting the rain-swollen Potomac River crossings at Williamsport, and waited for General George Meade's army to advance. Two days later, skirmishing was heavy along the lines as Meade positioned his forces for an attack. In the meantime, the river had fallen enough to allow the construction of a new bridge, and Lee's army began crossing the river after dark on July 13.

Fighting continued as the troops advanced on Shepherdstown. Unlike Gettysburg, the result was inconclusive, with more than 1,700 casualties.

When the Civil War ended in April 1865, Abraham Lincoln was hailed as a hero by most of the public. And following his assassination, he became a martyr and a symbol of Southern revenge.

That was bad news for his successor Andrew Johnson, who had to battle with uncooperative cabinet members like Secretary of War Edwin Stanton. His eventual impeachment meant that neither party wanted him as their candidate in 1868.

It was evident that Johnson would never escape Lincoln's shadow.

Brigham Young was the founder of Salt Lake City and served as the first governor of the Utah Territory.

However, his forgotten successor was a man named Alfred Cumming. He was a former mayor of Augusta, Georgia, who was appointed as the new governor of the territory in 1858 by President James Buchanan following the Utah War. He served as governor until 1861 and then returned to Washington, D.C.

Brigham Young got his name on a major university while Cumming is in a history book on the back shelf of the library.

The Wright Brothers' famous flight at Kitty Hawk, North Carolina, took place in 1903. But who was Traian Vuia?

He was a Romanian inventor and aviation pioneer who designed, built, and flew an early aircraft. His first flight was a distance of about forty feet at Montesson, France, on March 18, 1906. But as opposed to the Wright Flyer, Vuia's aircraft accomplished the first documented and unassisted takeoff and landing on a level surface by an engine-driven monoplane with a completely wheeled undercarriage.

Vuia's work in aviation is important, but in 1969 when Apollo 11 went to the moon, the astronauts took a small piece of the Wright Flyer with them. Too bad, Traian.

Henry Ford founded the Ford Motor Company and served as its first president. But on December 31, 1918, Henry's twenty-five-year-old son Edsel was named president of the business.

In 1943, Edsel died from stomach cancer at the age of forty-nine. His dad resumed his role as head of the company but was suffering from senility. The well known enterprise began to fall into decline, which led Edsel's widow to call for the ouster of the automotive legend. Her son, Henry Ford II, was then installed as president. He served in that post until 1960 and as CEO until 1979.

Charles Lindbergh will be remembered in aviation history as the first pilot to fly solo across the Atlantic Ocean. He landed safely in Paris on May 21, 1927, after a 33 hour 30 minute journey that covered 3,610 miles.

Two weeks later on June 6, aviator and stunt flier Clarence Chamberlin made a record nonstop transatlantic flight, with a passenger, in his monoplane *Columbia* from Roosevelt Field, Long Island (the same takeoff point as Lindbergh), to Eisleben, Germany, a distance of 3,911 miles, in 42 hours and 31 minutes.

But who remembers Clarence Chamberlin?

By the way, Chamberlain didn't do it for the money. He made several million dollars by salvaging ammunition after World War I.

Babe Ruth was the top baseball player of his era, setting season and career home-run records.

On February 26, 1935, the New York Yankees released the aging slugger who was past his prime. He was replaced as the team's right fielder by rookie George Selkirk. After seven years as a minor leaguer, the Canadian-born outfielder took advantage of the opportunity as he batted .312, hit 11 homers, and knocked in 94 runs in his first season as the legendary Bambino's successor.

Selkirk hit over .300 five times in nine seasons. He was also a key contributor to the Yankees' four consecutive World Series titles from 1936 to 1939. In 1983, he was inducted into Canada's Baseball Hall of Fame.

So, what was the problem? When Ruth departed, Selkirk donned the slugger's famous number 3 jersey, which didn't sit well with many Yankee fans.

He recalled, "I was just cocky enough to say, 'Wearing Babe's number won't make me nervous. If I'm going to take his place, I'll take his number too.' I got his [Ruth's] job and it took a long time for people to forgive me."

Since then, Ruth's number 3 along with the uniform numbers of several other star players have been retired by the team.

Al Capone, the boss of the Chicago Outfit, was convicted of tax evasion. He was the best-known mobster of all-time, attaining celebrity status in the media.

But in 1932 Capone went away to prison, which began a power struggle for control of his organization. Frank "The Enforcer" Nitti, who also served time for tax evasion, and Paul "The Waiter" Ricca each wanted to succeed their popular boss. But both lacked Capone's ability to elude justice and spent most of their time in courtrooms and jail cells.

World War II soldier Audie Murphy was a true legend, becoming one of the most decorated soldiers in history. During the war, the handsome major was featured on the cover of *Life* magazine, a place usually reserved for generals and presidents. In later years, he went on to become a popular movie star and best-selling author.

That was bad luck for Lieutenant Colonel Matt Urban, who actually garnered more medals than Murphy. He was belatedly awarded the Medal of Honor in 1980 for acts of heroism performed in 1944.

Urban died in 1995, thereby making him eligible for a commemorative stamp in 2005, which has yet to happen. Murphy was featured on a stamp in 2000.

Another outstanding soldier has also been largely ignored because of the unpopularity of the Vietnam War. Colonel Robert L. Howard received dozens of awards, including the Medal of Honor plus eight Purple Hearts.

But his Medal of Honor ceremony received no major television or newspaper coverage.

One of the highlights of every book that covers the Korean War is General Douglas MacArthur being relieved of command by President Harry Truman. But few of those ever covered the man who replaced the legend.

Matthew Bunker Ridgway had a successful career as a U.S. Army general. He held several major commands and was most famous for resurrecting the United Nations effort during the Korean War. Several historians have credited Ridgway with turning around the war in favor of the UN side. His long and prestigious military career was recognized when he was awarded the Presidential Medal of Freedom in 1986 by President Reagan.

Unfortunately for Ridgway, he followed the larger-than-life figure of Douglas MacArthur, who went home and received a ticker tape parade in New York City.

On Sunday February 9, 1964, the Beatles made their debut on American television. They performed five songs on the hour-long *Ed Sullivan Show*, which was watched by a record-smashing 73.7 million viewers. That was nearly 40 percent of the entire U.S. population.

But lost in history were the other acts that appeared on the show that evening. That group included British actors Georgia Brown and Davy Jones (before his days with the Monkees) performing two songs from the Broadway play *Oliver*, comedian and impressionist Frank Gorshin; and Welsh actress Tessie O'Shea, who later said, "The kids [in the audience] didn't know whether I was the Beatle's mother or a fifth Beatle."

The other acts should have all probably fired their agents for booking them on that program.

On April 4, 1968, Dr. Ralph Abernathy was with Martin Luther King Jr. when he was assassinated in Memphis, Tennessee. He was a close friend of Dr. King and replaced him as head of the Southern Christian Leadership Conference (SCLC).

Abernathy remained president of the SCLC for the next nine years. He had a distinguished career and was honored with more than three hundred awards and citations, including five honorary doctorate degrees.

But while there are a national holiday, streets, and schools named for Martin Luther King, his successor has been lost in the pages of history.

It's not much of a reach to remember that astronauts Neil Armstrong and Buzz Aldrin were the first two humans to walk on the moon on July 20,

1969, as part of the Apollo 11 mission. The landing is still a major topic of historical conversation.

Four months later, Apollo 12 became the second successful moon landing with Alan Bean and Pete Conrad strolling the lunar surface. It was a triumphant adventure, but it was a victim of bad timing.

Next up in April 1970 was the nearly disastrous journey of Apollo 13. The crew's dramatic effort to return safely to Earth was so noteworthy that it became a hit movie. Apollo 12 not only had the misfortune to follow a legend, it also preceded one.

Many fans consider John Wooden to be the greatest college basketball coach ever. Between 1964 and 1975, his UCLA (University of California, Los Angeles) teams won a remarkable ten NCAA (National Collegiate Athletic Association) Championships, spearheaded by future NBA (National Basketball Association) stars like Lew Alcindor (Kareem Abdul-Jabbar), Bill Walton, and Sidney Wicks.

When the "Wizard of Westwood" retired following the 1975 season and after winning his final title, Memphis State's successful coach Gene Bartow was tapped as his successor.

Over the next two seasons, Bartow's UCLA teams played well, compiling an impressive 52–9 record and garnering a pair of conference championships and a berth in the 1976 Final Four. Bartow is the second-winningest coach at UCLA by percentage of wins to losses at .852, but there were no national championships, and under intense pressure from fans and boosters, Bartow resigned after just two seasons.

It has been said that Benedict Arnold is the most famous American traitor of all time. That might be so, but he had nothing on Aldrich Ames.

Although not as famous as Arnold, Ames was just as devious. He was a CIA officer who, in 1985, began selling secrets to the Soviet Union. He earned about $4.6 million, and ten American agents were executed because their covers were exposed by Ames.

In time, he revealed the name of every U.S. agent operating in the USSR. His lavish lifestyle raised red flags for the CIA, and in February 1994, Ames was arrested and sentenced to life in prison. His wife, Rosario, was deported to South America.

Ronald Reagan was known as a relentless tax cutter and vocal opponent of Communism during his eight years in the White House. He had become a champion of the conservative movement in the 1980s.

In 1989, Reagan's departure paved the way for his vice president George H. W. Bush as his successor. Halfway through his term and with a victory in the Gulf War, Bush's approval ratings were higher than Reagan's at over 80 percent.

But a tax increase and higher unemployment spelled doom for the Bush campaign in 1992 as he joined the roster of one-term presidents.

On paper, the vice presidency is the second-highest office in the land. But being VP gives no guarantee of a promotion. The following individuals are examples of former second chairs who tried to take the next step but failed.

- George Clinton—Thomas Jefferson's VP, he failed to defeat James Madison in the primary (1808).
- Richard Johnson—Martin Van Buren's VP, he failed to defeat James Polk in the primary (1844).
- John Breckenridge—James Buchanan's VP, he ran as a National Democrat and failed to defeat Abraham Lincoln (1860).
- Henry Wallace—one of Franklin Roosevelt's VPs, he ran as a Progressive and failed to defeat Harry Truman (1948).
- Hubert Humphrey—Lyndon Johnson's VP, he failed to defeat Richard Nixon (1968).
- Walter Mondale—Jimmy Carter's VP, he failed to defeat Ronald Reagan (1984).
- Al Gore—Bill Clinton's VP, he lost the presidency to George W. Bush (2000).

WHAT IF?

We learn from history that we never learn anything from history.

—Hegel

Here are how some of history's best-known incidents have led to questions that can never be answered.

What if Benedict Arnold had not turned traitor during the Revolutionary War? Would he have gone down in history with the nation's greatest generals like Jackson, Grant, MacArthur, and Eisenhower?

What if John Parker, who was supposed to be guarding the presidential box at Ford's Theatre, hadn't left his post to go have a drink across the street? Would Booth have been able to kill Lincoln?

What if Adolf Hitler had achieved his dream of being admitted to art school in Vienna in 1907? Would there have been a Nazi regime and the Holocaust?

What if General George Patton had not been involved in a highly publicized incident for slapping a soldier? Would Eisenhower have allowed him to lead the D-Day invasion?

What if Harry Truman hadn't fired General MacArthur during the Korean War? Would MacArthur have run for president in 1952?

What if Rosa Parks had gone to the back of the bus when she was told to? Would there still have been a Montgomery Bus Boycott?

What if President Kennedy had not been assassinated? Would he have been reelected in 1964?

What if James Earl Ray had not escaped from prison in 1967? Would Martin Luther King Jr. be alive today?

What if Robert Kennedy had not been assassinated? Would he have been elected president in 1968?

What if the Watergate scandal had never happened? Would Richard Nixon have gone down in history as one of our ten best presidents? And would a Republican have been elected in 1976?

What if Timothy McVeigh had achieved his dream of making it into the U.S. Army's elite squad, the Green Berets? Would there have been an Oklahoma City Bombing?

What if the U.S. government had been able to capture or kill Osama bin Laden in the late 1990s? Would there have been the 9/11 attacks?

What if Saddam Hussein had been removed during the Gulf War of 1991? Would the United States have sent troops to Iraq in 2002?

Epilogue: The Last Word

It's a great invention but who would want to use it anyway?
—Rutherford B. Hayes, U.S. president, after a demonstration
of Alexander Graham Bell's telephone, 1877

The horse is here to stay but the automobile is only a novelty—
A fad.
—The president of the Michigan Savings Bank advising
Henry Ford's lawyer not to invest in the
Ford Motor Company in 1903

It is apparent to me that the possibilities of the aeroplane, which
two or three years ago were thought to hold the solution to the
[flying machine] problem, have been exhausted, and that we
must turn elsewhere.
—Thomas Edison, American inventor, 1895, eight years
before the Wright Brothers' historic flight

The cinema is little more than a fad. It's canned drama. What
audiences really want to see is flesh and blood on the stage.
—Charlie Chaplin, actor, producer, director,
and studio founder, 1916

A rocket will never be able to leave the Earth's atmosphere.
—*New York Times*, 1936

There is not the slightest indication that nuclear energy will ever be obtainable. It would mean that the atom would have to be shattered at will.

—Albert Einstein, 1932

There is no reason anyone would want a computer in their home.

—Ken Olson, president, chairman, and founder of Digital Equipment Corporation (DEC), maker of big business minicomputers, arguing against the personal computer in 1977

Sensible and responsible women do not want to vote.

—Grover Cleveland, former U.S. president, 1905

It doesn't matter what he does, he will never amount to anything.

—Albert Einstein's teacher to his father, 1895

Hurrah boys, we've got them!

—Lieutenant Colonel George A. Custer's final words to his troops at the Battle of the Little Bighorn, June 26, 1876

Acknowledgments

Thank you to the Lehman Institute and the Lincoln Institute.

References

ARTICLES CONSULTED

Allen, Richard V., "The Day Reagan was Shot," *Atlantic*, April, 2001.

Anthony, Carl Sferrazza, "A President of the Peephole," *Washington Post*, June 7, 1998.

Associated Press Pool Report, "Truman Always 'Captain Harry' to Battery," *Washington Observer-Reporter*, December 27, 1972.

Ayoob, Massad, "The Subtleties of Safe Firearms Handling," *Backwoods Home Magazine*, January/February, 2007.

Babbitt, James, and Deatrick, Tim, "The Last Mammoth: Lewis and Clark's Secret Mission," National Association of Tribal Historic Preservation Officers, March 10, 2010.

Bell, J. L., "Rachel Revere and Dr. Benjamin Church, Jr.," Boston 1775, November 11, 2009.

Blinderman, A., "John Adams: Fears, Depressions, and Ailments," *New York State Journal of Medicine*, 1977.

Booth, William, "Tabled Resolution," *Smithsonian Magazine*, June 2008.

Borade, Gaynor, "Lincoln Memorial Facts," Buzzle.com.

Bos, Carole D., "Daniel Boone," Awesome Stories, 1999.

Brown, L. Ames, "President Wilson the Motorist," *Northwestern Motorist*, September, 1916.

Brunker, Mike, "Illinois Has Long Legacy of Public Corruption," MSNBC, 2008.

Bruns, Roger A., " A More Perfect Union: The Creation of the United States Constitution," National Archives Trust Fund Board, 1986.

Butler, Anne M., and Wolff, Wendy, "United States Senate Election, Expulsion and Censure Cases," Government Printing Office, 1995.

Chan, Sue, "Guess Who Got the Key to Detroit?" CBS News, March 26, 2003.

Chen, Peter C., "Douglas MacArthur," World War II Database, 2008.

"Chinese Immigrants on America's Western Frontier," Wild West, June 12, 2006.

Chua-Eoan, Howard, "The Top 25 Crimes of the Century," Time.com, 2007.

Cooper, John S., "Presidential Feuds," Suite101.com, November 1, 2001.

Craven, Jackie, "12 Things You Didn't Know about the White House," About.com, 2010.

Dim, Joan Marans, "Robert Moses and the Second Avenue Subway," Huffington Post, February 27, 2012.

Drapkin, Jenny, "6 of LBJ's Favorite Things," Mental Floss, August 27, 2008.

Duncan, George, "George Duncan's Lesser Known facts of World War II," http://members.iinet.net.au/~gduncan/facts.html.

Feldman, Claudia, "Hail to the Chiefs: Presidential Historians Weigh In," Chron, February 14, 2010.

Ferhman, Craig, "First Lady Lit," *New York Times*, May 21, 2010.

Ferling, John, "Myths of the American Revolution," *Smithsonian Magazine*, January 2010.

Fowler, Philip, "Strange Political Pairings," President Elect, October 24, 2004.

Frail, T. A., "Top 10 Nation-Building Real Estate Deals," Smithsonian.com, September 7, 2009.

———, "Top 10 Historic Midterm Elections," Smithsonian.com, October 14, 2010.

Glass, Andrew, "FDR Inaugurated for Fourth Term, January 20, 1945," Politico, January 20, 2009.

Goldberg, Wendy H., and Goodwin, Betty, "Marry Me! Courtships and Proposals of Legendary Couples," About.com.

Goode, Stephen, "Little-Known Facts about U.S. Chief Executives," Insight on the News, January 8, 2001.

Goodheart, Adam, "10 Days That Changed History," *New York Times*, July 2, 2006.

Greene, David L., "Expect the Unexpected at Inaugurals," *New York Times*, January 19, 2005.

Griffith, Michael T., "Some Surprising Facts about the Confederacy," American Civil War, February 2008.

Hawk, Ruby, "How Did the Bay of Pigs Invasion Happen?" socyberty.com, September 18, 2009.

Headley, Susan, "The 1933 Saint-Gaudens Gold Double Eagle—World's Most Valuable Coin," About.com, September 15, 2006.

Henderson, Bruce, "Who Discovered the North Pole?" *Smithsonian Magazine*, April 2009.

Henderson, Jr., Robert W., "The Story of Old Glory," Battle of Nashville Preservation Society.

Holzel, David, "Five Feisty Presidential Daughters," Mental Floss, September 15, 2008.

Hopwood, Jon C., "The 10 Worst Vice Presidents of the United States," Associated Content, April 9, 2008.

Howard, Hugh, "Revolutionary Real Estate," *Smithsonian*, December 2007.

Hoyle, John, "From the Halls of Montezuma," Just One Opinion, April 25, 2009.

Italie, Leanne, "White House Romances," Associated Press, May 4, 2008.

Johnson, Eric, "7 Civil War Stories You Didn't Learn in High School," Mental Floss, June 10, 2009.

Johnston, Alexander, "Salary Grab," Library of Economics and Liberty, 1899.

Keck, Kristi, "First Daughters Balance Privilege and Pressure," CNN, August 7, 2009.

Kennedy, Bud, "The Great Hanging, Long Ignored, Now Immortalized," *Fort Worth Star-Telegram*, October 27, 2007.

Kenny, Kevin, "Irish Immigrants in the United States," America.gov, February 13, 2008.

Kovalchik, Kara, "8 Not-So-Famous Firsts," Mental Floss, November 12, 2009.

——, "Not-So-Famous Firsts, Arlington National Cemetery," Mental Floss, November 11, 2010.

Large, David Clay, "What If Annie Oakley Had Shot Kaiser Wilhelm II in 1889?" What If Diaries, January 3, 2007.

Leino, Gail, "Flag Day: History and Party Trivia," EzineArticles.com, November 8, 2006.

Lewis, Jone Johnson, "The Day the Suffrage Battle Was Won," About.com, June 27, 2010.

Linder, Doug, "John Scopes," University of Missouri, Kansas City School of Law, 2008.

Lippman, David H., "December 7th, 1941: The 55th Anniversary of the 'Day of Infamy,'" http://usswashington.com/worldwar2plus55/dl07de41.htm.

Lombardo, Robert M., "The Genesis of Organized Crime in Chicago," International Association for the Study of Organized Crime.

Longley, Robert, "From Time to Time: The State of the Union Address," About .com, January 27, 2010.

Lovgren, Stefan, "Election Is Crunch Time for U.S. Secret Service," *National Geographic News*, October 28, 2004.

Malloy, Betsy, "Golden Gate Bridge Facts," About.com, 2001.

Marotta, Michael E., "Mind Your Business," *Coin Collecting for Beginners*, 1998.

Martin, Paul, "Lincoln's Missing Bodyguard," Smithsonian.com, April 8, 2010.

Maurer, Mel, "There's Nothing Trivial about Him," Cleveland Civil War Round-table, 2003.

May, Allan, "The Brothers Capone," American Mafia, November 8, 1999.

McCain's Plane Crashes, FactCheck.org., October 12, 2008.

McPhee, Isaac M., "Taphephobia," Suite101.com, February 3, 2008.

Minard, Anne, "Apollo 11: 5 Little-Known Facts about the Moon Landing," *National Geographic News*, July 21, 2009.

Morens, D. M., "Death of a President," *New England Journal of Medicine*, April 20, 2000.

Mott, Frank Luther, "The Newspaper Coverage of Lexington and Concord," *New England Quarterly* 17, no. 4, 1944.

Naik, Abhijit, "Interesting Facts about the American Civil War," Buzzle.com.

Nevius, C. W., "Escaping the Glare of the Spotlight Isn't Easy for Kids Whose Dads Work in the Oval Office," *Hearst Newspapers*, January 22, 2004.

Perloff, James, "Pearl Harbor: Hawaii Was Surprised, FDR Was Not," *New American*, December, 2008.

Peters, Glen, "Brief Biographies of 19th-Century Vice Presidents," Associated Content February 21, 2008.

———, "Little Known Facts About the 20th-Century Presidents," Associated Content, July 20, 2007.

Petzal, David E., "David E. Petzal's Five Greatest Gunfights of the Old West," *Field & Stream*, February 13, 2009.

"President Monroe's Services in the Revolutionary War," *New York Times*, 1874.

Raab, Nathan, "A Library Thomas Jefferson Would Love," *Forbes*, June 22, 2010.

Rajeev, Loveleena, "History of the 13 Colonies," Buzzle, 2008.

Rosen, David, "America's Top Ten Sex Scandals," CounterPunch, August 1, 2007.

Rosenberg, Tina, "When Smallpox Struck During the Revolutionary War," *New York Times*, December 23, 2001.

Rushton, Bruce, "Ax Turns Out to Be Lincoln's Last Swing," Gatehouse News Service, February 22, 2008.

Ryan, Andrew, "Not Top Secret: Julia Child's Work for Spy Agency," *Boston Globe*, August 14, 2008.

Sabin, Greg, "Ten People Who Made a Fortune During the Depression," Mental Floss, Aug 12, 2009.

Sayers, Alethea, *eHistory's Civil War Newsletter*, July 1, 2000.

Schroeder, Joan Vannorsdall, "The Day They Hanged an Elephant in East Tennessee," *Blue Ridge Country*, May 1, 1997.

Sheeley, Rachel, "President Presence," *Palladium-Item*, July 18, 2010.

Shen Rastogi, Nina, "Dead by Inauguration Day," Slate, November 2008.

Smith, Craig R., "Lincoln and Habeas Corpus," California State University, Long Beach, April 16, 2007.

Smith, Elbert B., "President Harry S. Truman—Survived Assassination Attempt at the Blair House," HistoryNet.com, June 12, 2006.

Smith, Jacob, "The Dodge Brothers and Henry Ford," allpar.com.

Stahle, David W., Cleaveland, Malcolm K., Blanton, Dennis B., Therrell, Matthew D., and Gay, David A., "The Lost Colony and Jamestown Droughts," *Science*, 1998.

Stanley, Deb, "City Secret, Colorado, Was Almost Home to the Summer White House," Examiner.com, February 16, 2009.

Stephey, M. J., "America's Worst Vice-Presidents," *Time*, July 2008.

Taylor, Carl, "World Trade Center Facts," Harrow Group, April 1, 2002.

"The Old Man and the Mountain," *The Columbian*, April 1, 2010.

Trescott, Jacqueline, "A Signature Lincoln Artifact for the American History Museum," *Washington Post*, January 15, 2009.

Trex, Ethan, "Seven Historical Bans on Smoking," Mental Floss, January 21, 2010.

United States Congress, Congressional Record, House, 73rd Congress, 2nd session, March 21, 1934.

United States Government, "The Warren Report," 1964.

Ward, Geoffrey C., "A Wild Animal in Good Clothes," *American Heritage*, 1988.

Washington, Hugh S., "Roosevelt: Where's His Wheelchair?" *Time*, March 6, 1995.

BOOKS CONSULTED

Algeo, Matthew, *Harry Truman's Excellent Adventure: The True Story of a Great American Road Trip*, Chicago Review Press, 2009.

Arnold, Isaac, *The Life of Abraham Lincoln*, Bison Books, 1994.

Aurandt, Paul, *The Rest of the Story*, Bantam Books, 1984.

Ayres, Thomas, *That's Not in My American History Book*, Taylor Trade Publishing, 2004.

Benford, Timothy, *The World War II Quiz & Fact Book*, Harper & Row, 1982.

Beyer, Rick, *The Greatest Stories Never Told*, Harper, 2003.

Boller, Paul F. Jr., *Presidential Anecdotes*, Oxford University Press, 1996.

Browne, Francis Fisher, *The Every-Day Life of Abraham Lincoln*, University of Nebraska Press, 1995.

Bumgarner, John R., *The Health of the Presidents: The 41 United States Presidents through 1993 from a Physician's Point of View*, McFarland & Company, 2004.

Buschini, J., *A Splendid Little War*, Small Planet Communications, 2000.

Butt, Archibald W., *Taft and Roosevelt: The Intimate Letters of Archie Butt, Military Aide*, Kennikat Press, 1971.

Claiborne, John M., *Terry's Texas Rangers*, Confederate Veteran, 1911.

Cooper, L. Gordon, *Leap of Faith*, HarperCollins, 2000.

Crenshaw, Charles A., Hansen, Jens, Shaw, J. Gray, *JFK: Conspiracy of Silence*, Signet, 1992.

Cossley-Batt, Jill L., *The Last of the California Rangers*, Funk & Wagnalls, 1928.

Davis, Burke, *The Civil War: Strange and Fascinating Facts*, Wings, 1988.

DeGregorio, William A., *Complete Book of U.S. Presidents*, 6th ed., Barricade Books, 2005.

Department of Rare Books and Special Collections, Princeton University Library, Fuller Collection of Aaron Burr, 1756–1836.

Donald, David Herbert, *Lincoln*, Simon & Schuster, 1996.

Dwyer, John J., *The War between the States: America's Uncivil War*, Bluebonnet Press, 2005.

Ellis, Joseph, *American Sphinx: The Character of Thomas Jefferson*, Vintage, 1998.

Evans, Harold, *The American Century*, Knopf, 1998.

Farrand, Max, *The Framing of the Constitution of the United States*, Yale University Press, 1962.

Fawcett, Bill, *Oval Office Oddities*, Harper Paperbacks, 2008.

Fenn, Elizabeth Anne, *Pox Americana*, Hill and Wang, 2001.

Fischer, David Hackett, *Paul Revere's Ride*, Oxford University Press, 1995.

Fisher, Vardis, *Suicide or Murder? The Strange Death of Governor Meriwether Lewis*, Swallow Press, 1995.

Flexner, James Thomas, *Washington: The Indispensable Man*, Back Bay Books, 1994.

Foley, Hugh W. Jr., *Encyclopedia of Oklahoma History and Culture*, Oklahoma Historical Society, 2007.

Gaddis, John Lewis, *We Now Know*, Oxford University Press, 1998.

Gary, *Ralph, Following Lincoln's Footsteps*, Basic Books, 2002.

Gilbert, Robert E., *The Tormented President: Calvin Coolidge, Death, and Clinical Depression*, Praeger, 2003.

Gregory, Leland, *Stupid American History*, Andrews McMeel, 2009.

————, *Stupid Texas*, Andrews McMeel, 2010.

————, *Stupid California*, Andrews McMeel, 2010.

Grizzard, Frank Jr., *George Washington: A Biographical Companion*, ABC-CLIO, 2002.

Halberstam, David, *The Coldest Winter: America and the Korean War*, Hyperion, 2007.

Hall, Jonathan N., *The Revolutionary War Quiz and Fact Book*, Taylor Trade Publishing, 1999.

Havelin, Kate, *Ulysses S. Grant*, Twenty-First Century Books, 2004.

Haynes, George H., *Election of Senators*, Holt and Company, 1906.

Helm, Katherine, *Mary, Wife of Lincoln*, Harper, 1928.

Heysinger, Isaac W., *Antietam and the Maryland and Virginia Campaigns of 1862*, Neale Publishing, 1912.

Higginbotham, Don, *George Washington and the Colonial Military Tradition*, University of Virginia Press, March 2001.

Hoover, Irwin Hood, *Forty-Two Years in the White House*, Houghton Mifflin, 1939.

James, Marquis, *The Life of Andrew Jackson*, Bobbs-Merrill, 1938.

Kelly, C. Brian, *Best Little Stories from the Civil War*, Cumberland House, 1998.

Kingston, Mike, *The Texas Almanac*, Eakin Press, 1992.

Kleiman, Dave, *The Official CHFI Exam 312-49, for Computer Hacking Forensics Investigators*, Syngress, 2007.

Kunhardt, Dorothy M., and Philip B. Jr., *Twenty Days*, Harper & Row, 1965.

Kupperman, Karen Ordahl, *The Jamestown Project*, Belknap Press, 2007.

Kurland, Philip B., and Lerner, Ralph, *The Founders' Constitution*, University of Chicago Press, 1987.

Kurlansky, Mark, *The Big Oyster: History on the Half Shell*, Ballantine Books, 2006.

Lederer, Richard, *Presidential Trivia: The Feats, Fates, Families, Foibles, and Firsts of Our American Presidents*, Gibbs Smith, 2007.

Lehmann, Armin D., *In Hitler's Bunker: A Boy Soldier's Eyewitness Account of the Führer's Last Days*, Lyons Press, 2005.

Leuchtenburg, William E., *Franklin D. Roosevelt and the New Deal*, Harper Torchbooks, 1963.

Lienhard, John H., *The Engines of Our Ingenuity*, Oxford University Press, 2003.

Linder, Doug, *John Scopes*, University of Missouri, Kansas City School of Law, 2008.

McFeely, William S., *Grant*, W. W. Norton & Company, 2002.

Mitchell, Alexander D., *Washington D.C. Then and Now*, Thunder Bay Press, 2002.

Mitchell, Joseph, *Up in the Old Hotel*, Vintage Books, 1993.

Montgomery-Massingberd, Hugh, ed., *Burke's Presidential Families of the United States of American*, 2nd ed., Burke's Peerage, 1981.

Morris, Charles, *The Lives of the Presidents and How They Reached the White House*, John C. Winston, 1903.

Nagel, Paul C., *The Adams Women: Abigail and Louisa Adams, Their Sisters and Daughters*, Harvard University Press, 1999.

O'Brien, Cormac, *Secret Lives of U.S. Presidents*, Quirk Books, 2009.

O'Brien, Michael, *John F. Kennedy: A Biography*, St. Martin's Griffin, 2006.

Pendel, Thomas F., *Thirty-Six Years in the White House*, Applewood Books, 2008.

Peters, Charles, *Lyndon B. Johnson, the 36th President, 1963–1969*, Times Books, 2010.

Peterson, Merrill, *Thomas Jefferson and the New Nation: A Biography*, Galaxy Books, 1975.

Pringle, Henry F., *The Life and Times of William Howard Taft: A Biography*, Farrar & Rinehart, 1939.

Rehnquist, William H., *Grand Inquests: The Historic Impeachments of Justice Samuel Chase and President Andrew Johnson*, William Morrow, 1999.

Remini, Robert V., *The Life of Andrew Jackson*, Harper Perennial Modern Classics, 2010.

Ripley, Robert, *Ripley's Believe It or Not*, Ripley Publishing, 2004.

Rubenzer, Steven J., and Faschingbauer, Thomas R., *Personality, Character, and Leadership in the White House*, Brassey's, 2004.

Rutland, Robert Allen, *The Presidency of James Madison*, University Press of Kansas, 1990.

Sellers, Charles, *The Market Revolution: Jacksonian America, 1815–1846*, Oxford University Press, 1994.

Shalev, Eran, *Rome Reborn on Western Shores*, University of Virginia Press, 2009.

Shenken, Richard, *Legends, Lies & Cherished Myths of American History*, Harper & Row, 1989.

Simkins, Francis Butler, *Pitchfork Ben Tillman, South Carolinian*, University of South Carolina Press, 2002.

Smelser, Marshall, *The Democratic Republic, 1801–1815*, Waveland Press, 1992.

Smith, Marie, *Entertaining in the White House*, Macfadden-Bartell, 1971.

Sotos, John G., *The Physical Lincoln Sourcebook*, Mt. Vernon Book Systems, 2008.

Speakes, Larry, and Pack, Robert, *Speaking Out: The Reagan Presidency from Inside the White House*, Avon Books, 1987.

Sproule, Anna, *Thomas A. Edison: The World's Greatest Inventor*, Blackbirch Press, 2000.

Starchild, Adam, *History of the Income Tax*, International Law and Taxation Publishers, 2005.

Stern, C. C., *Braddock's Presidential Trivia*, Braddock Communications, 2000.

Stevenson, David, *1914–1918: The History of the Great War*, Penguin, 2005.

Stokesbury, James L., *A Short History of the Korean War*, Harper Perennial, 1990.

Sullivan, George, *Facts and Fun about the Presidents*, Scholastic Paperbacks, 1994.

True, Webster Prentiss, *The Smithsonian—America's Treasure House*, Sheridan House, 1950.

Tusa, John, and Tusa, Ann, *The Nuremberg Trials*, Skyhorse Publishing, 2010.

Walker, Martin, *The Cold War*, Holt Paperbacks, 1995.

Wallace, Irving, and Wallechinsky, David, *The People's Almanac*, Doubleday, 1975.

Wead, Doug, *The Raising of a President*, Atria, 2005.

Weinstein, Edwin A., *Woodrow Wilson: A Medical and Psychological Biography*, Princeton University Press, 1981.

Weintraub, Stanley, *MacArthur's War: Korea and the Undoing of an American Hero*, Free Press, 2008.

Zelden, Charles L., *Voting Rights on Trial: A Handbook with Cases, Laws, and Documents*, ABC-CLIO, 2002.

WEBSITES CONSULTED

www.alexandriava.gov
www.americancivilwar.com
www.americanheritage.com
www.americanhistory.si.edu
www.americanprofile.com
www.anecdotage.com
www.answers.com
www.archives.gov
www.associatedcontent.com
www.associatedpress.com
www.baic.house.gov
www.baseball-almanac.com
www.biography.com bookrags.com
www.boston-discovery-guide.com
www.bratoganibe.com
www.calgoldrush.com
www.cbs.news.com
www.centennialofflight.gov
www.chevroncars.com
www.cigaraficionado.com
www.cigarenvy.com
www.citytavernclubdc.org
www.civilwarwomenblog.com
www.clarksvillemainstreet.com
www.clerk.house.gov
www.Collectingpez.com
www.darrow.law.umn.edu
www.dcrepublican.com
www.deathpenaltyinfo.org
www.diagnose-me.com
www.discovery.com
www.driventotears.com
www.e-referencedesk.com

www.encyclopedia.com
www.essortment.com
www.failedsuccess.com
www.findingdulcinea.com
www.firstladies.org
www.FitCommerce.com
www.forgottenhsitroy.com
www.flyershistory.com
www.freerepublic.com
www.gallawa.com
www.glo-con.com
www.gustavewhitehead.org
www.gwpapers.virginia.edu
www.histclo.com
www.historichwy49.com
www.history.com
www.history.army.mil
www.historyconfidential.com
www.historyguide.org
www.historyguy.com
www.history.sandiego.edu
www.hnn.us
www.home.att.net
www.howstuffworks.com
www.hubpages.com
www.hueylong.com
www.ibiblio.org
www.ideafinder.com
www.inaugural.senate.gov
www.infoplease.com
www.inmamaskitchen.com
www.inn-california.com
www.interestingushistory.com

www.invent.org
www.j-grit.com
www.janessaddlebag.org
www.kerryr.net
www.legendsofamerica.com
www.lib.virginia.edu
www.libertyfund.org
www.Listverse.com
www.lou_ww1.tripod.com
www.medicinebow.org
www.michiganhistory.org
www.military.com
www.military-quotes.com
www.millercenter.org
www.monticello.org
www.mountvernon.org
www.neatorama.com
www.nebraskastudies.org
www.newworldencyclopedia.org
www.niagarafallsheritage.ca
www.nejm.org
www.noaa.gov notduck.com
www.nps.gov
www.nyhistory.com
www.nytimes.com
www.oddee.com
www.ohiohistorycentral.org

www.oldnewark.com
www.paul-revere-heritage.com
www.pawprints.com
www.pbs.org
www.peterson.org
www.politico.com
www.presidentsusa.net
www.purpletrail.com
www.rabbitworldview.com
www.randomhistory.com
www.raritanboro.org
www.RoadsideAmerica.com
www.Salon.com
www.seasky.org
www.secretservice.gov
www.senate.gov
www.sfmuseum.org
www.sfusd.edu
www.sonofthesouth.net
www.sparknotes.com
www.spartacus.schoolnet.co.uk
www.stephencarr.com
www.taxhistory.org
www.thecloroxcompany.com
www.thefoolsday.com
www.wikipedia.com

About the Author

For thirty-one years, **Mike Henry** taught American history to students at all levels of the educational spectrum, from elementary school to college. His technique of using the events of the past to show how they impact out lives in the present made him a popular classroom instructor and guest speaker. Since the inception of No Child Left Behind, he averaged a success rate of more than 80 percent on state mandated testing at a school where the majority of the students were at the poverty level.

Mike is a two-time award winner of Who's Who Among America's Classroom Teachers.

In 1994, he published his first work, a historical novel, called *Peacemaker: The Saga of an American Family*. Following his retirement, he wrote *Black History: More Than Just a Month* (Rowman & Littlefield, 2012), a book that has become popular among those wanting to learn more and for educators of African American history.

Mike and his wife Pamela, who is also a retired educator, reside near Dallas, Texas.